Experiments in

An Introductory Lab Manual

Experiments in ,
An Introductory Lab Manual

java ™

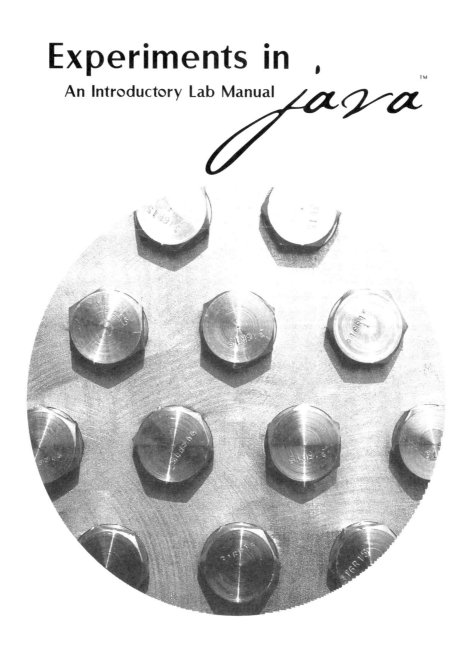

SAMUEL A. REBELSKY, Grinnell College

An imprint of Addison Wesley Longman, Inc.

Reading, Massachusetts • Menlo Park, California
New York • Harlow, England • Don Mills, Ontario
Sydney • Mexico City • Madrid • Amsterdam

Senior Acquisitions Editor	Susan Hartman
Assistant Editor	Lisa Kalner
Project Managers	The Publisher's Group
	Trillium Project Management
Executive Marketing Manager	Michael Hirsch
Compositor	Michael and Sigrid Wile
Proofreading	Trillium Project Management
Cover Designer	Joyce Cosentino

Library of Congress Cataloging-in-Publication Data
Rebelsky, Samuel A.
    Experiments in Java : an introductory lab manual / by Samuel A. Rebelsky.
        p.   cm.
    ISBN 0-201-61267-4
    1. Java (Computer program language)   I. Title.

QA76.73.J38 R43 2000
005.13'3—dc21   99-049190

Many of the designations used by manufacturers and sellers to distinguish their products are claimed as trademarks. Where those designations appear in this book, and Addison-Wesley was aware of a trademark claim, the designations have been printed in initial caps or all caps.

The programs and applications presented in this book have been included for their instructional value. They have been tested with care but are not guaranteed for any purpose. The publisher and author do not offer any warranties or representations, nor do they accept any liabilities with respect to the programs or applications.

Access the latest information about Addison-Wesley titles from our World Wide Web site: http://www.awlonline.com

This book was typeset in FrameMaker 5.5 on a Macintosh G3. The font families used were Sabon and Frutiger. It was printed on Lynx Opaque.

1 2 3 4 5 6 7 8 9 10–CRS–0302010099

To those who've mentored my career:
Don, Mike, Fillia, and Henry

Preface

Welcome to the fascinating world of computer science and to the art and craft of computer programming. Like many modern disciplines, computer science is broad and includes a variety of different (and sometimes difficult) topics. Many students learn computer science and computer programming better by experimenting with the topics in a laboratory setting, just as students in chemistry, physics, and biology benefit from labs in those disciplines.

While computer science is not the same as computer programming, computer programs and computer programming help ground many of the central ideas of computer science, from architecture to computational complexity. As such, it is important for students interested in computer science to have some experience reading, writing, and analyzing computer programs.

The best computer scientists and computer programmers regularly play with new ideas they encounter, whether these new ideas be language structures, algorithms, machines, or even theorems. However, few novices have the intuition or skills for such experimentation. Hence, in many of the experiments in this manual, you will play with various aspects of the Java programming language, as well as a few concepts in computing. For example, you may change your program slightly and see what happens. You may also try some things that the language definition is (or seems to be) unclear about. As you gain more experience with such experiments, it is likely that you will find new ways to test new ideas.

Java

This manual (and, presumably, your textbook and course) uses Java as the programming language, rather than one of the many other options, such as Ada, C, Pascal, C++, Scheme, or Haskell. Why? For a number of reasons. First, Java is one of the few truly platform-independent languages. A Java program written for one computer should run correctly and identically on almost any other modern computer. While programs written in other languages, such as Pascal and C, can be compiled on a variety of platforms, the same program will often behave differently on the different platforms because of inconsistencies in the designs of the compilers or machines. Second, the core of the Java language is relatively small, so that it is possible to learn all of the basics in a moderate number of laboratory sessions. Third, Java provides an extensive set of libraries, including standard libraries for graphical programs.

Different languages provide very different perspectives on programming and problem solving. In recent years, computer science educators have suggested that students should learn different *paradigms* early in their careers. Importantly, Java is both an *object-oriented* and an *imperative* programming language. Because Java is object-oriented, programmers can design Java programs that are collections of communicating objects. Because Java is imperative, it is possible to design programs or subprograms that look like traditional recipes in that they are a series of steps with some additional control. The exercises in the manual emphasize both aspects of the language.

Because Java has both imperative and object-oriented features, there are (at least) two approaches to teaching programming (and computer science) in Java. One can use an *objects-first* approach, in which objects are discussed and used as early as possible. Some claim that this helps students better understand and work with the object-oriented paradigm. One can also use an *objects-late* approach, in which objects are not introduced until students have mastered the basic imperative concepts, such as loops and conditionals. Some claim that this empowers students to work in a greater variety of language and helps ameliorate the sense of being overwhelmed that many students encounter in their introductory courses.

I will admit to being a proponent of the objects-first approach, and this lab manual reflects my preferences. As one reviewer notes, I use objects in the first program, even though they are not strictly necessary. However, I firmly believe that students better master the use of objects if they use them as early as possible.

Organization of the Manual

The manual is separated into a number of parts. The first part presents the core of the Java language. These eight sessions will give students experience with the core features and principles of the Java programming language. While these sessions do not cover the complete language, they will give students enough experience and breadth to learn more on their own or in further courses. Importantly, these sessions should give students the skills to experiment with new concepts they encounter so that they can learn more than just what they are told.

Computer science is more than computer programming. To many computer scientists, algorithms form the core of computer science. The second part of the manual helps you explore some issues pertaining to algorithms. You will begin by considering recursion, an important technique for algorithm design. You will then visit a few important searching algorithms. Finally, you will conclude this part by considering some ways in which one might analyze algorithms.

In the final part, a number of Java-oriented laboratory sessions cover additional topics not described in the core sessions. The additional topics include graphics, inheritance, and object design.

Applications and Applets

As you may know, Java supports at least two approaches to programming. In the *application model*, programs are written to operate by themselves without other supporting programs. (Of course, such applications still rely on an operating system and may communicate with other programs). In the *applet model*, programs are written to fit into other programs or documents. In particular, applets are often written for inclusion in Web pages.

This book primarily focuses on applications rather than applets. Why? As a teacher, I've found that students often encounter difficulty when dealing with the interaction between applets, the multiple versions of Java, and different mechanisms for running applets. For example, at the time I wrote this section, Java was at version 1.2 (at least on some platforms). However, some browsers, such as the standard version of Netscape Navigator 4.x, still seem to support only Java version 1.0. Unfortunately, the Java applet model changed significantly between Java 1.0 and Java 1.1, which means that applets written for the newer standards don't always work in older browsers. For that reason, I relegated Applets to optional exercises and an optional laboratory (G1).

I am the first to admit that there are a number of successful strategies for teaching Java. Hence, at the suggestion of some reviewers, I have also added some applet-based exercises to sections J1–J5. These applet-based exercises replicate G1 (or vice versa), and you are discouraged from doing both. If you do applets as part of J1–J5 (the first session), you may find it necessary to be quite selective in which parts to do/assign, or you may wish to spread J1 and J2 over four laboratory sessions rather than two.

Organization of Lab Sessions

As you may have noted, each laboratory has four or five sections, including an introductory cover page. The cover page presents a short introduction to the laboratory. This page typically includes one or two paragraphs of introductory material. A list of new skills you should develop while completing this laboratory follows. These are not the only skills you will develop, but they are the focus of the particular laboratory session. Next comes a list of prerequisite skills. When beginning a lab, you should review this list and make sure you have developed those skills (or at least understand what those skills should be). Because it is appropriate and necessary for you to use and modify existing programs, there are a number of required files.

The introductory section is followed by a discussion of the topic or topics covered in the laboratory session. *You should read the discussion section before coming to lab!* In fact, this lab manual separates the discussion from the experiments to encourage you to read first. During lab times, you will most likely want to refer back to the discussion section for ideas and suggestions.

The discussion is followed by a series of experiments. These experiments are intended to help reinforce the discussion and to give you more experience with the concepts. There are typically more experiments than one can complete in a typical laboratory session. Your instructor will tell you which of the proposed experiments to perform. If you finish early, you may decide to do others. While there is no answer key to the experiments, it is likely that you will be able to determine the correct answer in most cases. In some cases, experiments raise difficult issues. In many cases, you will find notes and solutions for such problems at the end of the laboratory. You should only refer to these notes after you attempt the problem on your own.

Laboratories typically include many post-laboratory problems, which are intended to help you enhance your skills and understanding. Your instructor may assign some of these, or you may choose to do them on your own. You can think of the experiments as tools to help you develop your understanding of concepts and the post-laboratory problems as tools to exercise your understanding.

Finally, selected problems have notes. A few of the problems are particularly difficult or may have particularly important implications. For these problems, you will find notes at the end of the section.

How do you use this manual? Before you go to lab, read the appropriate section and scan the experiments. When you come to lab, do the experiments. After lab, go home, relax, think about what you've learned, and consider the post-laboratory problems. Finally, come back to lab (or to some computer) and do the post-laboratory problems. More importantly, have fun and learn!

Formatting

All Java code and program output appear in a monospace font. Reserved words in the language are underlined to highlight them. Most comments are boldfaced to remind you that you should read comments before reading code. Comments that mark the end of a section are not boldfaced. Strings are italicized.

You may find that your editor or program development environment uses different choices (or perhaps none at all). *Do not worry if programs are formatted differently when you type them in; the appearance is secondary to the underlying meaning and often out of the control of the programmer.*

Warning!

As stated in the preface, this manual is intended to introduce you to a number of fundamental structures in Java. It is also intended to help you improve your understanding of these structures by encouraging you to experiment with them: trying variations of the same program or statement, testing limits, and otherwise experimentally exploring the meaning of the structures.

This manual is not a complete introduction to Java, to computer science, to structured or object-oriented design, or to the many other topics you will typically learn in an introductory computer science course. Your class and your textbook will provide additional information on everything from syntax (i.e., the way in which you write the various Java expressions) to philosophical underpinnings (e.g., why a language includes looping structures).

This manual is also intended to be textbook independent, except for its choice to approach Java objects-first. That is, to permit a wider variety of classes to benefit from these experiments, they are independent of any particular textbook. This means that some language structures will be used in different ways than you are accustomed to, that the layout of programs may be different, and that topics may be covered in a different order. Part of your growth as computer scientist and computer programmer involves being able to learn from these different perspectives, and I hope you will find these differences one of the benefits of this manual.

For Students

Computer science laboratories can and should be exciting, interesting, and fun. However, successful learning and enjoyment do require you to do some work outside of the laboratory session. You will need to *prepare* for each laboratory session in advance of that session and to *reflect* on each laboratory session after the session.

How should you prepare for a laboratory session? You should begin by reading over the instructions for the laboratory. Most of these laboratories include a few pages of text that introduce the topic. As your time in the lab will be limited, it is essential that you read and understand these pages in advance. You may also need to read some sections of the text to understand the discussion. It is important that you read the text actively: when you encounter a question, make sure you think about the answer before reading on. It is very important that you read the discussion section before you begin the laboratory. To reinforce this importance, I have separated discussion from experiments.

It will also be helpful if you read over the associated experiments, although the results and purposes of experiments are often best understood when you are conducting the experiment. You may want to ask yourself what the purpose of each experiment is and predict what is supposed to happen. Expect to spend at least one hour preparing for each lab.

During laboratory sessions, you should think about your background readings and predictions. Feel free to experiment when working on the exercises; many students learn best by developing their own variants of these exercises. The structure of lab sessions makes it impossible to cover all the details of any particular topic. To gain the most from a lab, you will need to experiment, discover, reflect, and refine.

In other sciences, you often write laboratory reports after a lab session. While these laboratories typically do not require reports, they do require you to reflect after the laboratory is complete. To help you reflect, each session ends with a number of post-laboratory problems. Those of you who work particularly quickly may want to consider working on some of these problems during the session. Depending on the number of post-laboratory problems your instructor assigns, plan to spend at least one hour on post-laboratory work.

For Instructors

Choosing Laboratories

As suggested above, this manual contains more laboratory sessions than can be covered in a typical course. I encourage you to pick the topics that best fit the intent of your course and the level of your students. If you want to give your students more experience with Java, add the optional Java laboratories. If you want to expose your students to some core algorithms, add those laboratories.

Here are a few sample laboratory sequences for courses with twelve lab meetings, one for orientation and eleven for sessions from this manual.

- The following organization includes the core Java topics, some additional Java, and a little bit of graphics for fun.
- J1 (An Introduction to Java), J2 (Objects and Methods), J3 (Building Your Own Classes), J4 (Boolean Expressions and Conditionals), J5 (Control Structures for Repetition), J6 (Arrays and Hash Tables), G1 (Graphics and Applets), A1 (Recursion), X1 (Primitive Types), X2 (Vectors) X3 (Input, Output, Files, and Exceptions).
- The following organization is appropriate for students who will benefit from increased exposure to data structures and algorithms.
- J1 (An Introduction to Java), J2 (Objects and Methods), J3 (Building Your Own Classes), J4 (Boolean Expressions and Conditionals), J5 (Control Structures for Repetition), J6 (Arrays and Hash Tables), A1 (Recursion), A2 (Searching), A3 (Analyzing Algorithms), O1 (Object-Oriented Design), X2 (Vectors).
- The following organization will give students broader exposure to object-oriented programming.
  J1 (An Introduction to Java), J2 (Objects and Methods), J3 (Building Your Own Classes), O2 (Inheritance), O3 (Interfaces and Polymorphism), J4 (Boolean Expressions and Conditionals), J5 (Control Struc-

tures for Repetition), J6 (Arrays and Hash Tables), O1 (Object-Oriented Design), A1 (Recursion), X3 (Input, Output, Files, and Exceptions).

By replacing lab O1 (Object-Oriented Design) in that organization with X1 (Primitive Types), you can cover more Java issues. Lab X1 might also be covered earlier in the sequence. Lab G1 (Graphics and Applets) might be used in place of another lab, preferably O3 (Interfaces and Polymorphism).

In addition to providing enough laboratories to allow you to customize your students' laboratory experience, I have also made the individual laboratories customizable. Each laboratory session contains a number of experiments, perhaps more than your students will need to complete in a two-hour laboratory session. You are encouraged to select the experiments that emphasize the topics you wish to cover. Each laboratory session also includes a number of post-laboratory problems. You may find it appropriate to assign select problems during laboratory and additional problems for later.

You may also find that it is possible to combine laboratory sessions through judicious selection of experiments. Particularly appropriate combinations are

- J2 (Objects and Methods) and J3 (Building Your Own Classes),
- O2 (Inheritance) and O3 (Interfaces and Polymorphism),
- A2 (Searching) and A3 (Analyzing Algorithms), and
- G2 (Java's Abstract Windowing Toolkit) and G3 (Java's Abstract Windowing Toolkit, Continued).

Preparing for the Laboratories

All of the laboratories are designed to be run with Sun's Java Development Kit (JDK), version 1.1. While other development environments are available, the JDK provides a standard development platform that is relatively easy to learn, that is free, and that is generally available. If you do not use the JDK, you may need to provide custom instructions for some of the laboratories. You will also have to provide some custom instructions for the first laboratory, which is intended to get students familiar with the local computing environment.

If your students will have regular web access, it may be useful to install local copies of the Java API

`http://java.sun.com/products/jdk/1.1/docs/api/packages.html`

and *The Java Tutorial*

`http://java.sun.com/docs/books/tutorial/index.html`

Many of the laboratories rely on existing classes. The source and compiled versions of all of these classes are available on the lab web site at

`http://www.math.grin.edu/~rebelsky/ExptInJava/Code/`

You are encouraged to make a local copy of those classes.

Library Java files to accompany the book can be downloaded from

`ftp://ftp/cseng/authors/rebelsky`

Acknowledgments

Thanks to Julie Dunn of Addison Wesley Longman for suggesting that I develop this laboratory manual and for providing ready assistance during its development. When Julie left AWL to pursue her interests in editing history, Lisa Kalner took over. Amy Rose of The Publisher's Group also helped guide me through many of the final stages. Vivek Venugopal of Grinnell helped me check over copyedits. I appreciate their help and patience.

Many of the ideas and exercises in this manual are based, in part, on exercises in *Experiments in Computer Science: A C++ Laboratory Manual*. I thank Mary P. Boelk and J. Glenn Brookshear for those contributions.

Clif Flynt tested many of the experiments before we unleashed them on our students. I thank him for his valuable comments, particularly his real programmer's insights. Ryan Gerling provided additional comments on a number of laboratories.

Clif's students and my students beta tested many of these experiments. I thank them for their enthusiasm, patience, and suggestions. Oleksiy Andriychenko, Erik Hanson, Rachel Heck, Eric Otoo, Paul Carlson, Justin Rose, Shekhar Shah, and Siera Soleil gave the manuscript a particularly careful and insightful reading and caught many small and subtle errors. Henry Walker of Grinnell College used the draft versions of some experiments in his classes. I thank him for his comments and contributions.

A number of anonymous reviewers provided suggestions on everything from the organization of the manual to particular wording. They were particularly helpful in making me think about different development environments and different course organizations. I thank those reviewers for their help.

The development of this manual was supported, in part, by Addison Wesley Longman, Grinnell College, the Technology Studies concentration at Grinnell College, and by the National Science Foundation's Division of Undergraduate Education through grant DUE#98-50546. Any opinions, findings, conclusions, or recommendations expressed in this material are those of the author and do not necessarily reflect the views of the National Science Foundation or the other supporters.

Finally, thanks to my family, Michelle, William, and Jonathan, for their patience during the time spent writing this manual.

Further Reading

This manual is not intended to provide a comprehensive introduction to the Java language. Rather, it is intended to give students sufficient experience that they can read more on their own. Among the topics *not* covered in this manual are

- many of the standard Java classes
- abstract classes

- protection levels
- enumerations
- graphical user interfaces
- threads
- anonymous and inner classes (and anonymous inner classes)
- and many, many more.

A number of excellent tutorial guides to Java are available. Two that I have found particularly useful are

- Mary Campione and Kathy Walrath, *The Java Tutorial*, Second Edition. Reading, Massachusetts: Addison-Wesley, 1998.
- Judy Bishop, *Java Gently: Programming Principles Explained*, Second Edition. Reading, Massachusetts: Addison-Wesley, 1998.

For programmers moving on in Java, I'd recommend some standard references. The first provides a great deal of detail about each of the library classes that are part of the standard Java distribution. The second simply lists all those methods (with some introductory examples), but is nonetheless surprisingly useful, particularly if you don't quite remember the calling strategy for a method.

- Patrick Chan, Rosanna Lee, and Douglas Kramer, *The Java Class Libraries*, Second Edition (two volumes). Reading, Massachusetts: Addison-Wesley, 1998.
- Patrick Chan, *The Java Developers Almanac 1999*. Reading, Massachusetts: Addison-Wesley, 1999.

Contents

Session G2:   Java's Abstract Windowing Toolkit   259

Session J1: An Introduction to Java

In this laboratory session you will begin reading Java programs and writing your own Java programs. The goals of this laboratory are to

- give you experience compiling and running Java programs;
- orient you to the form of Java programs;
- introduce variables in Java;
- describe input and output in Java;
- introduce some of the primitive types in Java.
- introduce the `String` class, one of the core Java classes; and
- introduce the <u>int</u> and <u>double</u> data types, two of Java's primitive data types.

Your instructor will tell you which of the proposed experiments you are to perform.

Because each computer system is structured differently, your instructor will supplement this laboratory session with guidelines for compiling and executing programs in your environment.

Prerequisite skills:

- Editing files

Required files:

- `BasicComputations.java`
- `Greetings.java`
- `HelloWorld.java`
- `SimpleInput.java`
- `SimpleOutput.java`

Optional applet files:

- `HelloWorldApplet.java`
- `helloworld.html`

Discussion

- A hello world program
- Compilation
- Reading input
- Concatenating strings
- Variables
- Numeric input and output
- Applets

A hello world program

Many people begin working in a new programming language by writing a short program that prints the words "Hello World". Here's one such program, written in Java.

```java
import SimpleOutput;
/**
 * A simple Java program that illustrates textual output.
 *
 * @author Samuel A. Rebelsky
 * @version 1.1 of March 1998
 */
public class HelloWorld {
  /**
   * Print the string "Hello world." to standard output.
   */
  public static void main(String[] args) {
    // The object we're using to print output.
    SimpleOutput out = new SimpleOutput();
    // And print
    out.println("Hello world");
  } // main(String[])
} // class HelloWorld
```

Let's examine the pieces of this program.

The `import` statement

```java
import SimpleOutput;
```

This statement tells the Java compiler that we'll be using one or more `SimpleOutput` objects to support our program. The name of that class suggests that we will be using the objects to print output (to the screen or elsewhere).

Introduction

```java
/**
 * A simple Java program that illustrates textual output.
 * <p>
 * Copyright (c) 1998 Addison Wesley Longman.  All rights reserved.
 *
 * @author Samuel A. Rebelsky
```

```
 * @version 1.1 of March 1998
 */
```

These lines are a comment about the program. A comment is a note for the reader of the program (rather than for the computer). Java supports a variety of commenting styles. The preceding comment is an introductory one. Every introductory comment begins with a slash and two stars and ends with a star and a slash. Every class should have an introductory comment that consists of a few-sentence summary of the intent of the class, a blank line, and the author and version (as above).

Class header

```
public class HelloWorld {
```

The class header begins the real code. We're defining a class named `HelloWorld` that can be used anywhere (because it is `public`). The left curly brace begins the definition (or code) for the class. You'll see a corresponding closing brace later.

What is a *class*? The notion of "class" is one of the central components of object-oriented programming, and classes are used for many purposes. Classes serve as *templates* to guide the creation of objects. Classes gather *methods* that provide functionality for objects. Classes can suggest or limit usage.

In this case, the `HelloWorld` class is used to gather methods. In particular, it has a single method, called "`main`".

Method summary

```
/**
 * Print the string "Hello world" to standard output.
 */
```

This method summary is another introductory comment. Each component of a program or class (you'll learn more about these components and classes later) should have an introductory comment.

Method header

```
public static void main(String[] args) {
```

This header starts a method (also known as a function or procedure) definition. In particular, we're defining a method called `main`. Every Java program must have one main function that begins just like this. For now, we won't worry about why it looks like this; it just does. When you execute a Java program, execution begins at the start of your main method. The curly brace begins the code for the main method.

Comment

```
// The object we're using to print output.
```

This line shows another way to comment. The earlier comments began with a slash and a star and ended with a star and slash. You can also begin a comment with two slashes and end it with the end of the line. Generally, you use the slash-star comments for longer descriptions (outside of components and classes) and the double-slash comments for shorter descriptions (usually for a few lines of code).

This particular comment indicates that the following line creates and names an object that we'll be using to print output.

Variable declaration and creation

```
SimpleOutput out = new SimpleOutput();
```

This variable declaration says that out refers to a new object of type SimpleOutput. SimpleOutput objects provide mechanisms for writing to the screen.

Output

```
// And print
out.println("Hello world");
```

This line says to print the string "Hello World." More precisely, we use this line to call the println method of the out object we've just created and to pass it the string "Hello world." Note that the ordering here is similar to that we'd use if we were talking to someone, as in "Sam, write 'Hello World' on the board."

End of method definition

```
} // main(String[])
```

This line matches the brace that opened the body of main. For every opening brace you write, you'll need a corresponding closing brace. The comment isn't strictly necessary, but it makes it easier to read the program. I'd recommend making it a point to comment every end brace to indicate what you are ending.

End of class definition

```
} // HelloWorld
```

This line matches the brace that opened the definition of HelloWorld. Again, the comment isn't strictly necessary, but it makes the program more readable.

Compilation

Computers typically cannot execute programs written in source text (such as the Java program above). Before being executed, these programs must be *translated* or *compiled* into a form the computer can better understand. Hence, you will need to execute the *Java compiler* to translate any Java program to an executable form. The executable form of a Java program is called a "class" file and has the suffix `.class`. For example, if I compile the program `HelloWorld.java`, the compiled program will be called `Hello-World.class`.

Java differs from many languages in what you do with the translated program. Typically, programs are compiled to machine code, which the computer can then execute directly. In Java, programs are compiled to *Java machine code,* which "Java machines" can execute directly. Most computers cannot directly execute such code. Hence, you must run a *Java machine simulator* (also known as an *interpreter*) to execute your Java programs. Why the difference? Because Java provides many features (typically having to do with security) that typical machines do not provide directly.

In Experiment J1.1 you will execute `HelloWorld` and consider some principal issues in Java development. In Experiment J1.2 you will extend `Hello-World`.

Reading input

We've seen how to print output and a sketch of the overall structure of a simple Java program. Now, let's move on to one that also reads input.

```java
import SimpleInput;
import SimpleOutput;
/**
 * A simple Java program that illustrates textual input and output.
 *
 * @author Samuel A. Rebelsky
 * @version 1.1 of March 1998
 */
public class Greetings {
  /**
   * Prompt for the user's name and print a greeting.
   */
  public static void main(String[] args) {
    // The object we're using to read input.
    SimpleInput in = new SimpleInput();
    // The object we're using to print output.
    SimpleOutput out = new SimpleOutput();
    // The user's name.
    String name;
    // Prompt for the name.
    out.print("What is your name? ");
    // Get the name.
    name = in.readString();
    // Print a friendly message.
    out.print("Hello ");
    out.print(name);
```

```
        out.println(", welcome to the joys of Java.");
    } // main(String[])
} // Welcome
```

Again, we'll look at it, line by line (or at least chunk by chunk).

```
import statements
import SimpleInput;
import SimpleOutput;
```

Here, we indicate that we're using two different library objects. The first does simple input; the second does simple output.

Introductory material

```
/**
 * A simple Java program that illustrates textual input and output.
 * <p>
 * Copyright (c) 1998 Samuel A. Rebelsky.  All rights
 * reserved.
 *
 * @author Samuel A. Rebelsky
 * @version 1.1 of March 1998
 */
public class Greetings {
```

Again, we begin with an introductory comment that describes the program and lists author and version. Next is a class header, indicating that the class is named `Greeting`. Finally, we have an open brace that begins the class.

Introduce `main`

```
/**
 * Prompt for the user's name and print a greeting.
 */
public static void main(String[] args) {
```

We begin with an introductory comment describing the purpose of the method. Then we have the method header, which gives the name and some related information. Finally, we have an open brace to begin the definition.

While methods can have many names, the name "`main`" has particular meaning to Java. In fact, the `main` method is the core of any Java application. Java uses the `main` method as the starting place for the program.

You may be wondering about the other parts of the method declaration (the `public`, `static`, and such). Unfortunately, at this stage of your career, you are best served by accepting that this code is just how you indicate the start of your program. For those of you who can't wait for more explanation, you can find a basic explanation in the notes at the end of this section.

Object declarations and initialization

```
// The object we're using to read input.
SimpleInput in = new SimpleInput();
// The object we're using to print output.
SimpleOutput out = new SimpleOutput();
// The user's name.
String name;
```

This time, we have three named objects. One will be used for reading input, one for writing output, and one to store the user's name (since we're reading the user's name, we need to store it somewhere).

`String` is a special type of class, used to describe collections of letters and numbers. Strings appear regularly in Java programs. For example, "*Hello world*" is a string (with eleven characters). When you deal with textual input and output, you will need strings. Note that we were able to use the type `String` without <u>import</u>ing it. This is because strings are built into Java. Note also that we did not use <u>new</u> to create a new `String` object. This is because we will be getting a string later in the program, and the method we use to get the string will create the new string.

Prompt

```
// Prompt for the name.
out.print("What is your name? ");
```

Note that `SimpleOutput` permits you to use both `println` (which includes a carriage return) and `print` (which does not include a carriage return).

Input

```
// Get the name.
name = in.readString();
```

`SimpleInput` provides a number of methods for reading values. The simplest is `readString`, which reads and returns one line of text.

Output

```
// Print a friendly message.
out.print("Hello ");
out.print(name);
out.println(", welcome to the joys of Java.");
```

Again, we print with `print` and `println`.

Cleanup

```
  } // main(String[])
} // Welcome
```

As before, we need to close the definitions of `main` and the complete class.

In Experiment J1.3, you will execute `Greetings` and learn about some of the ways that programmers inadvertently break programs. In Experiment J1.4, you will extend `Greetings` to read and print additional information.

Concatenating strings

As you may have noted from the prior example, it can become tedious to print a sequence of outputs. In that example, we needed separate calls to the `println` method for the greeting, the name, and the welcome. It would be useful to be able to print all three with one statement. Fortunately, Java permits you to concatenate (join) strings together with the plus (+) operation. For example, I could rewrite the three lines above as

```
out.println("Hello " + name + ", welcome to the joys of Java.");
```

Variables

When programming, it is often necessary to store and name values temporarily. In most languages (including Java), we need to create a storage cell for the value, name that storage cell, and store and retrieve values. Such storage cells are typically called *variables*.

In Java, all variables are typed. That is, you must describe what type of values are stored within the variables. You might store numbers, strings, or even objects. In our first program, we needed to work with an object of type `SimpleOutput`, so we created a variable called `out` of that type. In subsequent programs, you will create variables of other types.

Note that we can get the value stored in a variable by using the name of the variable and we can store values in variables by writing the name of the variable, an equals sign, and an expression. For example, we can declare `alpha` and `beta` to be string variables with

```
String alpha;
String beta;
```

We can assign the string `"Java"` to `alpha` with

```
alpha = "Java";
```

We can assign two copies of `alpha` to `beta` with

```
beta = alpha + alpha;
```

Numeric input and output

Our previous programs worked with text. A great deal of computation uses numbers instead of text. Let's move on to some programs that read and write numbers. Our basic program will prompt for a number and print the square of that number.

```
import SimpleInput;
import SimpleOutput;

/**
 * A simple Java program that illustrates numeric input and output.
 *
 * @author Samuel A. Rebelsky
 * @version 1.1 of March 1998
```

```
  */
public class BasicComputations
{
  /**
   * Prompt for a number and print the square of the number.
   */
  public static void main(String[] args)
  {
    // The object we're using to read input.
    SimpleInput in = new SimpleInput();
    // The object we're using to print output.
    SimpleOutput out = new SimpleOutput();
    // The value entered.
    double val;
    // Prompt for the value.
    out.print("Please enter a value and I will square it: ");
    // Get the name.
    val = in.readDouble();
    // Print a friendly message.
    out.println(val + " squared is " + (val*val));
  } // main
} // class BasicComputations
```

This time, we'll only look at the "new" lines (the ones that differ significantly from those in previous programs).

Numeric variables

```
double val;
```

You declare numeric variables by writing the keyword `double` and the name of the variable, which says that val is a variable that stores numbers. You will soon discover that `double` variables store numbers that include a fractional portion (e.g., 3.5 and 1.2). If you only want to store integers (numbers without a fractional portion; some people call these whole numbers), you can use `int`.

Numeric input

```
val = in.readDouble();
```

`SimpleInput` also supports a `readDouble` method that reads a number. This line says to read a number and store that number in val. If you want to read an integer, you can use `readInt`.

Output and computation

```
out.println(val + " squared is " + (val*val));
```

This line illustrates one of the oddities of Java (or comes close to illustrating one of those oddities). The meaning of some symbols is *context-dependent*. Usually, we think of the plus sign as being used to add two numbers. However, as we've already seen, it can also be used to join strings. In this case, it is being used for the latter purpose. Surprisingly, when you add a string and a number, Java automatically converts the number to a string and adds as if they were both strings.

In Experiment J1.5, you will explore numeric input and output, as well as some simple numeric computation.

Applets

This section is optional and is intended for classes emphasizing applets or pursuing a simultaneous discussion of applications and applets.

In addition to supporting the standard application model of programming, Java also supports a variant model, known as the *applet* model. Applets are programs that are designed to be run within other programs. Most often, applets are graphical programs that run within Web pages. In the first lab session, you may have experimented with applets that drew pictures on the screen or animated balls or balloons. In this session, we'll focus on the static applets.

Interestingly, the structure of an applet differs from that of an application. In particular, applets typically do not contain constructors or a `main` method. You also declare applets in a somewhat different way than you declare applications.

The following is a small Java applet that prints the words "Hello World".

```java
import java.applet.Applet;
import java.awt.Graphics;
/**
 * A simple Java applet that illustrates textual output.
 *
 * @author Samuel A. Rebelsky
 * @version 1.0 of June 1999
 */
public class HelloWorldApplet
  extends Applet
{
  /**
   * Print/draw the string "Hello world".
   */
  public void paint(Graphics paintBrush) {
    paintBrush.drawString("Hello world", 10, 20);
  } // paint(Graphics)
} // class HelloWorldApplet
```

You might include this applet in a Web page as follows.

```html
<html>
  <head>
    <title>A Sample Applet</title>
  </head>
  <body>
    <applet code="HelloWorldApplet.class" width="400" height="300">
    </applet>
  </body>
</html>
```

As you may have noticed, many things set `HelloWorldApplet.java` apart from our `HelloWorld.java` application:

- There is no `main` method.
- There is, instead, a `paint` method.
  - While `main` has `String[] args` as a parameter, `paint` has `Graphics paintBrush` as a parameter.
  - While `main` is <u>static</u>, `paint` is not.
- While `HelloWorld` imports `SimpleOutput`, `HelloWorldApplet` imports both `java.applet.Applet` and `java.awt.Graphics`.
- While `HelloWorld` must declare and create a new `SimpleOutput` object, `HelloWorldApplet` does not declare any variables and never calls <u>new</u>.
- While the `println` method took only the string to print as a parameter, `drawString` takes two numbers in addition.

Let's consider these differences. We begin by noting the way in which Web browsers and other things that run applets operate.

- First, the browser loads the class specified in an HTML file (or elsewhere, if appropriate).
- It then creates a new object corresponding to that class. (Recall that a class can act as a template for the object.)
- If the class has an `init` method, the browser calls that. Our `HelloWorldApplet` does not, so the browser ignores it.
- Finally, the browser calls the `paint` method and supplies a `Graphics` object. A `Graphics` object, like a `SimpleOutput` object, is a utility object that helps you put information on the screen. (`Graphics` is a standard object; `SimpleOutput` was developed for this laboratory manual.)

We are now ready to look at the individual parts.

Imported classes

```
import java.applet.Applet;
import java.awt.Graphics;
```

These statements tell Java that you will be using two helper classes. One, called `Applet`, is part of the standard Java distribution (specified by `java.`) and is one of the applet classes (specified by `applet.`). The other, called `Graphics`, is also part of the standard Java distribution, and is one of the abstract windowing toolkit classes (specified by `awt.`).

Class header

```
public class HelloWorldApplet
   extends Applet
```

This class header looks a lot like our other class declarations, but adds the "<u>extends</u> `Applet`". This new phrase tells Java that your new class is an applet rather than an application. Whenever you write an applet, you need to include this phrase.

Method header

```
public void paint(Graphics paintBrush) {
```

Many applets paint/draw pictures on the screen. They know when to do so because the browser calls their `paint` method. They use a `Graphics` object (which we call `paintBrush`) to do the actual painting.

Method body

```
paintBrush.drawString("Hello world", 10, 20);
```

This statement tells the Graphics object to draw the string *"Hello world"* ten units from the left of the applet's drawing area, and twenty units from the top of the applet's drawing area.

HTML code

```
<applet code="HelloWorldApplet.class" width="400" height="300">
</applet>
```

This HTML tag tells the browser to load the applet named `HelloWorldApplet`, which is stored in the file `HelloWorldApplet.class`. The tag gives the applet a space in the Web page with a width of four-hundred units and a height of 300-hundred units.

We have neither time nor space here to introduce HTML, the Hypertext Markup Language used for the World Wide Web. You can use the document above as a template and experiment on your own.

In Experiment J1.6, you will begin your exploration of applets. In Experiment J1.7, you will explore some of the things that can go wrong when you use applets.

Experiments

Name: _____

ID: _____

**Experiment J1.1:
Executing your
first program**

Required files:

- `SimpleOutput.java`
- `HelloWorld.java`

Step 1. Make a copy of the two required programs, compile them, and execute `HelloWorld`. Record the results. Your instructor will provide you with information on copying files, compiling Java programs, and executing compiled Java programs.

Step 2. Rename `HelloWorld.java` as `helloworld.java` (i.e., change the capitalization) and try to recompile it. Record any error messages you observe. What do those error messages suggest about Java?

When you have entered your response, rename `helloworld.java` to `HelloWorld.java`.

The following steps are primarily applicable to command-line development environments, like Sun's JDK.

Step 3. Remove `SimpleOutput.java` (source code) but keep `SimpleOutput.class` (compiled code) and the two versions of `HelloWorld`. (Your directory or folder should contain only `HelloWorld.java`, `HelloWorld.class`, and `SimpleOutput.class`.) Execute `HelloWorld`. Record the results. If the program doesn't work, suggest why not. If the program continues to work, suggest why.

Step 4. Make another copy of `SimpleOutput.java` (source code) and delete `SimpleOutput.class` (compiled code). (Your directory or folder should contain only `HelloWorld.java`, `HelloWorld.class`, and `Simple-Output.java`.) Execute `HelloWorld`. Record the results. If the program doesn't work, suggest why not. If the program continues to work, suggest why.

Step 5. Compile `SimpleOutput.java`. Delete the line from `Hello-World.java` that reads

<u>import</u> SimpleOutput;

Try to recompile and execute the program. If the program successfully recompiles, suggest why. If it does not, suggest why not.

After entering an answer, you may wish to read the notes on this problem.

Step 6. Remove `SimpleOutput.java` (source code), `SimpleOutput.class` (object code), and `HelloWorld.class` (object code). You should now have only `HelloWorld.java` in your directory or folder. Attempt to recompile and execute `HelloWorld`. If the program successfully recompiles, suggest why. If it does not, suggest why not.

Step 7. Make a copy of `SimpleOutput.java`. Delete `HelloWorld.class` if it exists. You should now have `SimpleOutput.java` and `Hel-loWorld.java` in your folder or directory. Try to recompile and execute `HelloWorld`. Does it compile successfully? Did you expect it to? Did any new files appear in your directory? What does this suggest about Java?

Experiment J1.2: Extending your first program

Required files:

- `SimpleOutput.java`
- `HelloWorld.java`

Before you begin, if you have not done so already, make copies of `Simple-Output.java` and `HelloWorld.java` and compile them.

Step 1. Insert the following lines to `HelloWorld.java` right before the end of the main method.

```
out.print("Welcome to Java.");
out.println("We hope you enjoy yourself.");
```

Execute `HelloWorld`. Record the output. Is this what you expected? If not, suggest why not.

Step 2. Recompile `HelloWorld.java` and then execute it. Record the output. Did you get what you expected? If not, suggest why not.

Step 3. What do the results of the first two steps suggest?

Step 4. What is the difference between `print` and `println`?

Step 5. Replace the line in `HelloWorld.java` that reads

```
out.println("Hello World");
```

with one that reads

```
println("Hello World");
```

Recompile and execute the program. What happens? What does this suggest about Java?

If you introduced any errors in this step, repair them.

Step 6. Replace the line in `HelloWorld.java` that reads

```
SimpleOutput out = new SimpleOutput();
```

with one that reads

```
SimpleOutput out;
```

Recompile and execute the program. What happens? What does this suggest about Java? If you introduced any errors, repair them.

Experiment J1.3: When things go wrong

Required files:

- `SimpleInput.java`
- `SimpleOutput.java`
- `Greetings.java`

In case you've forgotten, here is the code for `Greetings.java`.

```java
import SimpleInput;
import SimpleOutput;
/**
 * A simple Java program that illustrates textual input and output.
 *
 * @author Samuel A. Rebelsky
 * @version 1.1 of March 1998
 */
public class Greetings {
  /**
   * Prompt for the user's name and print a greeting.
   */
  public static void main(String[] args) {
    // The object we're using to read input.
    SimpleInput in = new SimpleInput();
    // The object we're using to print output.
    SimpleOutput out = new SimpleOutput();
    // The user's name.
    String name;
    // Prompt for the name.
    out.print("What is your name? ");
    // Get the name.
    name = in.readString();
    // Print a friendly message.
    out.print("Hello ");
    out.print(name);
```

```
    out.println(", welcome to the joys of Java.");
  } // main(String[])
} // Welcome
```

Step 1. If you have not already done so, make a copy of the required programs, compile them, and execute Greetings. Record the results.

Step 2. At times, programmers forget to enter the quote that ends a string. Replace the line that reads

```
out.print("Hello ");
```

with one that reads

```
out.print("Hello );
```

(i.e., remove the ending quotation mark). What difference do you expect this change to make?

Step 3. Attempt to recompile and execute Greetings. What happened? Why?

After entering your answers, correct the error.

Step 4. Another common mistake is to leave out semicolons. Replace the line that reads

```
String name;
```

with one that reads

```
String name
```

(i.e., drop the semicolon). What difference do you expect this change to make?

Step 5. Attempt to recompile and execute `Greetings`. What happened? Why?

After entering your answers, correct the error.

Step 6. Replace the line that reads

```
out.print("What is your name? ");
```

with one that reads

```
out.print("What is your name? ")
```

(that is, drop the semicolon). What difference do you expect this change to make? After recording your answer, attempt to recompile and execute `Greetings`. Explain what happened.

After entering your answers, correct the error.

Step 7. What do your answers to Steps 5 and 6 suggest?

Step 8. Another common mistake is to mistype a variable name. For example, we might decide to use `output` instead of `out`. Change only the line that reads

```
SimpleOutput out = new SimpleOutput();
```

to read

```
SimpleOutput output = new SimpleOutput();
```

What difference do you expect this change to make? After recording your answer, attempt to recompile and execute `Greetings`. Explain what happened.

After entering your answers, correct the error.

Step 9. Yet another common mistake is to forget to end multi-line comments. Remove the `*/` that appears just before

<u>public</u> <u>class</u> Greetings {

What difference do you expect this change to make? After recording your answer, attempt to recompile and execute Greetings. Explain what happened.

After entering your answers, correct the error.

Step 10. Remove the "`*/`" that appears just before

<u>public</u> <u>static</u> <u>void</u> main(String[] args) {

What difference do you expect this change to make? After recording your answer, attempt to recompile and execute Greetings. Explain what happened.

After entering your answers, correct the error.

Step 11. It is likely that your answers for Steps 9 and 10 were different. Can you explain why?

Experiment J1.4: Executing and extending a program with input

Required files:

- SimpleInput.java
- SimpleOutput.java
- Greetings.java

Step 1. If you have not already done so, make a copy of the required programs, compile them, and execute Greetings. Record the results.

Step 2. Extend the program to read in some other fact about the user (e.g., a major or home town) and to print out a response to that fact. Before making the changes, write down the new lines of code. After extending the program, you should recompile and execute the program.

If you make mistakes, the Java compiler will print some error messages. Write down any error messages you receive and a possible explanation of those errors.

Step 3. Remove the semicolon after

```
import SimpleInput;
```

Try to recompile the program. Record the error messages. Reinsert the semicolon to repair the error you just created.

Step 4. Remove other semicolons from the program and try to recompile. What semicolons did you remove and what error messages did you get? Record the error messages and corresponding semicolons. Repair those errors.

Experiment J1.5: Numeric input and output

Required files:

- `BasicComputations.java`
- `SimpleInput.java`
- `SimpleOutput.java`

Before you begin, if you haven't done so already, obtain copies of `SimpleInput.java` and `SimpleOutput.java` and compile them.

Step 1. Obtain a copy of `BasicComputations.java`, compile it, and execute it. Try a variety of inputs (small numbers, large numbers, positive numbers, negative numbers, things that aren't numbers) and record the results for each input. What do the results suggest about Java's treatment of numbers?

Step 2. After the line that prints the square in `BasicComputations.java`, add lines that read

```
out.print(val);
out.print(" + 1 is ");
out.println(val+1);
```

What do you think this will do? Compile and execute the program to test your hypothesis. Record any discrepancies and suggest why such discrepancies might occur.

Step 3. Change all the instances of `double` to `int`. Change `readDouble` to `readInt`. Recompile the program. Execute the program and enter the value `2`. Record the output. Execute the program and enter the value `2.4`. Record the output. What does this suggest?

Experiment J1.6:
Your first applet

Optional applet experiment

Required files:

- `HelloWorldApplet.java`
- `helloworld.html`

Step 1. Make a copy of the two files. Compile `HelloWorldApplet.java`. Load the applet, using whatever technique your instructor specifies. (You might load it in a browser like Netscape Navigator or Microsoft Internet Explorer; you might run an application like Sun's appletviewer.) Describe the output.

Step 2. In `helloworld.html`, change the width of the applet from 400 to 20. What do you expect will happen when you reload the applet?

Step 3. Reload the applet, using the modified `helloworld.html`. What happened? Explain why.

After recording your answer, restore the width to 400.

Step 4. Explain how to update this program to print *"Hi there!"* rather than *"Hello world"*.

Step 5. Make the change you suggested in the previous step, recompile `HelloWorldApplet`, and run it. If you did not get the expected results, update your answer to Step 4, and try again.

Step 6. Change the line that reads

`paintBrush.drawString("Hello world", 10, 20);`

to one that reads

`paintBrush.drawString("Hello world", 100, 20);`

What effect do you expect this change to have?

Step 7. Recompile `HelloWorldApplet` and run it. What results did you observe? What do these results tell you about the second parameter to `drawString`?

When you are done, change that parameter from 100 back to 10.

Step 8. Change the line that reads

```
paintBrush.drawString("Hello world", 10, 20);
```

to one that reads

```
paintBrush.drawString("Hello world", 10, 100);
```

What effect do you expect this change to have?

Step 9. Recompile `HelloWorldApplet` and run it. What results did you observe? What do these results tell you about the third parameter to `drawString`?

When you are done, change that parameter from 100 back to 20.

Step 10. What code might you write to print `"Hello"` at the top left of the screen and `"Goodbye"` at the bottom right?

Step 11. Try including that code in `HelloWorldApplet`. Recompile and run it. If necessary, keep experimenting until you get it right.

Experiment J1.7: Some common applet errors

Optional applet experiment

Required files:

- `HelloWorldApplet.java`
- `helloworld.html`

Before you begin, if you have not already done so, make a copy of the required files, compile `HelloWorldApplet`, run it, and record the results.

Step 1. Remove the line that reads

`extends Applet`

What effect do you expect this change to have?

Step 2. Attempt to recompile and execute `HelloWorldApplet`. What happens? Explain why.

After you are done, restore the line that reads

`extends Applet`

Step 3. Remove the line that reads

`import java.awt.Graphics;`

What effect do you expect this change to have?

Step 4. Attempt to recompile and execute `HelloWorldApplet`. What happens? Explain why.

After you are done, restore the line that reads

`import java.awt.Graphics;`

Step 5. Change the line that reads

`public void paint(Graphics paintBrush) {`

to one that reads

`public static void paint(Graphics paintBrush) {`

What effect do you expect this change to have?

Step 6. Attempt to recompile and execute `HelloWorldApplet`. What happens? Explain why.

After you are done, restore the line that reads

`public void paint(Graphics paintBrush) {`

Step 7. Make a copy of `HelloWorldApplet.java` called `Example.java`. Replace the body of `paint` with

`paintBrush.drawString("An example applet");`

What do you expect to happen when you try to compile `Example.java`? Try to compile it and explain the error messages.

Step 8. Replace all the instances of `HelloWorldApplet` in `Example.java` with `Example`. What do you expect to happen when you try to compile it? Verify your answer by trying to compile it.

Step 9. Hopefully, `Example` compiled successfully. Next, make a copy of `helloworld.html` called `example.html`. Run your new applet using `example.html`. What happens? Why?

Step 10. If you have not already realized that you need to do so, update `example.html` so that it uses `Example.`<u>`class`</u> instead of `Hello-World.`<u>`class`</u>.

Post-Laboratory Problems

Problem J1-A:
Generating verse

Write a Java program that prints your favorite poem or short piece of verse. If you have no favorite writing, consider using Lewis Carroll's *Jabberwocky*.

> 'Twas brillig and the slithy toves
>   did gyre and gimble in the wabe.
> All mimsy were the borogoves
>   and the mome raths outgrabe.

Problem J1-B:
Name replication

Write a Java program that asks for a person's name and then prints the name one time, then two times, then three times, and then four times. For example, if the user entered `William`, your program would print

```
William
William William
William William William
William William William William
```

Problem J1-C:
Errors galore

The following Java program contains a large number of errors. Identify as many as you can by hand and suggest how to correct them. Once you have done so, enter the revised program in the computer and attempt to compile it. Record any errors the compiler reports and attempt to correct those errors. Note that once you have corrected some errors the compiler may then report additional errors.

```
impart SimpleInpt
import SimpleOutput();
/**
 * A very erroneous program.
 *
 * @author Samuel A. Rebelsky
 * @version 1.0 of March 1998
public class Erroneous (
  /**
   * Do something.
   */
  public void main(String() args) {
    SimpleInput in = new SimpleInput;
    SimpleOutput out = old SimpleOutput;
    double val
    Out.print("Please enter a number: );
    val - in.readdouble();
    in.print(val - 1 + " is " + val - 1);
  { / /main(String[])
}}
```

**Problem J1-D:
Predicting
output**

What do you think will happen when a user runs the following program and enters `Lewis Carroll` on one line? Separate lines?

```java
import SimpleInput;
import SimpleOutput;
/**
 * Illustrate textual input and output.
 *
 * Copyright (c) 1998 Samuel A. Rebelsky.  All rights reserved.
 *
 * @author Samuel A. Rebelsky
 * @version 1.0 of March 1998
 */
public class Namer {
  /**
   * Ask for a name and do some funny things with it.
   */
  public static void main(String[] args) {
    // Set up input and output.
    SimpleInput in = new SimpleInput();
    SimpleOutput out = new SimpleOutput();
    // The person's first name
    String first_name;
    // The person's last name
    String last_name;
    // Get the name
    out.print("Please enter your full name: ");
    first_name = in.readString();
    last_name = in.readString();
    out.println("I will record your name in my database as " +
            last_name + ", " + first_name + ".");
  } // main(String[])
} // Namer
```

**Problem J1-E:
Temperature
conversion**

Reflect on the previous programs and see if you can design a program that converts Celsius to Fahrenheit. Use the conversion formula

$$F = C * (9.0/5.0) + 32.0$$

Begin by designing your program on paper, rather than on the computer! Experience shows that we do much better when we design before coding. At this stage in your career, you should first design on paper, then sketch your code on paper. Only once you've sketched the code should you move to the computer.

**Problem J1-F:
Bar graphs**

Write a program that creates a bar graph for the following fictitious data on Web browser usage:

```
Internet Explorer35%
Netscape Navigator40%
HotJava10%
Other10%
```

Model your output after the following example:

```
   Lines of code in "Hello World"
C:****
C (w/comments):*******
Java:*******
Java (w/comments):********************
Pascal:******
Pascal (w/comments):**********
Scheme:*
Scheme (w/comments):**
|   |    |    |    |
1   5    10   15   20
```

Notes

The `main` method. You may recall that a class's `main` method is declared as

`public static void main(String[] args)`

What does everything mean?

The "`main`" names the method. Every Java application needs a `main` method. When you execute a Java application, the Java interpreter knows to start with `main`.

The `main` method must be `public`, which means that the method can be called by other classes and other objects. Arguably, something else (the Java interpreter) is calling this class, so it must be public.

The `main` method must be `static`, which means that it is associated with the class as a whole and not just with individual objects. In general, Java methods are associated with objects, and can only be used if you've created a corresponding object. Since we don't always want to create objects for our applications, `main` is `static`.

The `main` method has type `void`, which means that the method does not return a value. Many methods are like mathematical functions. For example, we might say that a square-root function (method) returns a number, and a "make up a nonsense word" method returns a word. Because our program will not "return" values (simply interact with the user), it needs this `void`.

The terms in parentheses are the parameters to the method. Many methods have parameters. For example, a square-root function would take a number as a parameter, and a "translate to Pig Latin" function might take a word as a parameter. The `args` gives us a name for the parameter. The `String[]` says that this parameter is a list of words ("`Strings`" in Java parlance).

Where do these strings come from? Java, at least in part, comes from an environment (Unix) in which programs are typically invoked from a command line (as in DOS). In addition to specifying the name of the program, you can add information that helps the program work. For example, the

Unix "print" command accepts files to print as parameters and can also accept information on which printer to use. The designers of Java knew that many programmers would need similar capabilities. You won't need those capabilities in your early programs, but you might need them later.

Aren't you sorry you didn't wait?

Experiment J1.1, Step 4. In some cases, the Java interpreter is smart enough to find related classes, even without an explicit `import` statement. However, good practice dictates that you use such statements.

Session J2: Objects and Methods

In this laboratory session, you will build and use your first Java objects and develop your first Java classes. The purposes of this lab session are to

- introduce object-oriented programming, including the concepts of *object* and *class;*
- introduce Java's version of modular programming, in which different portions of a program are placed in different files;
- introduce *methods,* small subprograms that you write and include in classes; and
- prepare you for some of the difficulties of dealing with objects.

Your instructor will tell you which of the proposed experiments you are to perform.

Prerequisite skills:

- Editing, compiling, and executing Java programs
- Basic Java programming (including the `main` method)

Required Java files:

- `AverageTester.java`
- `JustPlaneFun.java`
- `Plane.java`
- `Point.java`
- `PointFun.java`
- `PointPrinter.java`
- `PointReader.java`
- `SimpleInput.java`
- `SimpleOutput.java`
- `TextPlane.java`
- `TextPlaneFun.java`

Optional applet files:

- `circle.html`
- `CircleApplet.java`

- `helloworld.html`
- `HelloWorldApplet.java`

Discussion

Objects

You may have heard that Java is an *object-oriented* language. What does that mean? Being an object-oriented language means that Java programs are collections of *objects* that communicate with each other. An object can be almost anything, from a number to a virtual person. Each object has certain attributes, such as the value of the number or the eye color of the virtual person. In addition, each object has certain abilities, which are provided by *methods*. For example, a number might be able to add itself to another number, a virtual person might be able to blink, and an electronic book might be able to tell you where to find information on a particular topic.

In Java, objects are grouped into *classes*. A class specifies the methods each object provides and the kinds and names of attributes each object in the class has. Objects differ in the particular values associated with attributes. In addition, objects with different values for their attributes will most likely work differently. For example, adding the number 2 is different from adding the number 3.

What does this mean in terms of the nitty-gritty details? In particular, how do you use objects when you are programming? As you've seen, Java programs are based on a `main` method. You can use this method to create objects and then tell them to do things (you ask them to execute methods). In fact, in the experiments you did in the previous lab, you may have created `SimpleInput` and `SimpleOutput` objects. You then used the `SimpleOutput` objects to write output to the computer screen and the `SimpleInput` objects to read input from the keyboard. You've also used Java's built-in `String` objects.

What objects can you use other than these three objects? Java comes with thousands of built-in objects. More importantly, you can define your own objects. Today, you will use and extend an existing class, `Point`. You will also build your own very simple classes, `PointPrinter` and `PointReader`.

Creating objects

To use an object in Java, you must first create the object and make a variable refer to that object. For example, to create a new `SimpleOutput` object and have `out` refer to it, we use

```
SimpleOutput out = new SimpleOutput();
```

As this suggests, you need the `new` command to create objects. In addition, you need to *construct* the object you are creating. A *constructor* is a method used to create new objects that initializes the values of the object.

For example, suppose we had a class of objects representing dates, with corresponding year, month, and day. In order to create a new date, we'd need to specify the year, month, and day. Hence, the constructor would need three values. Here's an example in which we create the date April 1, 1998.

```
SimpleDate date = new SimpleDate(1998, 4, 1);
```

Note that the year, month, and day are given as values in parentheses following the name of the class. These are called the *parameters* to the constructor. (You may also see them referred to as *arguments, actual parameters,* or *actuals.*)

How did I know which order to use when building the object? I looked at the <u>documentation</u>. The person who designs a class determines the available constructors and the order in which *parameters* to constructors are supplied. The clients of a class must consult documentation to determine which constructors are available and how they should be used.

Similarly, if we were to create the point (2,3) in the plane, we might write

```
Point pt = new Point(2,3);
```

Note that we didn't need any parameters when creating a new `SimpleOutput` object. That's because the default for these objects is to print to the screen and they don't need any other information. There is also a no parameter constructor for `Point` that creates a point at (0,0).

What can you do with a point once you've created one? It's somewhat up to the designer. You might move it left, right, up, or down. You might ask for its value or its distance from the origin.

The following is a simple program that creates a point, moves it a little, and then prints out a little bit of information about it.

```
import Point;

/**
 * Build a point and move it around.
 *
 * @version 1.1 of September 1998
 * @author Samuel A. Rebelsky
 */
public class PointFun {
  /**
   * Build a point and move it around.
   */
  public static void main(String[] args) {
    // We'll be generating some output.
    SimpleOutput out = new SimpleOutput();
    // The point we'll be playing with.
    Point pt = new Point(2,3);
    // Print some basic information.
    out.println("(" + pt.getX() + "," + pt.getY() + ")");
    out.println("  distance from origin: " +
            pt.distanceFromOrigin());
    // Move it right a little bit.
    out.println("Shifting right by 0.7");
    pt.shiftRight(0.7);
```

```
    // Print current information.
    out.println("(" + pt.getX() + "," + pt.getY() + ")");
    out.println("  distance from origin: " +
                pt.distanceFromOrigin());
    // Move it up a little bit.
    out.println("Shifting up by 2.5");
    pt.shiftUp(2.5);
    // Print current information.
    out.println("(" + pt.getX() + "," + pt.getY() + ")");
    out.println("  distance from origin: " +
                pt.distanceFromOrigin());
    // Move it left a little bit.
    out.println("Shifting left by 10.2");
    pt.shiftLeft(10.2);
    // Print current information.
    out.println("(" + pt.getX() + "," + pt.getY() + ")");
    out.println("  distance from origin: " +
                pt.distanceFromOrigin());
  } // main(String[])
} // class PointFun
```

What should you observe about this? First, that whenever we need information from an object we need to request it by calling a method. Second, that the ability to get information does not tell us much about how the object is designed (we'll come back to this later). For example, is the distance of the point from the origin stored within the point or only computed on demand?

In Experiment J2.1 you will consider some issues in using and printing points.

Coordinating objects

While it is certainly useful to deal with points numerically, many times we want to see them plotted on the plane. If we were given a `Plane` class, how might we plot some points?

```
Build a new Plane object.
For each point,
  Build a new point.
  Plot it.
```

Here is a simple class that does just that.

```
import Plane;

/**
 * A simple attempt to play with the Plane and Point classes.
 *
 * @version 1.0 of May 1998
 * @author Samuel A. Rebelsky
 */
public class JustPlaneFun {
  /**
   * Build a plane and display it.
   */
  public static void main(String[] args) {
```

```
   // Build the plane.
   Plane plane = new Plane();
   // Plot a few points.
   plane.plot(new Point(1,3));
   plane.plot(new Point(-2.5,4));
   plane.plot(new Point(4,-5.2));
 } // main(String[])
} // class JustPlaneFun
```

You should observe a number of things about this class.

- It contains only a `main` method. In general, this design is a good one to follow. One class will contain only the `main` method. The other classes will do the actual work.
- The `main` method creates a number of objects in different contexts (not only a `Plane`, but also `Points`).
- It is possible to create objects without naming them. Since `plot` requires a `Point`, we can create one on the fly.
- We don't need to know about the implementation of `Plane` in order to use it successfully. All we need to know is that we can add points with `plot`.

In Experiment J2.2, you will consider how one uses the `Point` and `Plane` classes together, using the `JustPlaneFun` class to coordinate the two.

Building your own methods

Note that in our experiments and programs above, we had a number of operations in common. In `PointFun.java`, we printed the point in the same way again and again and again. If we made a change in the way we decided to print points, we'd need to modify a great deal of code. It would be useful to write the instructions once and then simply say something like "print out this point."

Similarly, in the experiments we needed to write instructions for reading in a point in different programs (both in `PointFun.java` and `JustPlane-Fun.java`). Here it would be useful to just write "read in a point."

Can we create such shorthands? Yes! We will make a copy of `Point.java` and develop *methods* that provide the shorthands.

What is involved in a method definition? Four things:

- The keyword `public`, which indicates that the method is generally accessible. (That is, any program that creates an appropriate object can use this method of the object.)
- The *type* of the method. Many methods return values. The *type* indicates what is returned. If the method doesn't return anything, we say that the type is `void`.
- The *name* of the method. Method names traditionally begin with a lowercase letter and consist of lowercase letters, uppercase letters, and numbers.
- The *formal parameters* (also *formals* or *parameters*) of the method. The method uses these "inputs" to do computation. A method that prints a

point will use a `SimpleOutput` object. (It also uses the point to be printed, but that will be handled implicitly.) A method that reads in a point will need a `SimpleInput` object. Each formal parameter is described with (1) a *type* and (2) a *name*. Note that the formal parameter gives a name to the parameter for use within the method. The names of the formal and actual parameters do not need to match.

It is also helpful to begin each method with a short comment that describes what the method does.

We now have the tools to build a method that prints out a point and its distance from the origin. We will add this method to the `Point` class. What parameters will this method need? The `SimpleOutput` object that does the printing. Why is there no parameter for the point to print? Because Java's object-oriented design suggests that each point will provide this method, hence the point to print is implicit. (Just as we write `pt.getX()`, we'll write `pt.print(out)`.)

The method header therefore begins

```
public void print(SimpleOutput out) {
```

What does the body of the method look like? More or less like the code we used elsewhere.

```
out.println("(" + this.getX() + "," + this.getY() + ")");
out.println("  distance from origin: " +
            this.distanceFromOrigin());
```

The `this` refers to the current object. Since `getX` and `getY` must be called for a particular object, we need to specify that object. Since we want to print the current object, we use `this`.

As always, you must end the method with a right curly brace.

How do we use our new method? Just like the methods we've used in the past. We create the object and then call the method.

```
Point pt = new Point(2,3);
pt.print(out);
Point another = new Point(4,2);
another.print(out);
```

What should you observe about this new method? First, we've added a name to some common code and *parameterized* that common code, which means that we can use it even with points with different names.

In Experiment J2.3 you will add the new `print` method to the `Point` class.

Creating your own classes

What if you'd like to write `print`, but you do not have access to the source code for `Point`? (In commercial settings, you will rarely have access to the source code for the classes you use.) As you will see in a later session, you can extend existing classes. However, that is beyond this introductory session. For now, the best solution may be to create your own new class that knows how to print points. Whenever you want to print a point, you create an object in this class. Some programmers consider such *helper classes* an odd design tactic. However, at this point in your career, you will find many benefits from using them.

How do we begin a new class? As in past experiments, begin with

```
public class PointPrinter {
```

In this case, the `print` method will need to take two parameters: not just the output object, but also the explicit point to print. The method will begin

```
public void print(SimpleOutput out, Point pt) {
```

What does the body of the method look like? More or less like the code we used elsewhere.

```
out.println("(" + pt.getX() + "," + pt.getY() + ")");
out.println("  distance from origin: " +
            pt.distanceFromOrigin());
```

And, as always, we end our method with a right curly brace. Putting it all together and adding a few short comments, we get

```
import Point;
import SimpleOutput;

/**
 * Some utilities for printing points.
 */
public class PointPrinter {

  // +---------+-----------------------------------------------
  // | Methods |
  // +---------+
  /**
   * Print a point using a particular output object.    */
  public void print(SimpleOutput out, Point pt) {
    out.println("(" + pt.getX() + "," + pt.getY() + ")");
    out.println("  distance from origin: " +
                pt.distanceFromOrigin());
  } // print(SimpleOutput, Point)
} // class PointPrinter
How do we use our new class? We create a new object in the class and
then call its method, as in
PointPrinter printer = new PointPrinter();
Point pt = new Point(2,3);
printer.print(out,pt);
Point another = new Point(4,2);
printer.print(out,another);
```

What should you observe about this new class? First, we've once again added a name to some common code and *parameterized* that common code, which means that we can use it even with points with different names. Second, in order to use the new method, we need to create an object that provides that method. For now, this will be your model for programming in

Java: when you need a new method, you'll need to put it in a class and create an object that provides the method, which fits in well with Java's object-oriented paradigm.

In Experiment J2.4 you will experiment with this newly-created class.

Return values

So far, all of the methods we've created have modified the object or printed output. At times, we want to write methods that return values. For example, we might want to write methods that give the x coordinate of a point or the distance of a point from the origin.

How do we write methods that return values? It turns out that it's not much different than writing methods that do not return values. First, you need to determine what type will be returned (e.g., integer, string, etc.). In the declaration for the method, you need to write that type, as in

```
public type method(...) {
  ...
} // method(...)
```

For example, we might declare getX as

```
public int getX() {
  ...
} // getX()
```

Next, we need to specify which value to return from the method. We do this with a return statement, as in

```
public int getX() {
  return xcoordinate;
} \\ getX()
```

Similarly, to return the average of two numbers, you might write

```
/**
 * Compute the average of two doubles.
 */
public double average(double a, double b) {
  double ave (a + b) / 2;
  return ave;
} // average(double,double)
```

In Experiment J2.5 you will create a simple class that can compute averages.

Static methods

You may have found it awkward to need to create a new helper object (in this case PointPrinter) every time you needed a helper method (in this case, print). This may be especially true if you've worked in other languages in which it is possible to define methods separate from objects and classes.

If you are sure that you need an object-independent method, Java permits you to create so-called *static methods* (also called *class methods*). Such methods are associated with particular classes, but do not require the creation of objects to use them.

For example, let's suppose that we wanted to write a method that reads in x and y coordinates and returns a point. Here's a sketch of the body of that method.

```
float x;  // The x coordinate
float y;  // The y coordinate
out.print("Enter the x coordinate: ");
x = in.readFloat();
out.print("Enter the y coordinate: ");
y = in.readFloat();
return new Point(x,y);
```

We'll place this method in a class called `PointReader`. Now, suppose that we want to be able to use that method without creating a new `PointReader`. We can declare the method as `static`, as in

```
static public Point read(SimpleOutput out, SimpleInput in) {
```

If you place this method within `PointReader`, you can refer to it as `PointReader.read`. If you create an object, `reader`, of class `PointReader`, you can also refer to this method as `helper.read`.

Experience shows that static methods often lead to problems for beginning programmers. Hence, static methods will be used rarely, if at all, in subsequent exercises.

In Experiment J2.6, you will consider some issues pertaining to static methods.

Detour: The main method

By now, you may have realized that all of those `main` methods you've been creating are, in fact, `static` methods. As you might guess, Java's `main` is `static` so that you do not need to create a new object in order to run it. In fact, when you execute a class, you are actually telling the Java virtual machine to call the `main` method of that class.

Assigning objects

One of the more confusing aspects of Java is the treatment of variables that store references to objects. Objects, like `Point`s and `String`s, are treated differently than primitive values, like integers. In particular, when you assign integer variables, the value is copied from one to another. However, when you assign objects, a *reference* is copied. In effect, Java allows multiple variables to refer to the same object.

For example, consider the following code:

```
SimpleOutput out = new SimpleOutput();
int a;
int b;
a = 3;
b = a;
a = 2;
```

```
out.print("a = " + a);
out.print(", ");
out.println("b = " + b);
b = 10;
out.print("a = " + a);
out.print(", ");
out.println("b = " + b);
```

This code will print out

```
a = 2, b = 3
a = 2, b = 10
```

This suggests that the value stored in variable a is copied to variable b in the line

```
b = a
```

but that no relationship between the two is maintained.

As a contrast, consider the following code:

```
SimpleOutput out = new SimpleOutput();
Point p1 = new Point(2,3);
Point p2 = p1;
out.println("Originally");
out.println("p1: (" + p1.getX() + "," + p1.getY() + ")");
out.println("p2: (" + p2.getX() + "," + p2.getY() + ")");

p1.shiftLeft(4);
out.println("After shifting p1 left 4");
out.println("p1: (" + p1.getX() + "," + p1.getY() + ")");
out.println("p2: (" + p2.getX() + "," + p2.getY() + ")");

p2.shiftUp(3);
out.println("After shifting p2 up 3");
out.println("p1: (" + p1.getX() + "," + p1.getY() + ")");
out.println("p2: (" + p2.getX() + "," + p2.getY() + ")");
```

This code will print out

```
Originally
p1: (2,3)
p2: (2,3)
After shifting p1 left 4
p1: (-2,3)
p2: (-2,3)
After shifting p2 up 3
p1: (-2,6)
p2: (-2,6)
```

In this case, both p1 and p2 refer to the same Point object. Hence, a change made to that object through p1 is reflected in p2 and vice-versa.

In many ways, this corresponds to our normal sense of objects. Each "real world" object has many names. For example, you might call your teacher "Professor Smith" and one of your fellow students might call your teacher "Teach". If you give "Professor Smith" an apple, then your fellow student will still be able to note that "Teach" has an apple.

But this association is not permanent. You are free to change which object a variable refer to. For example, consider the following code

```
Point p1 = new Point(2,3);
Point p2 = p1;
out.println("(" + p1.getX() + "," + p1.getY() + ")");
out.println("(" + p2.getX() + "," + p2.getY() + ")");
p2 = new Point(1,1);
out.println("(" + p1.getX() + "," + p1.getY() + ")");
out.println("(" + p2.getX() + "," + p2.getY() + ")");
```

This code will print

```
(2,3)
(2,3)
(2,3)
(1,1)
```

This output happens because the assignment to `p2` changed the reference and not the object. Again, this effect corresponds to our normal sense of naming. If you take computer science from Professor Smith and mathematics from Professor Jones, then you might use "Teach" to refer to Professor Smith during computer science and Professor Jones during mathematics. When you ask "Teach" a question, who you ask depends on who "Teach" currently refers to.

In Experiment J2.7, you will consider some issues relating to assigning objects.

Fonts and graphics for applets

This section is optional and is intended for classes emphasizing applets or pursuing a simultaneous discussion of applications and applets.

The applets you created in the first laboratory session were relatively primitive. All they did was print a simple message, in some font that the applet viewer or Web browser selected. Obviously, you'd like more abilities and control. In particular, most programmers expect to be able to draw pictures in their applets and to select the color and typeface for text.

As you might expect, much of this control has to do with objects and methods. In particular, there is a `Font` class (more particularly, `java.awt.Font`) that lets you create new objects for controlling the appearance of text. In addition, objects in the `java.awt.Graphics` class provide a number of methods for drawing other objects.

When you want to write text in a new font, you must first create a new `Font` object (or reuse an existing `Font` object) that specifies basic details of the font: the logical name (SansSerif, Serif, Monospaced, etc.), the size (10pt, 12pt, etc.), and the style (plain, bold, italic, or bold-italic). The command to create a new `Font` is

```
Font myFont = new Font(name, style, size)
```

where the style must be selected from `Font.PLAIN`, `Font.BOLD`, `Font.ITALIC`, or `Font.BOLD+Font.ITALIC`. For example,

```
Font myFont = new Font("Serif", Font.BOLD, 24);
```

Once you have selected a font, you must tell the graphics object to use that font with `setFont`. For example, the following `paint` method paints the string "Hello World" in a 24-point, bold, serif font.

```
public void paint(Graphics paintBrush) {
  Font myFont = new Font("Serif", Font.BOLD, 24);
  paintBrush.setFont(myFont);
  paintBrush.drawString("Hello World", 10, 40);
} // paint(Graphics)
```

Note that you cannot specify color as part of a font selection. Color is determined by the graphics object that does the actual drawing. You tell the graphics object what color to use with the `setColor` method. What colors can you use? The basic set consists of: `Color.black`, `Color.blue`, `Color.cyan`, `Color.darkGray`, `Color.gray`, `Color.green`, `Color.lightGray`, `Color.magenta`, `Color.orange`, `Color.pink`, `Color.red`, `Color.white`, and `Color.yellow`. For example, to draw the word "Hello" in green and "Goodbye" in red, I might write

```
paintBrush.setColor(Color.green);
paintBrush.drawString("Hello", 10, 30);
paintBrush.setColor(Color.red);
paintBrush.drawString("Goodbye", 15, 60);
```

What are all these `Color.xxx` things? They are *predefined* objects, specified within the library class `java.awt.Color`. Hence, in order to use any of these colors, you must import that class.

But these colors do not give you a very rich pallet. What if you want more colors? You can create your own colors. That is, you can create your own objects that are members of `java.awt.Color` and that give you more precise control than the basic colors. The easiest way to create a new color is by specifying red, green, and blue components (each a value between 0 and 255). For example,

```
Color myPurple = new Color(...);
```

You are encouraged to experiment with these components to see how they are used to form different colors.

But what about drawing something other than pieces of text? Java's `Graphics` objects provide a number of methods to support drawing shapes, including

- `paintBrush.drawOval(int left, int top, int width, int height)`
- `paintBrush.drawRect(int left, int top, int width, int height)`
- `paintBrush.fillRect(int left, int top, int width, int height)`
- `paintBrush.drawLine(int x1, int x2, int y1, int y2)`

In Experiment J2.8, you will make use of Java's `Font` and `Color` classes. In Experiment J2.9, you will test the various drawing primitives.

Experiments

Name: _____

ID: _____

Experiment J2.1: Printing out a point

Required code files:

- `Point.java`
- `PointFun.java`

Step 1. Make a copy of `Point.java`. Compile it. Try to execute it. Record your results. Compare your notes with the notes at the end of this lab.

Step 2. Make a copy of `PointFun.java`. Compile and execute it and record the results. Do you observe anything odd? What do you think is going on? For an explanation, turn to the end of this lab.

Step 3. Update the `main` method of `PointFun.java` so that it shifts the point five spaces right, five spaces up, ten spaces left, five spaces down, and then five spaces right, printing the position and distance from the origin each time. Record your code.

Step 4. Run your code and record any observations.

Step 5. Update the `main` method of `PointFun.java` to read in the initial x and y coordinates. Record your solution.

Experiment J2.2: Coordinating classes

There are two versions of this experiment. Experiment J2.2A is designed for students working on computers that include graphics displays. Experiment J2.2B is designed for students working on computers that only support textual displays (or for other classes that do not wish to use graphics).

Experiment J2.2A: Coordinating classes (graphical application)

Required code files:

- `Point.java`
- `Plane.java`
- `JustPlaneFun.java`

Step 1. Make copies of `Point.java`, `Plane.java`, and `JustPlaneFun.java`. Compile all three. Execute `JustPlaneFun` and record the results.

Step 2. Modify `JustPlaneFun` to use only one point that you move around. Start the point at (1,1) and shift the point right five, up five, left ten, down five, and right five, plotting it after each step. Execute the modified version and record the results. What do these results suggest?

Step 3. Modify `JustPlaneFun` to input the point to plot. Note that the point won't be plotted until after the `main` method terminates. Why? Because `main` just sets things in motion and `Plane` waits until `main` is done to display itself. Record your code.

Experiment J2.2B: Coordinating classes (textual application)

Required code files:

- `Point.java`
- `TextPlane.java`
- `TextPlaneFun.java`

Step 1. Make copies of `Point.java`, `TextPlane.java`, and `TextPlane-Fun.java`. Compile all three. Execute `TextPlaneFun` and summarize the output.

Step 2. Modify `JustPlaneFun` to use only one point that you move around. Start the point at (1,1) and shift the point right five, up five, left ten, down five, and right five, plotting it and displaying the plane after each step. Execute the modified version and record the results. What do these results suggest?

Step 3. Modify `JustPlaneFun` to input the point to plot. Record your code.

Step 4. Plot points at (0.5,0.5) and (1.2,2) and display the plane. Where does the point appear? What does that suggest?

**Experiment J2.3:
Your own
method**

Required code files:

- `Point.java`
- `PointFun.java`

Step 1. Modify `Point` so that it includes the new `print` method we developed earlier. Here is the code for that method.

```
/**
 * Print information about the current point.
 */
public void print(SimpleOutput out) {
  out.println("(" + this.getX() + "," + this.getY() + ")");
  out.println("  distance from origin: " +
              this.distanceFromOrigin());
} // print(SimpleOutput)
```

Step 2. Modify `PointFun` so that it uses the new `print` method to print the various points. Compile the various files and then execute `PointFun`. Summarize your changes to the program. Record the output from the program.

Step 3. Modify `Point` so that it prints out points as `<X,Y>` rather than `(X,Y)`. Recompile just `Point` and then execute `PointFun`. Record the results.

Step 4. Change all instances of `out` to `screen` in the `print` method of `Point`. Recompile just `Point` and then execute `PointFun`. Record the results. What happened? Was that what you expected?

After you have written down your observations, you may wish to look at the notes on this problem.

Experiment J2.4:
Your own class

Required code files:

- `Point.java`
- `PointFun.java`
- `PointPrinter.java`

Step 1. Modify `PointFun` so that it creates a `PointPrinter` object called `printer` and uses `printer` to print the various positions of the point. Compile the various files and then execute `PointFun`. Summarize your changes to the program. Record the output from the program.

Step 2. Modify `PointPrinter` so that it prints out points as `<X,Y>` rather than `(X,Y)`. Recompile just `PointPrinter` and then execute `PointFun`. Record the results.

Step 3. Change all instances of `pt` to `apoint` in `PointPrinter`. Recompile just `PointPrinter` and then execute `PointFun`. Record the results. What happened? Was that what you expected?

You may wish to look at the notes on this problem.

Step 4. Change all instances of out to screen in PointPrinter. Recompile just PointPrinter and then execute PointFun. Record the results. What happened? Was that what you expected?

You may wish to look at the notes on this problem.

Experiment J2.5: Return values

Step 1. Create a new class, AverageComputer (stored in AverageComputer.java) with the following method.

```
/**
 * Compute the average of two doubles.
 */
public double average(double a, double b) {
  double ave = (a + b) / 2;
  return ave;
} // average(double,double)
```

Step 2. Make a copy of AverageTester.java, which reads as follows.

```
import AverageComputer;
import SimpleInput;
import SimpleOutput;

/**
 * Some simple tests of the AverageComputer class.
 *
 * @author Samuel A. Rebelsky
 * @author Your Name Here
 * @version 1.0 of January 1999
 */
public class AverageTester {
  /**
   * Test away!
   */
  public static void main(String[] args) {
    // Prepare for reading input and printing output.
    SimpleOutput out = new SimpleOutput();
    SimpleInput in = new SimpleInput();
    // Build a new computer.
    AverageComputer computer = new AverageComputer();
    // The two values we'll be reading.
    double first;
    double second;
```

```
  // Read the two values.
  out.print("Enter a number: ");
  first = in.readDouble();
  out.print("Enter another number: ");
  second = in.readDouble();
  // Compute the average and print the result.
  out.println("The average of " + first + " and " + second + " is " +
              computer.average(first,second));
  } // main(String[])

} // AverageTester
```

Compile both `AverageComputer` and `AverageTester`. Execute `AverageTester`. Record the results.

Step 3. Change the `average` method of `AverageComputer` to read

```
public double average(double a, double b) {
  double ave = (a + b) / 2;
} // average(double,double)
```

What do you expect to happen when you try to recompile `AverageComputer`?

Step 4. Recompile `AverageComputer` and record the error messages you receive. What do the error messages suggest?

Step 5. Change the `average` method of `AverageComputer` to read

```
public double average(double a, double b) {
  double ave = (a + b) / 2;
  return 0;
} // average(double,double)
```

What do you expect to happen when you try to execute `AverageTester` with the modified `AverageComputer`?

Step 6. Recompile `AverageComputer` and execute `AverageTester`. Use 1 and 2 as the inputs. What is the output? What does this suggest?

Step 7. Change the `average` method of `AverageComputer` to read

```
public double average(double a, double b) {
  double ave = (a + b) / 2;
  return 0;
  return ave;
} // average(double,double)
```

Try to recompile `AverageComputer` and record the error messages. What do these messages suggest?

Experiment J2.6:
Static methods

Required code files:

- `Point.java`
- `PointFun.java`
- `PointPrinter.java`
- `PointReader.java`

Step 1. Make a copy of `PointReader.java`, which is defined as follows.

```
import SimpleInput;
import SimpleOutput;
import Point;

import SimpleOutput;
import SimpleInput;
```

```
/**
 * Simple methods for reading in points.  Arguably, these could also
 * be part of the Point class, but some issues have dictated that we
 * use a separate class.
 *
 * Developed as an illustration of static methods.
 *
 * @author Samuel A. Rebelsky
 * @version 1.0 of January 1999
 */
public class PointReader {
  // +---------------+-----------------------------------------
  // | Static Methods |
  // +---------------+

  /**
   * Prompt for and read one point.
   */
  static public Point read(SimpleOutput out, SimpleInput in) {
    float x;   // The x coordinate
    float y;   // The y coordinate
    out.print("Enter the x coordinate: ");
    x = in.readFloat();
    out.print("Enter the y coordinate: ");
    y = in.readFloat();
    return new Point(x,y);
  } // read(SimpleOutput, SimpleInput)
} // class PointReader
```

Note that `PointReader.java` contains a `PointReader` class with only one method, a static `read` method. Compile `PointReader`.

Step 2. Add the following lines to the `main` method of `PointFun`.

```
PointReader reader = new PointReader();
PointPrinter printer = new PointPrinter();
Point zebra = reader.read(out,in);
printer.print(out,zebra);
```

If your copy of `PointFun` does not create a `SimpleInput` object called `in`, you should insert the following line before those lines.

```
SimpleInput in = new SimpleInput();
```

What do you expect these lines to do?

Step 3. Recompile and execute `PointFun`. Record the new results. Were they what you expected? Explain the results.

Step 4. Add the following lines to the `main` method of `PointFun`.

```
Point stripes = PointReader.read(out,in);
printer.print(out,stripes);
```

Recompile and execute `PointFun`. Record the new results. Were they what you expected?

Step 5. Add the following lines to the `main` method of `PointFun`

```
Point white = PointReader.read(out,in);
PointPrinter.print(out,white);
```

Try to recompile and execute `PointFun`. What happens? What does this suggest?

After recording your answer, you may wish to look at the notes on this problem. You should also remove these lines from the program.

Step 6. Add the following lines to the `main` method of `PointFun`

```
Point black = PointReader.read(in,out);
printer.print(out,black);
```

Try to recompile and execute `PointFun`. What happens? What does this suggest?

After recording your answer, you may wish to look at the notes on this problem. You should also remove these lines from the program.

**Experiment J2.7:
Copying objects**

Required code files:

- `Point.java`

Step 1. Write a class, `PointExperiment`, that imports the `Point` class and has an empty `main` method. Compile and execute the program. Your program should do nothing. You need not enter any results for this step.

Step 2. Add the following lines to the `main` method. Recompile and execute the program. Record the output. Is this what you expected? Why or why not?

```
SimpleOutput out = new SimpleOutput();
int a;
int b;
a = 3;
b = 2*a;
out.println("a = " + a + ", b = " + b);
a = 1;
out.println("a = " + a + ", b = " + b);
```

Step 3. Add the following lines to the `main` method. Recompile and execute the program. Record the output. Explain why the program generated that output.

```
Point p1 = new Point(1,1);
Point p2 = p1;
out.println("(" + p1.getX() + "," + p1.getY() + ")");
out.println("(" + p2.getX() + "," + p2.getY() + ")");
p1.shiftLeft(1);
out.println("(" + p1.getX() + "," + p1.getY() + ")");
out.println("(" + p2.getX() + "," + p2.getY() + ")");
p2.shiftDown(1);
out.println("(" + p1.getX() + "," + p1.getY() + ")");
out.println("(" + p2.getX() + "," + p2.getY() + ")");
```

Step 4. Add the following lines to the `main` method. Recompile and execute the program. Record the new output. Explain why the program generated that output. Explain why this output differs from that of the previous segment.

```
Point p3 = new Point(1,1);
Point p4 = new Point(1,1);
out.println("(" + p3.getX() + "," + p3.getY() + ")");
out.println("(" + p4.getX() + "," + p4.getY() + ")");
p3.shiftLeft(1);
out.println("(" + p3.getX() + "," + p3.getY() + ")");
out.println("(" + p4.getX() + "," + p4.getY() + ")");
p4.shiftDown(1);
out.println("(" + p3.getX() + "," + p3.getY() + ")");
out.println("(" + p4.getX() + "," + p4.getY() + ")");
```

Step 5. Consider the following code, which is missing some parts.

```
Point p5 = new Point(0,0);
  ...
Point p6 = _____;
out.println("Initially ...");
out.println("  difference in X values is " + (p5.getX() -
p6.getX()));
out.println("  difference in Y values is " + (p5.getY() -
p6.getY()));
p6.shiftUp(1);
out.println("After shifting p6 up 1 ...");
out.println("  difference in X values is " + (p5.getX() -
p6.getX()));
out.println("  difference in Y values is " + (p5.getY() -
p6.getY()));
p5.shiftRight(3);
out.println("After shifting p5 right 3 ...");
out.println("  difference in X values is " + (p5.getX() -
p6.getX()));
out.println("  difference in Y values is " + (p5.getY() -
p6.getY()));
```

What expression should be used in the blank so that the output is as follows?

```
Initially ...
  difference in X values is 0
  difference in Y values is 0
```

```
After shifting p6 up 1 ...
  difference in X values is 0
  difference in Y values is -1
After shifting p5 right 3 ...
  difference in X values is 3
  difference in Y values is -1
```

Your code should generate this output no matter how p5 changes in the section marked by ellipses.

Enter the expression assigned to p6 here.

Experiment J2.8: Changing the font

Optional applet experiment

Required files:

- `HelloWorldApplet.java`
- `helloworld.html`

Before you begin, if you have not already done so, please familiarize yourself with the applet and HTML file. Make a copy of the two files. Read the code to make sure you understand the various parts. Compile `HelloWorldApplet.java`. Load the applet, using whatever technique your instructor specifies. (You might load it in a browser like Netscape Navigator or Microsoft Internet Explorer; you might run an application like Sun's appletviewer.)

Step 1. Add the following lines to the top of `HelloWorldApplet.java`.

```
import java.awt.Font;
import java.awt.Color;
```

Why do you think you were asked to add those lines?

After recording your answer, you may wish to consult the notes on this step.

Step 2. Replace the `paint` method of `HelloWorldApplet` with the following.

```
public void paint(Graphics paintBrush) {
  Font myFont = new Font("Serif", 24, Font.BOLD);
  paintBrush.setFont(myFont);
  paintBrush.drawString("Hello World", 10, 30);
} // paint(Graphics)
```

Recompile `HelloWorldApplet` and load the applet from `helloworld.html`. **Record the result.**

Step 3. Remove the line that reads

```
import java.awt.Color;
```

What do you expect will happen when you try to recompile `HelloWorldApplet` and load the applet from `helloworld.html`?

Confirm your answer by recompiling and loading the applet. You may also wish to consult the notes on this step.

Reinsert the line that you just deleted.

Step 4. Remove the line that reads

```
import java.awt.Font;
```

What do you expect will happen when you try to recompile `HelloWorldApplet` and load the applet from `helloworld.html`?

Confirm your answer by recompiling and loading the applet. You may also wish to consult the notes on this step.

Reinsert the line that you just deleted.

Step 5. What changes would you have to make for the message to be printed in 14pt sans serif italic?

Confirm your answer by making those changes to `HelloWorldApplet`, recompiling, and loading the applet with `helloworld.html`.

Step 6. Replace the `paint` method of `HelloWorldApplet` with the following

```
public void paint(Graphics paintBrush) {
  paintBrush.setFont(new Font("Serif", 18, Font.ITALIC));
  paintBrush.drawString("Hello World", 10, 30);
} // paint(Graphics)
```

Recompile `HelloWorldApplet` and load the applet from `helloworld.html`. What does this result suggest?

Warning! This is a conceptually difficult problem.

After entering your answer, you may wish to consult the notes on this step.

Step 7. Add the following line to the beginning of the `paint` method of `HelloWorldApplet` (before the call to `setFont`).

```
paintBrush.setColor(Color.red);
```

What effect do you expect this change to have?

Confirm your answer by compiling `HelloWorldApplet` and loading the applet from `helloworld.html`.

Step 8. Move the `setColor` line to the *end* of the `paint` method of `HelloWorldApplet` (after the call to `drawString`). The body of this method should now read

```
paintBrush.setFont(new Font("Serif", 18, Font.ITALIC));
paintBrush.drawString("Hello World", 10, 30);
paintBrush.setColor(Color.red);
```

What effect do expect this change to have?

Confirm your answer by compiling `HelloWorldApplet` and loading the applet from `helloworld.html`. You may also wish to consult the notes on this step.

Step 9. Add the following line to the start of the `paint` method.

```
paintBrush.setColor(new Color(255, 0, 255));
```

What effect do you expect this change to have?

Confirm your answer by compiling `HelloWorldApplet` and loading the applet from `helloworld.html`.

Step 10. Update the `paint` method to read

```
paintBrush.setFont(new Font("Serif", Font.PLAIN, 24));
paintBrush.setColor(Color.red);
paintBrush.drawString("Hello world", 10, 30);
paintBrush.setColor(Color.blue);
paintBrush.drawString("Hello world", 12, 32);
```

What do you expect the new applet to show?

Confirm your answer by compiling `HelloWorldApplet` and loading the applet from `helloworld.html`.

Step 11. Update the `paint` method to read

```
paintBrush.setFont(new Font("Serif", Font.PLAIN, 24));
paintBrush.setColor(Color.blue);
paintBrush.drawString("Hello world", 12, 32);
paintBrush.setColor(Color.red);
paintBrush.drawString("Hello world", 10, 30);
```

How will this applet differ from the one in the previous step?

Confirm your answer by compiling `HelloWorldApplet` and loading the applet from `helloworld.html`.

**Experiment J2.9:
Some simple
pictures**

Optional applet experiment

Required files:

- `circle.html`
- `CircleApplet.java`

Step 1. Make copies of <u>`CircleApplet.java`</u> and <u>`circle.html`</u>. Read both files. What do you expect the applet to do?

Step 2. Compile `CircleApplet`. Load the applet using `circle.html`. Note what you see.

Step 3. Indicate what you expect to happen if you change the line that reads

`paintBrush.fillOval(0,0,40,40);`

to instead read

`paintBrush.fillOval(0,0,50,30);`

Confirm your answer by compiling `CircleApplet` and loading the applet from `circle.html`.

Step 4. Change that line to read

`paintBrush.drawOval(0,0,50,30);`

What effect do you expect this change to have?

Confirm your answer by compiling `CircleApplet` and loading the applet from `circle.html`.

Step 5. Change that line to read

```
paintBrush.fillRect(10,0,50,30);
```

What effect do you expect this change to have?

Confirm your answer by compiling `CircleApplet` and loading the applet from `circle.html`.

Step 6. Change that line to read

```
paintBrush.fillOval(10,-25,50,50);
```

What effect do you expect this change to have?

Confirm your answer by compiling `CircleApplet` and loading the applet from `circle.html`.

Step 7. Modify `CircleApplet` so that it draws a red circle of radius 25 centered at (30,30). Enter your code here.

Step 8. Modify `CircleApplet` so that it draws both the red circle and a blue circle of radius 10 centered at (30,30). Enter the new code here.

Step 9. What happens if the `paint` method draws the blue circle before drawing the red circle?

Step 10. Draw a series of five concentric circles centered at (50,50), using a different color for each circle. Enter your code here.

Post-Laboratory Problems

**Problem J2-A:
Shifting points**

Add a `shiftAndPrint` method to `PointPrinter` that moves a point right 3, up 3, left 6, down 6, right 6, up 3, and left 3, printing the result at each step.

**Problem J2-B:
Shifting points,
revisited**

Add a `shiftAndPlot` method to `PointPrinter` that moves a point right 3, up 3, left 6, down 6, right 6, up 3, and left 3, plotting the result at each step. Write a program that reads in the point and uses the helper to plot the point at each position.

**Problem J2-C:
Drawing a grid**

Write a program, `Grid.java`, that prints out a 3 by 3 grid of points on the plane. Make the spacing in the grid one unit.

**Problem J2-D:
Drawing a grid,
revisited**

Write a program, `Grid.java`, that prints out a 3 by 3 grid of points on the plane. Input the spacing in the grid and the center point in the grid.

**Problem J2-E:
Happiness**

Write a program, `Smiley.java` that draws a smiley face by plotting points appropriately.

**Problem J2-F:
Initials**

Write a program, `Initials.java`, that draws your initials by plotting points appropriately.

**Problem J2-G:
Rainbow Text**

Using the techniques from Experiment J2.8, draw your name in a rainbow of colors. (Your name will appear in each color.)

**Problem J2-H:
Other Drawing
Methods**

In this session, you learned about six methods provided by `java.awt.Graphics` for drawing basic shapes: `drawString`, `drawLine`, `drawRect`, `drawOval`, `fillRect`, and `fillOval`. Are these all that's available? Consult the Java documentation and write short summaries of the other drawing methods.

**Problem J2-I:
Determining Text
Width**

Instead of the rainbow-drawing technique from Problem J2-G, you might want to draw each letter in a different color. However, this makes it necessary for you not only to change the color before drawing each letter, but also to determine the correct place to draw each letter. Does Java give you the tools for doing so? Yes. There is a `FontMetrics` class that helps you determine the width of strings. Read the documentation on that class and write instructions that a classmate could use to write his or her name with each letter in a different color.

Notes

Experiment J2.1, Step 1. You won't be able to execute `Point`. Why not? Because it doesn't include a `main` method. `Point`s can be used to manipulate points on the plane, but they won't work by themselves; they need to be coordinated by a separate `main` routine.

Experiment J2.1, Step 2. Why are the numbers so strange? Because Java, like many programming languages, tends to approximate numbers. However, the internal working of the computer lead to different approximations than we normally get. So, when we subtract 10.2 from 2.7, we should get -7.5. However, the approximation leads to the strange number you see.

Experiment J2.3, Step 4. Experiment J2.4, Step 3. Experiment J2.4, Step 4. All of these cases show that the name used within a method is independent of the name used outside the method. In effect, Java *renames* any arguments used in a method call so that they correspond to the parameter names in the method. As long as you are consistent within the method, you should be fine.

Experiment J2.6, Step 5. If you call a nonstatic method (a normal method) and don't provide an accompanying object, the Java compiler will issue an error message. In this case, `print` is not a static method, but it's being used as if it were a static method.

Experiment J2.6, Step 6. The parameters are being passed to the method in the wrong order. The `read` method is designed to take a `SimpleOutput` object as its first parameter and a `SimpleInput` object as its second parameter.

Experiment J2.8, Step 1. It's likely we'll be creating new `Font` objects and new `Color` objects, so we import those two classes.

Experiment J2.8, Step 3. We have yet to make explicit use of a `Color`, so there is no immediate harm in removing the line. However, since we expect to use colors in the near future, it behooves us to reinsert the line once we are done testing.

Experiment J2.8, Step 4. Because we use the `Font` class and do not import that class, Java is likely to complain that the class has been used without a corresponding import statement.

Experiment J2.8, Step 6. In effect, the one line

```
paintBrush.setFont(new Font("Serif", Font.ITALIC, 18));
```

replaces the two lines

```
Font myFont = new Font("Serif", Font.ITALIC, 18));
paintBrush.setFont(myFont);
```

That is, it creates a new `Font` object and then immediately passes it to `set-Font`, rather than storing it in a variable and then passing it with that variable.

If you are only creating a new `Font` to use with `setFont`, you can use this technique to avoid the intermediate step and the otherwise-unused variable. You'll find that many experienced Java programmers use similar shortcuts.

Experiment J2.8, Step 9. Since the paint color is only changed after the text has been drawn, there is no visible effect.

Session J3: Building Your Own Classes

In this laboratory session, you will learn more about the capabilities of objects and extend your skills at building and using objects and classes. The goals of this laboratory are to

- introduce the *state* of an object;
- demonstrate how to describe and manipulate the state of an object;
- consider *overloading,* in which multiple methods in the same class can have the same name; and
- show you how to develop your own *constructors* for creating and initializing objects.

Your instructor will tell you which of the proposed experiments you are to perform.

Prerequisite skills:

- Fundamentals of Java
- Building simple objects
- Using objects
- Methods

Required files:

- `AverageComputer.java`
- `AverageTester.java`
- `Point.java`
- `PointFun.java`
- `PointPrinter.java`
- `PointReader.java`
- `ReadTester.java`
- `SimpleInput.java`
- `SimpleOutput.java`

Optional applet files:

- `borderedsquare.html`
- `BorderedSquareApplet.java`
- `bsquaretester.html`
- `BorderedSquare.java`
- `BorderedSquareTester.java`

Discussion

Class capabilities

In the previous laboratory session, we used a number of classes including a `Point` class that represented points on the Euclidean plane. We also developed our own class, `PointPrinter`, which provided a simple method for printing information about points.

You may have noted that `Point` provided many capabilities that we have not yet seen how to add to `PointPrinter`. In particular, you may have noted that `Point`s have a *state:* each point has x and y coordinates and maintains those coordinates throughout the execution of the program. In addition, `Point`s have *parameterized constructors:* when you create a new point, you can specify the initial position of the point. Most classes provide a number of *methods,* some of which have *return values:* when you call a method such as `getX()`, the method not only gets the x coordinate, but also returns it to the calling method. We will consider each of these issues in this laboratory session.

Program state

Before we look into the state of objects, let us think a little bit about the state of a program. For example, suppose you were asked to describe everything that should be known about the following function at the point the "What do we know?" comment appears. What would you say?

```
public void doStuff(SimpleOutput out) {
  int a = 1;
  int b = 3;
  int d = a + b * 2;
  a = d + 2;
  // What do we know?
  b = a + a;
  out.println("b is " + b);
} // doStuff()
```

Hopefully, you would have described the values of the variables and parameters. For example, you might say something like "d has the value 7, a has the value 9, b has the value 3, and `out` has an unknown value, corresponding to the `SimpleOutput` object passed as a parameter to the function".

In Experiment J3.1 you will investigate program state.

Object state

It turns out that the state of an object is also represented by things that are very similar to the variables that we use in methods. These "things" are often called *attributes* or *fields*. Fields look very much like variables except that they are associated with classes (and objects), rather than methods. To declare a field in a class, write

- the keyword protected,
- the *type* of the field, and
- the *name* of the field.

Are there any fields that we might use with PointPrinter? Yes. We might want to keep track of the number of points that we have printed out, so that we print out not only the point, but also a number of each point. For our PointPrinter class, we would define this field with

```
public class PointPrinter {
  /**
   * The number of points we've printed.
   */
  protected int numprinted = 0;
  ... }
// PointPrinter
```

What can we do with this field now that we've added it? We need to update it and perhaps even use it. When referring to the fields of an object, you use the keyword this, a dot, and the name of the field. For example, we'll update the numprinted field in the print method of PointPrinter by adding the line

```
this.numprinted = this.numprinted + 1;
```

The this indicates that the field belongs to the current object. While not strictly necessary, usage improves clarity. You should always use this in your code.

How might we use the new numprinted field? We can print it out whenever we print a point. For example, we might use

```
out.print(this.numprinted + ": ");
...
```

In Experiment J3.2 and Experiment J3.3 you will investigate fields.

Constructors

In our example above, we *initialized* the numprinted field to give it an initial value. You may have noted that it is often the case when we create an integer variable, we initialize it. Often, you will initialize your fields to a default value.

However, this does lead to a question. When we create a new object, how do we specify what we want the value of that object to be? That is, if we can create an integer with initial value 1, shouldn't we also be able to create a Point with initial value (2,3) or a PointPrinter that starts numbering points at 10?

You may recall that we used constructors to set the initial values for the `Point`s we created in a previous session. For example, to create a new `Point` with the initial value (2,3), we might use

```
Point p = new Point (2,3);
```

Similarly, if there was an appropriate constructor defined for `Point-Printer` (we have not yet defined one, but we will), one might write

```
PointPrinter start_with_10 = new PointPrinter(10);
```

We will now consider how one defines constructors. In effect, a constructor is simply a method that uses its parameters to set the values of an object's fields. If you've done experiment J3.4, you've already created a method that does that. So, how do constructors differ from regular methods? They differ in their name and their type. When you create a constructor for a class,

- the name of the constructor must be the same as the name for the class and
- you do not specify a type for the constructor.

For example, we might declare a constructor for `PointPrinter` as follows

```
public class PointPrinter {
  ...
  /**
   * Create a new PointPrinter that counts printed points
   * starting with value start_val.
   */
  public PointPrinter(int start_val) {
    this.numprinted = start_val;
  } // PointPrinter(start_val) ...
} // class PointPrinter
```

Can we declare constructors with no parameters? Certainly. For `Point-Printer`, we might build a constructor that initializes `numprinted` to 1 with

```
public class PointPrinter {
  ...
  /**
   * Create a new PointPrinter that numbers points starting at 1.
   */
  public PointPrinter()  {
    this.numprinted = 1;
  } // PointPrinter()
  ...
} // class PointPrinter
```

Note that there are two ways to initialize fields to default values: we can use assignment statements (using equals signs), or we can use parameterless constructors (constructors without parameters). Using constructors is the preferred mechanism.

We have defined two constructors for `PointPrinter`, one that has a single integer parameter and one that has no parameters. Both seem to have the same name. Is this legal? Yes. Java permits multiple constructors provided it is possible to tell them apart by the parameters. If you could think of a reason, it would be legal to create additional constructors with two integer parameters or with a string parameter. However, it would not be legal to create another constructor with a single integer parameter, because Java would not be able to tell which one to use.

What happens if we do not define constructors for one of our classes? It turns out that Java creates a default constructor with no parameters that, in effect, sets all fields to "reasonable" defaults. This is why we did not need to create a constructor for `PointPrinter` or `MyPoint`. These default constructors are nice, but they also have some drawbacks. In particular, if you define your own constructors, then the default constructor is no longer available. This point is an important enough point that we'll repeat it: if you define any constructor for a class (even a parameterized constructor), then there is no longer a default, parameterless constructor for the class. We will explore this issue further in the experiments.

In Experiment J3.4 you will add constructors to the `PointPrinter` class and investigate some of the issues surrounding the no-argument constructors. In Experiment J3.5, you will consider other issues relating to constructors.

Overloading

You've seen that it's possible to have multiple constructors for the same class. Since the name of a constructor is the same as the name of the class, it seems like we have two "methods" (constructor methods) in the same class with the same name.

Similarly, we've seen that different classes can provide methods with the same name. For example, there is a `print` method in the `SimpleOutput` class and a `print` method in the `PointPrinter` <u>class</u>.

Can we have two methods with the same name in the same <u>class</u> (other than constructors)? Yes! This is a common programming technique called *overloading*.

Would we ever want to have different methods in the same <u>class</u> with the same name? Yes. Consider the `SimpleOutput` class. This class provides a different `print` method for `String`s, <u>int</u>s, <u>long</u>s, <u>double</u>s, and all the other things you might need to print. Imagine what would happen if you needed to use a different method name for each type. Not only would you often need to look up the appropriate name, depending on what you wanted to print, you would also find it difficult to modify your code to work in slightly different situations.

How do you overload a method? You simply define the method multiple times, using different types of arguments each time. For example, we might want to add a `read` method to `PointReader` that reads the X and Y coordinates without prompting. Here is such a method.

```
/**
 * Read a point without prompting.
 */
public static Point read(SimpleInput in) {
  float x;// The x coordinate.
  float y;// The y coordinate.
  x = in.readFloat();
  y = in.readFloat();
  return new Point(x,y);
} // read(SimpleInput)
```

How does Java decide which version of an overloaded method to use? First, it looks at the class of the object whose method it calls. For example, if you ask for `printer.print` and `printer` is a `PointPrinter`, then it will look in `PointPrinter`. If, however, `printer` is a `SimpleOutput`, then it will look in `SimpleOutput`. After determining which class to use, Java looks at the *signature,* the name of the method plus the types of the arguments. For example, if we call the `print` method of a `SimpleOutput` object with an `int` as a parameter, then Java looks for a method with signature `print(int)`.

If Java can't find an exact match, it looks for an approximate match. For example, if there is no `print(int)` method, but there is a `print(double)`, Java will use that instead because Java knows how to convert `int`s to `double`s.

In Experiment J3.6, you will add the overloaded `print` method to `PointReader`. In Experiment J3.7, you will investigate some of the limitations of overloading.

Creating a bordered square class

This section is optional and is intended for classes emphasizing applets or pursuing a simultaneous discussion of applications and applets.

How can objects and classes help us as we build applets? We've already seen that it's helpful to have the predefined `Font` and `Color` classes. It is also useful to create our own classes. For example, we can use classes to make it easier to draw repeatedly a greater variety of figures. For example, we might create classes that represent stick figures, more-interesting basic shapes, and similar components for our drawings. We'll begin with a simple shape: a filled square with a different-color border.

When designing a class, we need to consider fields, constructors, and methods.

What fields will a `BorderedSquare` class need? It will certainly need the color of the square and the color of the border. It is also helpful to have the left edge, the top edge, and the length of each side. (You may want to consider how we'd do without those values.)

What constructors will this class need? We'll start with one. It will take five parameters, corresponding to the five fields.

```
public BorderedSquare(
  int left, int top,
  int side,
  Color mainColor, Color border)
{
  ...
} // BorderedSquare(int,int,int,Color,Color)
```

What methods will this class need? We'll start with one. We'll need a way to paint the square. We'll call this method `paint`. What parameters does it need? It needs the graphics paintbrush for doing the actual painting.

```
public void paint(Graphics paintBrush) {
  ...
} // paint(Graphics)
```

How do we paint the square? We'll simply use `fillRect` filling in the left edge, top edge, and side length.

```
paintBrush.fillRect(left, top, sideLength, sideLength);
```

How might we draw a border around the square? You might assume that we can use similar dimensions for a call to `drawRect` that you were using for `fillRect`, decreasing the left and top edges by 1 and increasing the width and height by 2. For example, suppose we wanted to explicitly draw a 40x40 black square with a red border. We might write

```
public void paint(Graphics paintBrush) {
  paintBrush.setColor(Color.black);
  paintBrush.fillRect(5,5,40,40);
  paintBrush.setColor(Color.red);
  paintBrush.drawRect(4,4,42,42);
} // paint(Graphics)
```

However, this is not precisely correct.

As you may recall, Java's coordinate system is somewhat odd, with the upper-left-corner being (0,0) and coordinates increasing to the right and downward. This should not affect our border. However, this is also not the only way in which Java's drawing conventions defy many beginning programmers' initial assumptions.

Surprisingly, the coordinates on the grid are not where the ink appears. Rather, the ink appears between these points. For example, the top-left pixel is not *at* (0,0). Rather, it appears between the four points (0,0), (0,1), (1,0), and (1,1). In fact, the "graphics pen" is placed down and to the right of the path it traverses.

Why does this make a difference? Because `fillRect` and `fillOval` color only the pixels within the area described by the parameters, whereas `drawRect` and `drawOval` color the pixels to the left and down from the object described. For example, the lower-right pixel drawn by `fill-Rect(0,0,3,2)` is bounded by (2,1), (2,2), (3,1), and (3,2). However, the lower-right pixel drawn by `drawRect(0,0,3,2)` falls to the right of and below the lower-right corner (3,2) and therefore is bounded by (3,2), (3,3), (4,2), and (4,3). What is the moral? *Filled shapes are typically one pixel smaller horizontally and vertically than drawn shapes.*

In Experiment J3.8, you will consider this drawing difficulty. In Experiment J3.9, you will create and use a bordered square class.

Experiments

Name: _____

ID: _____

**Experiment J3.1:
Program state**

Consider the following fragment of Java code

```java
int x = 0;
int y = 0;
int z = 0;
...
// potential changes to x, y, and z
...
// position 1 (before the following steps)
x = 2 * y;
y = 5;
z = x + y;
// position 2 (after the first set of steps)
x = 2 * y;
y = 5;
z = x + y;
// position 3 (after both sets of steps)
```

What do you know about the values of x, y, and z at positions 1, 2, and 3?

**Experiment J3.2:
Fields**

Required code files:

- `Point.java`
- `PointFun.java`
- `PointPrinter.java`

Step 1. Make copies of the required code files. Modify `Point-Printer.java` so that it includes a `numprinted` field which it prints and updates every time it prints a point. Modify `PointFun.java` so that it creates and uses a `PointPrinter` object for output. Compile the various files, execute `PointFun`, and record the results. Are they what you expected? Why or why not?

Step 2. Rename `numprinted` to `printed` everywhere that it appears in `PointPrinter.java` and recompile. Execute `PointFun` and record the results. Are they what you expected? Why or why not?

After recording your answer, you may wish to look at the notes on this step.

Experiment J3.3:
Fields, revisited

Step 1. Create a new class, `MyPoint`, that contains two integer fields, `xcoordinate` and `ycoordinate`. Note that all you will need for this class (at least at this point) are the class declaration and the field declarations. (Do not initialize the fields, just declare them.) Compile your class and correct any errors reported by the compiler. Enter the code for your class here.

Step 2. Create a `print(SimpleOutput out)` method for your `MyPoint` class. This method should print out the point in a reasonable format. Recompile your class and correct any errors reported by the compiler. Enter the code for that method here.

Step 3. Create a `TestMyPoint` class with a `main` method that creates a `MyPoint` and asks it to print itself out. Compile and execute `TestMyPoint`. What values are printed for the x and y coordinates? Why do you think this is?

If you encounter problems with this step, please read the notes on this problem.

Step 4. Create a `setLocation(int x, int y)` method for the `MyPoint` class. This method will set the `xcoordinate` and `ycoordinate` fields to the corresponding parameters. Recompile `MyPoint` and correct any compiler errors.

Extend `TestMyPoint` to test this method by setting the x coordinate to 2 and the y coordinate to 3 and then asking the point to print itself. Recompile and run `TestMyPoint` and correct any errors.

Enter the code for the `setLocation` method here.

Experiment J3.4: Constructors

Required code files:

- `Point.java`
- `PointFun.java` (as modified in Experiment J3.2)
- `PointPrinter.java` (as modified in Experiment J3.2)

Step 1. Create a constructor for the `PointPrinter` class that takes no parameters and initializes any fields to appropriate values. Recompile `PointPrinter` and execute `PointFun`. What happens? Is that what you expected? Why or why not?

Step 2. In Step 1, you recompiled `PointPrinter` but executed `PointFun`. Why didn't you need to recompile `PointFun`?

Step 3. Create a one-parameter constructor for the `PointPrinter` class that initializes the count of points printed. (Do not delete your other constructor!) Recompile `PointPrinter` and correct any errors. Enter your code for the constructor here.

Step 4. `PointFun` to use that constructor and to use 100 as the first value. Recompile and execute `PointFun`. Did the modifications have the expected impact?

Step 5. Update `PointFun` to use a zero-parameter constructor, as in

```
PointPrinter printer = new PointPrinter();
```

Recompile and test. What happens? Is that what you expected? Why or why not?

Step 6. Delete the zero-parameter constructor for the `PointPrinter` class (leaving you with just the one-parameter constructor). Recompile `Point-Printer` and try to execute `PointFun` (you should not need to recompile `PointFun`). What happens? Is that what you expected? Why or why not?

Step 7. Delete the one-parameter constructor for the PointPrinter class (leaving you with no constructors). Recompile PointPrinter and try to execute PointFun (you should not need to recompile PointFun, but you may do so if you wish). What happens? Is this the same as in the previous step? Why or why not?

Experiment J3.5: Constructors, revisited

Required code files:

- MyPoint.java (created in Experiment J3.3)
- TestMyPoint.java (created in Experiment J3.3)

Step 1. Create a constructor for the MyPoint class that takes two parameters: the initial x value and the initial y value. Recompile MyPoint and correct any errors.

Update TestMyPoint to use that constructor (and only that constructor). For example, you might write

MyPoint pt = new MyPoint(2,3);

Recompile and run TestMyPoint.

Enter your code for the constructor here.

Step 2. Update TestMyPoint to use a parameterless constructor for MyPoint. For example, you might write

MyPoint pt2 = new MyPoint();

What happens when you try to compile and run TestMyPoint? Why?

Step 3. Create a parameterless constructor for `MyPoint` that initializes both coordinates to 0. Recompile `MyPoint` and correct any errors. What happens when you try to compile and run `TestMyPoint`? Is your result the same as or different from the result in Step 2? Why?

Step 4. Make a copy of `MyPoint` named `MyPt` (when making the copy, you will need to change the file name to `MyPt.java` and the class name to `MyPt`). Try to compile the new class. What happens? Why? How can you correct that problem?

Experiment J3.6: Overloading read methods

Required files:

- `Point.java`
- `PointPrinter.java`
- `PointReader.java` (if you've modified this in a previous part of this lab, do not make another copy)
- `ReadTester.java`

Before you begin, make a copy of `Point.java`, `PointReader.java`, and `PointPrinter.java`. Compile the three files.

Step 1. Make a copy of `ReadTester.java`, which contains

```java
import SimpleInput;
import SimpleOutput;
import Point;
import PointReader;
import PointPrinter;

/**
 * A simple test of the various methods provided by the PointReader
 * class.  Used as an illustration of method overloading.
 */
public class ReadTester {
  /**
   * Run the thrilling tests.
   */
```

```
public static void main(String[] args) {
  SimpleInput in = new SimpleInput();
  SimpleOutput out = new SimpleOutput();
  PointReader reader = new PointReader();
  PointPrinter printer = new PointPrinter();
  Point pt = reader.read(out,in);
  printer.print(out,pt);
} // main(String[])
} // class ReadTester
```

Compile and execute `ReadTester`. Record the output.

Step 2. Add the following lines to the `main` method of `ReadTester`.

```
// Step 2.  Read a point without prompting.
pt = reader.read(in);
printer.print(out,pt);
```

What do you expect to happen when you compile the modified `ReadTester` class?

Step 3. Attempt to compile the modified `ReadTester`. Record any errors. What do these errors suggest?

Step 4. Add the following method to `PointReader`.

```
/**
 * Read a point without prompting.
 */
public static Point read(SimpleInput in) {
  float x;    // The x coordinate.
  float y;    // The y coordinate.
  x = in.readFloat();
  y = in.readFloat();
  return new Point(x,y);
} // read(SimpleInput)
```

What do you expect to happen when you compile the modified `PointReader` class?

After entering your answer, compile the modified class and correct any errors.

Step 5. What do you expect to happen when you now try to compile `ReadTester`?

After entering your answer, compile the modified class.

Step 6. Execute `ReadTester` and record the results. Note that you will have to enter the two components of the second point without being prompted.

Experiment J3.7: Overloading

Required files:

- `AverageComputer.java` (created in a previous laboratory).
- `AverageTester.java`

Before you begin, make sure you have a fresh copy of `AverageComputer.java`, which you should have created in a previous lab. If not, here is the code for it.

```
/**
 * Methods for averaging two numbers.  Intended as an illustration of
 * function return values.  Will also be used as an example of
 * overloading.  Might also be used as an example of overflow.
 *
 * @author Samuel A. Rebelsky
 * @version 1.0 of January 1999
 */
public class AverageComputer {
  /**
   * Compute the average of two doubles.
   */
  public double average(double a, double b) {
    return (a + b) / 2;
  } // average(double,double)
} // class AverageComputer
```

Also make sure that you have a copy of `AverageTester.java`.

Step 1. Compile the two files and execute `AverageTester`. When prompted for input, enter 2 and 3 and record the results.

Step 2. Add the following lines to the end of the `main` method of `Average-Tester`.

```
// Step 2.  Average two integers.
int firstInt;
int secondInt;
out.print("Enter an integer: ");
firstInt = in.readInt();
out.print("Enter another integer: ");
secondInt = in.readInt();
out.println("The average of " + firstInt + " and " + secondInt +
            " is " + computer.average(firstInt,secondInt));
```

What do you think will happen when you try to compile and execute the modified `AverageTester`? Why? If it executes successfully, what will the output be?

Step 3. Compile and execute the modified `AverageTester`, using 2 and 3 as the pair of numbers in each case. Record and explain the output. Pay close attention to differences in the output.

After recording your answer, you may wish to look at the notes on this problem.

Step 4. Add the following lines to the end of the `main` method of `Average-Tester`.

```
// Step 4.  Compute the average in a different way.
out.print("That average might also be stated as ");
out.println((firstInt + secondInt) / 2);
```

What do you expect the new output to be?

Step 5. Compile and execute the modified `AverageTester`, using 2 and 3 as the pair of numbers in each case. Record and explain the output.

After recording your answer, you may wish to look at the notes on this problem.

Step 6. Add the following method to `AverageComputer`.

```
/**
 * Compute the average of two integers.
 */
public int average(int a, int b) {
  return (a + b) / 2;
} // average(int,int)
```

What effect, if any, do you expect this modification to have on the output of `AverageTester`?

Step 7. Recompile `AverageComputer` and `AverageTester`. (Even though you have not modified `AverageTester`, you should recompile it because you've overloaded a method it uses in `AverageComputer`.) Execute `AverageTester`. Enter 2 and 3 for each pair of numbers. Record your output. Does this output differ from that in Step 5? If so, why?

After recording your answer, you may wish to look at the notes on this problem.

Step 8. Remove the `average(int,int)` method from `AverageComputer`. Then add the following methods to `AverageComputer`.

```
/**
 * Compute the average of an integer and a double.
 */
public double average(int a, double b) {
  return (a + b) / 2;
} // average(int,double)

/**
 * Compute the average of a double and an integer.
 */
public double average(double a, int b) {
  return (a + b) / 2;
} // average(double,int)
```

Do you expect this modification to have any effect on either program?

Step 9. Compile `AverageComputer`. If that succeeds, compile `Average-Tester`. If that succeeds, execute `AverageTester`. What happened? Why?

After recording your answer, you may wish to look at the notes on this problem.

Experiment J3.8: Borders

Optional applet experiment

Required files:

- `borderedsquare.html`
- `BorderedSquareApplet.java`

Step 1. Make copies of `borderedsquare.html` and `BorderedSquareApplet.java`. Read the two files. In your own words, explain what should happen when your run the applet.

Step 2. Compile `BorderedSquareApplet`. Load the applet using `borderedquare.html`. Describe the output.

Step 3. What do you expect to happen if you paint the border before painting the main body of the square?

Confirm your answer by making the appropriate changes, recompiling `BorderedSquareApplet`, and reloading the applet.

Step 4. You may have noted that while the left and right borders appear correct, there is a gap between the black square and the red border on the right and bottom. It makes no difference whether we draw the border first or the outline first. Change the line that reads

```
paintBrush.drawRect(4,4,42,42);
```

to read

```
paintBrush.fillRect(4,4,42,42);
```

(This should now be the first rectangle you draw.) What effect do you expect this change to have?

Confirm your answer by making the appropriate changes, recompiling `BorderedSquareApplet`, and reloading the applet.

Step 5. Change the line that reads

```
paintBrush.fillRect(4,4,42,42);
```

to read

```
paintBrush.drawRect(4,4,41,41);
```

What effect do you expect this change to have?

Confirm your answer by making the appropriate changes, recompiling `BorderedSquareApplet`, and reloading the applet.

Step 6. Are there differences between the previous two solutions? If so, what are they? Does it matter whether the border is drawn first or second in either case?

Experiment J3.9: A bordered-square class

Optional applet experiment

Required files:

- `bsquaretester.html`
- `BorderedSquare.java`
- `BorderedSquareTester.java`

Step 1. Make copies of the three files. Explain, in your own words, what the role of each file is or might be. You may wish to compile certain files or load applets.

After recording your answer, you may wish to consult the notes on this problem.

Step 2. We already know how to paint a "normal" square. We use `paintBrush.fillRect(...)`. How might we paint a bordered square we've just created called `mySquare`?

Step 3. In your own words, summarize the changes you'll need to make to `BorderedSquare` in order to support different colors, sizes, and positions of bordered squares.

Step 4. Add five fields to `BorderedSquare`:

- an integer field, `left`, for the left edge of the square;
- an integer field, `top`, for the top edge of the square;
- an integer field, `side`, for the side length of the square (this will serve as the square's width and height);
- a `Color` field, `mainColor`, for the primary color of the square; and
- a `Color` field, `border`, for the border's color.

Compile `BorderedSquare` and verify that you have declared the fields correctly. Once you have done so, record the field declarations here.

Step 5. Add a zero-argument constructor to `BorderedSquare`. This constructor should initialize all of the fields to reasonable default values. Once you verify that the constructor works correctly, enter the code for the constructor here.

Step 6. Update the `paint` method to paint the main body of the square (not the border), using the fields for the various information. Once you verify that the method works correctly, enter the code for the method here.

Step 7. Add a five-argument constructor to `BorderedSquare`. The constructor should take the form

```
public BorderedSquare(
  int left, int top,
  int side,
  Color mainColor, Color border)
{
...
} // BorderedSquare(int,int,int,Color,Color)
```

Once you verify that the constructor works correctly, enter the code for the constructor here.

Step 8. Add the following lines to the `paint` method of `Bordered-SquareTester`.

```
BorderedSquare redblack =
    new BorderedSquare(10,10,50,Color.red,Color.black);
BorderedSquare blackred =
    new BorderedSquare(80,20,30,Color.black,Color.red);
redblack.paint(paintBrush);
blackred.paint(paintBrush);
```

What effect will this change make?

Step 9. What changes must we make to the `paint` method of `Bordered-Square` in order for the border to appear? You may need to refer to the steps in this experiment and the previous experiment.

Step 10. What other methods would you recommend we add to the `BorderedSquare` class? You might want to consider whether we should be able to change fields, move the square, or update colors.

Step 11. In your own words, what are the advantages of having a `BorderedSquare` class?

Post-Laboratory Problems

Problem J3-A:
Shifting points

Add `shiftLeft(int amt)`, `shiftRight(int amt)`, `shiftUp(int amt)`, and `shiftDown(int amt)` methods to the `MyPoint` class. Write an appropriate test procedure that demonstrates the use of these methods.

Problem J3-B:
Refined points

We designed the `MyPoint` class so that points have integer values, which means that it is impossible to have a point at positions with fractional components, such as (1.5, 3.2). Update `MyPoint` to permit such positions.

Problem J3-C:
Distance from origin

Add a `distance` method to the `MyPoint` class. This method should compute the distance from the origin (traditional distance, involving diagonals). Note that to compute a square root in Java, you should use `Math.sqrt(...)`. Write an appropriate series of tests for this method.

Problem J3-D:
A date class

Create a `Date` class with three fields, `year`, `month`, and `day`. Your class should include at least one constructor as well as methods to extract the year, month, and day from a date. Write an appropriate `TestDate` class to test the methods and constructors of the `Date` class.

Problem J3-E:
Converting dates to strings

Add a `String toString()` method to the `Date` class. Your method should return a string corresponding to the date. For example, if the year were 1998, the month 6, and the day 12, you might return the string `6/12/1998` (for American users). Write appropriate tests for this method.

Problem J3-F:
Stick Figures

Create a `StickFigure` class, similar in purpose to our bordered-square class.

Problem J3-G:
House Components

Create a number of classes (`Window`, etc.) that one might use to aid in drawing houses.

Problem J3-H:
Boxed Text

Create a class, `BoxedText`, whose objects display not only a colored string, but an appropriate rectangle around the string. That is, the rectangle should precisely surround the text. Longer messages should have bigger rectangles.

Warning! You will need the answer from Problem J2-I in order to solve this problem. You will also need to read more about `java.awt.FontMetrics`.

Notes

Experiment J3.2, Step 2. This is an instance of the power of *information hiding*. Since other classes don't know what you've named the field, changes to the name of the field don't affect the operation of your program.

Experiment J3.3, Step 3. Observe that there are two ways in which you might print out a point,

```
out.println(pt);
```

or

```
pt.print(out);
```

The first reads (informally), "Ask the output object to print point `pt`". The second reads (informally), "Ask `pt` to print itself, using output object `out` as a helper".

Which is more appropriate? The second is clearly better. Why? Because points know about output objects (you've specifically written the method so that it understands them), while output objects don't necessarily know about points.

You can observe the difference in the output. The first technique will print out something odd, such as `MyPoint@12345`, indicating that it's printing all that it knows (the class and some other information). The second should print something like `(0,0)`.

Experiment J3.7, Step 3. Although there is not an `average(int,int)` method, Java knows how to convert `int`s to `double`s and does so.

Experiment J3.7, Step 5. We get two different results because the inputs are treated as different types in the two different computations. In the first case, both inputs are converted to `double` before computing the average, so the average will be a `double` (including a fractional part). In the second case, the average is computed by adding two `int`s and then dividing by two. In this case, *integer division* is done, so there is no remainder.

Experiment J3.7, Step 7. The results are different because in the earlier step, the call to `average(firstInt,secondInt)` used `average(double,double)` and returned a `double`. This time, the call uses `average(int,int)` and returns an `int`.

Experiment J3.7, Step 9. Surprisingly (or not so surprisingly), Java can no longer tell which version of `average` you intend to use when you call `average(firstInt,secondInt)`. Why? Because there are two versions of `average` that seem to match equivalently well.

Experiment J3.9, Step 1. This experiment uses a base class, an applet for testing, and a corresponding HTML file.

`BorderedSquare.java` is a class that will be used to create drawable objects. Since they're called "bordered squares," we can assume that they will be colored squares that have a corresponding border. Right now, the class is mostly unimplemented (although it will draw something).

`BorderedSquareTester.java` is an applet that will be used to test the new `BorderedSquare` class as we develop it. Given past experience, it is likely that we will modify and extend the one method contained within this class.

`bsquaretester.html` is the HTML file used to load the testing applet.

Experiment J3.9, Step 2. We call the square's `paint` method. In this respect, `BorderedSquare`s are a lot like applets. To get them to draw themselves, you need to call their paint method and give them a paintbrush.

Session J4: Boolean Expressions and Conditionals

In this laboratory session, you will learn about conditional control structures that permit your Java programs to select which actions to perform. You will learn about control structures as we develop a more useful `SimpleDate` class that permits us to represent and manipulate dates. The goals of this laboratory are to

- motivate and describe the `boolean` type;
- motivate the need for conditional control structures;
- introduce the primary Java conditional control structures: `if` and `switch`;
- consider the development of a `SimpleDate` object; and
- enhance your understanding of Java objects and methods.

Your instructor will tell you which of the proposed experiments you are to perform.

Prerequisite skills:

- Basic Java programming, up to and including objects and classes

Required files:

- `DateTester.java`
- `SimpleDate.java`
- `SimpleInput.java`
- `SimpleOutput.java`

Optional applet files:

- `ConfigurableGreeting.java`
- `greeting.html`

Discussion

Let us turn our attention to the creation of a simple class to represent dates. We will call this class `SimpleDate`. You may have created such a class in a previous lab. In case you haven't (or in case you are not confident in your code), here is a sample one.

```java
/**
 * A very simple implementation of dates using Gregorian-style
 * calendars (with year, month, and day).
 *
 * @author Samuel A. Rebelsky
 * @version 1.2 of September 1998
 */
public class SimpleDate {

  // +--------+--------------------------------------------------
  // | Fields |
  // +--------+
  /** The year. */
  protected int year;
  /** The month.  Use 1 for January, 2 for February, ...  */
  protected int month;
  /** The day in the month.  */
  protected int day;

  // +--------------+--------------------------------------------
  // | Constructors |
  // +--------------+
  /**
   * Build a new date with year, month, and day.  The month should be
   * between 1 and 12 and the day between 1 and the number of days in
   * the month.
   */
  public SimpleDate(int y, int m, int d) {
    this.year = y;
    this.month = m;
    this.day = d;
} // SimpleDate(int,int,int)

// +------------+--------------------------------------------------
// | Extractors |
// +------------+
/**
 * Get the year.
 */
public int getYear() {
  return this.year;
} // getYear()
  /**
   * Get the month.
   */
  public int getMonth() {
    return this.month;
  } // getMonth()
```

```
/**
 * Get the day.
 */
public int getDay() {
  return this.day;
} // getDay()

/**
 * Convert to a string (American format: MM/DD/YYYY)
 */
public String toString() {
  return this.month + "/" + this.day + "/" + this.year;
} // toString()
} // class SimpleDate
```

At present, this class is relatively primitive. All we can do is create new dates, check on their various components, and convert dates to strings. Good object design dictates that we think about some other things we might want to do with dates, such as check whether the current year is a leap year or determine the number of days in the month.

In Experiment J4.1 you will extend this SimpleDate class.

Boolean expressions

While there are a number of different methods we might add to the SimpleDate class, we will begin with some relatively basic ones (in terms of the complexity of implementation) and move on to more complicated ones.

To begin with, we'll look at a very simple question: "Does this date occur in January?" While it is not a very sophisticated question, it will help us get started with more advanced questions. It might even be used in support of other questions. For example, in order to determine whether a date is in winter, we might want to check if it's in January.

How do we determine if the date occurs in January? Fairly easily: all we need to do is compare the month field to the value we use for January (1).

Now, how might we express this as a Java method? By this point, you should know that every method begins with the keyword public, a return type, a method name, and a parameter list. Each method also has a body that describes how to implement the method.

What *name* should we give our method that checks whether the current date falls in January? Perhaps inJanuary.

What *type* should inJanuary return? It shouldn't return a number, since numbers aren't used to answer questions like "Is this day in January?" (If you don't understand this, think about how you'd react to "four" as an answer to "Is it sunny today?") Strings seem like they might be appropriate, since "Yes" and "No" are valid responses. However, these are really the only responses that we would accept (e.g., "Zebra" is not a response we would be very happy with). Because there are many cases in which we accept only two answers, Java provides a primitive type, boolean, which only has two legal values. The two legal values are true (corresponding to "yes") and _false_ (corresponding to "no"). The type is named _boolean_ after George Boole, a logician who developed a system of reasoning about these two values.

What parameters do we send to `inJanuary`? None, it turns out. While you may be tempted to give `inJanuary` a `SimpleDate` as a parameter, in the object-oriented perspective, we will ask each date whether it occurs in January. A small difference, but an important one.

Putting it all together, we get the following:

```
/**
 * Determine whether the current date falls in January.
 */
public boolean inJanuary() {
  ...
} // inJanuary()
```

If the `month` field has the value 1, then it is January. The "is" operator in Java is written `==` and, as you might guess, returns a _boolean_ value. We write this as

```
return this.month == 1;
```

In addition to `==` for "is", Java also supports

- `!=` for "is not";
- `<` for "is less than";
- `<=` for "is less than or equal to";
- `>` for "is greater than"; and
- `>=` for "is greater than or equal to".

For example, you might check if `x` is negative with `x<0`. Similarly, you might check if `x` is non-negative with `x>=0`.

In Experiment J4.2 you will develop some simple boolean methods.

Operations on Booleans

As you might guess, we can be somewhat limited if all we can do is one comparison. In particular, you may want to _use_ the results of a comparison and you may want to do _multiple comparisons_. We will examine the second issue first and write _boolean_ expressions that involve multiple comparisons. In particular, we will look at three new questions we might ask about a date:

- "Is this the first day of the year?"
- "Does this date occur in winter?"
- "Does this date occur in a leap year?"

These questions have some other appropriate aspects. Our previous question ("Does this date occur in January?") is at least partially involved in the answer to two of these questions ("Does this date occur in winter?" and "Is this date the first day of the year?"). The last two questions also have simple approximate answers (e.g., "It's winter if it's December, January, or February.") and more complex correct answers (e.g., "It's winter if it's after the winter solstice and before the vernal equinox."). Note also that these questions are used to answer more complex questions, like "How many days are there in this year?" and "How likely is it to be cold on this day?"

How do we know that a day is the first day of the year? It's the first day of the year if it's in January and it's the first day of the month. You'll note that we have two tests we want, and we'd like both of them to hold. Just as we said *and* in the sentence above, we use an *and* operator in Java. Surprisingly, *and* is written `&&` in Java. Using that operator, we can write

```
/**
 * Is this day the first day of the year?
 */
public boolean isFirstDay() {
   return (this.month == 1) && (this.day == 1);
} // isFirstDay
```

Note that we could also have used `inJanuary()` in place of `(this.month == 1)`. Note also that we used parentheses to gather together the subexpressions. Such parentheses aren't always necessary, but we recommend that you use them as they keep your code clearer.

Is `isFirstDay` strictly necessary? Probably not, as we could just use the test that forms the one line of its body. However, using `isFirstDay` can make our code more readable, shorter, and more supportive of change. For example, if it were somehow decreed that July 31 were the first day of the year, we would only need to change `isFirstDay` and not hundreds or thousands of lines of code.

Now let us move on to the next method. How do we determine if a date occurs in winter? We'll use the simple view that a month is in winter if it is in December, January, or February. Note that here we used the word *or*. Java includes an *or* operator that holds if either argument holds. In Java, *or* is written `||`. Using that operator, we can write the simple `isWinter` as follows.

```
/**
 * Is this day in winter?
 */
public boolean isWinter() {
   return (this.month == 12) ||
          (this.month == 1) ||
          (this.month == 2);
} // isWinter
```

You might want to think about how to write a more sophisticated version of this method that only returns true when it's between the winter solstice and the vernal equinox.

How do we determine whether it's a leap year? For the modern Gregorian calendar, it involves a relatively simple calculation. You might think that this calculation as "a year is a leap year if the year is divisible by 4." However, the designers of the Gregorian calendar realized that such a calculation would lead to some inaccuracy as the centuries marched on. In fact, years divisible by 100 are not leap years, unless they are also divisible by 400. So,

1900 is not a leap year, but 2000 is. Is such precision necessary in a computer program? Certainly. For example, computer programs are responsible for computing interest on bank accounts, and you wouldn't want the bank to pay you one less day of interest in some years (and, conversely, the bank wouldn't want to pay all of its customers for an extra day of interest). More importantly, if you claim that a leap year isn't a leap year, then you'll misidentify which day of the week most days of the year fall on. So, we can say that a year is a leap year if is divisible by 400 or if it is divisible by 4 and not divisible by 100.

So, how do we determine if a year is evenly divisible by 4 (or 100 or 400). We can use the *modulus* or *remainder* operator, `%`. To express "the remainder after dividing x by 4" in Java, we would write `x%4`. A number is evenly divisible by 4 if the remainder after dividing by 4 is 0, hence `year` is divisible by 4 if `(year%4 == 0)`.

Putting it all together, we get

```
/**
 * Determine if the current year is a leap year.
 */
public boolean isLeapYear() {
  return (this.year % 400 == 0) ||
    ((this.year % 4 == 0) && (this.year % 100 != 0))
} // isLeapYear
```

Note that we used the "is not" operator, `!=`. We can also use the boolean not operator, which is written `!`. So, we could also write "this year is not divisible by 100" as

```
!(this.year % 100 == 0)
```

In Experiment J4.3 you will develop additional boolean methods for the `SimpleDate` class.

Conditionals

By this point, you may have noted that we are not doing much with the results of all the methods we have developed. If you have done the experiments, you will have noted that you can use them to print `true` or `false`, but not much else. So, how do we use `boolean` variables and methods? Most typically, we use them in *conditional expressions*. For example, if someone asked how many days there are in the year, you might say to yourself "If it is a leap year, then there are 366 days; otherwise, there are 365 days". Java provides an `if` statement that does something similar.

The `if` statement has the form

```
if (condition) {
  statement-list;
}
else {
  statement-list;
}
```

To execute an `if` statement, Java first evaluates the condition (a boolean expression). If the condition holds (evaluates to true), Java then executes the statements in the first statement list. If the condition does not hold, Java then executes the statements in the second list.

For example, to print meaningful text about whether or not a day falls in winter, we might write

```java
if (day.isWinter()) {
  out.println(day.toString + " falls in winter.");
}
else {
  out.println(day.toString + " does not fall in winter.");
}
```

Similarly, to write a function that returns the number of days in the current year we might write

```java
/**
 * Determine the number of days in the current year.
 */
public int daysInYear() {
  if (this.isLeapYear()) {
    return 366;
  }
  else {
    return 365;
  }
} // daysInYear()
```

Note that you do not need to include the `else` portion of the `if` statement. If you leave out the `else` and the condition fails, Java simply goes on to the next statement. For example, if you only want to print a comment about winter days, you might write

```java
// Say something about cold winter days.
if (day.isWinter()) {
  out.println("Brr ... I'll bet it's cold on " +
              day.toString() + ".");
} // if the day is in winter
```

We are now ready to consider a more complicated method, one that determines whether or not the current date precedes another date. This method requires us to do a sequence of tests. One might say

- If the year corresponding to this date precedes the year corresponding to the other date, then return true.
- Otherwise, if the year corresponding to this date follows the year corresponding to the other date, then return false.
- Otherwise, we know the two dates are equal.
  - If the month corresponding to this date precedes the month corresponding to the other date, then return true.
  - ...

Note that if we wrote this using the indentation method given above, we would indent fairly far. Hence, custom dictates that in a series of *nested* ifs, you maintain the same indentation, as in

```
/**
 * Determine if the current date precedes the parameter.
 */
public boolean precedes(SimpleDate other) {
  if (this.year < other.year) {
     return true;
  }
  else if (this.year > other.year) {
   return false;
  }
  else if (this.month < other.month) {
     return true;
  }
  else if (this.month > other.month) {
     return false;
  }
  else if (this.day < other.day) {
     return true;
  }
  else if (this.day > other.day) {
     return false;
  }
  else {
     return false;
  }
} // precedes(SimpleDate)
```

In Experiment J4.4 you will improve the output from this class. In Experiment J4.5 you will investigate comparison of dates.

The switch statement

Let us now consider how one might compute the number of days until the end of the month. If we had a daysInMonth function, we might simply write

```
/**
 * Compute the number of days until the end of the month.
 */
public int daysLeftInMonth() {
  return this.daysInMonth() - this.day;
} // daysLeftInMonth()
```

If you've done Experiment J4.5, you may even have started to write such a method. However, we will assume that no such method is available. What should we do? It seems like a series of nested `if` statements is necessary, as in

```java
/**
 * Compute the number of days until the end of the month.  Return
 * -1 if it is not possible to determine this value.
 */
public int daysLeftInMonth() {
  if (this.month == 1) {
    return 31 - this.day;
  } // January
  else if (this.month == 2) {
    if (this.isLeapYear()) {
      return 29 - this.day;
    } // A leap year
    else {
      return 28 - this.day;
    } // Not a leap year
  } // February
  ...

  else if (this.month == 11) {
    return 30 - this.day;
  } // November
  else if (this.month == 12) {
    return 30 - this.day;
  } // December
  else { // Aagh!  Not a month I recognize.
    return -1;
  } // Troubles
} // daysLeftInMonth()
```

Such a solution is rather cumbersome. To handle some of these cumbersome cases, Java provides the `switch` statement, which has the following form

```java
switch (expression) {
  case val-1:
    statement-list-1;
    break;
  case val-2:
    statement-list-2;
    break;
  ...
  case val-n:
    statement-list-n;
    break;
  default:
    statement-list;
    break;
} // switch
```

This statement has the meaning "Evaluate the *expression*. If it is equal to *val-1*, then execute *statement-list-1*. Otherwise, if it is equal to *val-2*, then execute *statement-list-2*. If the *expression* is not equal to any of the values, execute the default statement list."

Using this statement, we can rewrite `daysLeftInMonth` as

```
/**
 * Compute the number of days until the end of the month.  Return
 * -1 if it is not possible to determine this value.
 */
public int daysLeftInMonth() {
  int daysLeft;
  switch (this.month) {
    case 1:  // January
      daysLeft = 31 - this.day;
      break;
    case 2:  // February
      if (this.isLeapYear()) {
        daysLeft = 29 - this.day;
      }
      else {
        daysLeft = 28 - this.day;
      }
      break;
  ...

    case 12:  // December
      daysLeft = 31 - this.day;
      break;
    default:
      daysLeft = -1;
      break;
  } // switch(this.month)
  return daysLeft;
} // daysLeftInMonth()
```

Note that you can only use `switch` statements with primitive types, like integers, boolean values, and real numbers.

It is possible to use multiple *labels* (the lines that read `case`) for each statement sequence. If any of the corresponding values match, then the statement is executed. Using this feature, we can rewrite `daysLeftInMonth` a final time.

```
/**
 * Compute the number of days until the end of the month.  Return
 * -1 if it is not possible to determine this value.
 */
public int daysLeftInMonth() {
  int daysLeft;
  switch (this.month) {
    case 1:  // January
    case 3:  // March
    case 5:  // May
    case 7:  // July
    case 8:  // August
```

```
        case 10: // October
        case 12: // December
          daysLeft = 31 - this.day;
          break;
        case 4:  // April
        case 6:  // June
        case 9:  // September
        case 11: // November
          daysLeft = 30 - this.day;
          break;
        case 2:  // February
          if (this.isLeapYear()) {
            daysLeft = 29 - this.day;
          }
          else {
            daysLeft = 28 - this.day;
          }
          break;
        default:
          daysLeft = -1;
          break;
      } // switch(this.month)
      return daysLeft;
    } // daysLeftInMonth()
```

We will not cover many subtleties to the switch statement. For example, you can leave out the break statements, in which case you "fall through" to the next bit of code.

In Experiment J4.6 you will investigate the switch statement.

Applet parameters

This section is optional and is intended for classes emphasizing applets or pursuing a simultaneous discussion of applications and applets.

As you may have noticed, the applets that we've built so far are limited. If you want an applet to do something slightly different (e.g., display a different piece of text), you need to change the source code of the applet. Is this the only way to configure an applet? No. You can also use the HTML page to set other attributes of the applet. These are often called the applet's *parameters*. What can the parameters be? Anything you think is appropriate: colors, text, more general instructions, and so on and so forth.

How do you set a parameter? With a param tag (another HTML tag). The param tag goes between your applet tags. For example, to indicate that the message should be "Reconfigured," one might write:

```
<param name="message" value="Reconfigured">
```

How can you access that parameter? With a getParameter method. The getParameter method always returns a string (even if you want a number).

If the HTML code does not include a `param` tag with the appropriate name, `getParameter` returns the special `null` value.

Here is the `paint` method of a simple applet that draws a selected string in green.

```
public void paint(Graphics paintBrush) {
  String msg;
  msg = getParameter("message");
  paintBrush.setColor(Color.green);
  paintBrush.drawString(msg, 10, 14);
} // paint(Graphics)
```

If the `message` parameter is set to "Hello World", then this will display "Hello World". If the `message` parameter is set to "Java Rules", then this will display "Java Rules".

But what if the page does not set a parameter? Then `msg` will by `null`. We don't know what `drawString` does with `null` messages, but it's unlikely to be pleasant. Hence, we should specify a *default* message that the applet uses when no parameter is supplied. How do we know when to use the default? Conditionals help us tell.

```
String msg = getParameter("message");
if (msg == null) {
  msg = "No message selected";
}
```

Conditionals can also help you help you convert strings to other objects. As an example of conversion, consider how one might allow the Web page to set the color that text is displayed in. As before, `getParameter` will return a string. Presumably, the string for the color will be "blue", "red", "yellow", or other colors you wish to support. Yet `setColor` needs a color. Hence, we compare the string for the color to members of a fixed set of strings, and when we find which it matches, we select the appropriate color. For example,

```
Color color = Color.black;  // Default
String colorName = getParameter("color");
if ("blue".equals(colorName)) { color = Color.blue; }
else if ("red".equals(colorName)) { color = Color.red; }
else if ("yellow".equals(colorName)) { color = Color.yellow; }
```

Note that we compare strings with the `equals` method rather than `==`.

What about numeric parameters? Since your applet receives the parameter as a string, you need a way to convert strings to numbers. Unfortunately, while Java includes a standard conversion mechanism, that mechanism is somewhat confusing for novices. Conversion involves the use of the `Integer.parseInt` method along with a `try`/`catch` clause. For example,

```
int fontSize;
String sizeParam = getParameter("Size");
try {
  fontSize = Integer.parseInt(sizeParam);
}
```

```
catch (Exception e) {
  fontSize = 12;
}
```

What does this say? As you might guess, the first line is a declaration of the variable `fontSize` and the second line reads in the string used for the font size. The line that reads `fontSize = Integer.parseInt(sizeParam);` does the conversion.

So, what is a `try`/`catch` clause? It's a kind of conditional. Java cannot convert all strings to integers. For example, what integer should it use for the string "Hello?" Hence, you'd like to write a conditional that says something like "if the conversion fails, use a default." The `try` indicates that you're doing something that might fail. The `catch` is the "if it fails, do this."

In effect, the code above says "try to convert `sizeParam` to an integer and then assign it to `fontSize`; if that fails, assign 12 to `fontSize`."

In a subsequent lab, you will consider `try`/`catch` clauses in more depth. For now, just model your code on this example. You are now ready to build parameterized applets. In Experiment J4.7 you will consider the basics of applet parameters. In Experiment J4.8 you will use conditionals to improve applet customization.

In both labs, you will use and extend the following customizable applet.

```java
import java.applet.Applet;
import java.awt.Color;
import java.awt.Font;
import java.awt.Graphics;

/**
 * A simple illustration of applet parameters.
 * Will eventually support the following parameters:
 *   message: the message to print
 *   font: the base font (Serif, SansSerif, etc.)
 *   size: the size of the font
 *   style: the style (plain, bold, italic, bolditalic)
 *   color: the color of the message
 *   shadow: the color of a shadow behind the message
 * The initial version supports only the message parameter.
 *
 * @author Samuel A. Rebelsky
 * @version 1.0 of August 1999
 */
public class ConfigurableGreeting
  extends Applet
{
  /** Paint the greeting. */
  public void paint(Graphics paintBrush) {
    // Begin with reasonable defaults
    String message = "A configurable message";
    String fontName = "Serif";
    int fontSize = 14;
    int fontStyle = Font.PLAIN;
```

```
      Color fontColor = Color.red;
      Color shadowColor = Color.gray;

      // Read information from the parameters.
      message = getParameter("message");

      // Set the font in preparation for writing.
      paintBrush.setFont(new Font(fontName, fontStyle, fontSize));

      // Paint the shadow first.  The vertical offset is based on
      // the size of the font.  This allows the message to appear
      // at the top of the applet.
      paintBrush.setColor(shadowColor);
      paintBrush.drawString(message, 12, fontSize+6);

      // Paint the message.
      paintBrush.setColor(fontColor);
      paintBrush.drawString(message, 10, fontSize+4);
   } // paint(Graphics)
} // class ConfigurableGreeting
```

Experiments

Name: _____

ID: _____

Experiment J4.1: Extending the `SimpleDate` class

Step 1. Make a list of at least three capabilities you might want to include in the `SimpleDate` class. You might consider changing dates, getting other types of information about dates, or working with multiple dates.

Step 2. Express each of the capabilities described in Step 1 as a Java method. For each method, you need only provide type, name, and parameters. You need not provide any code in the bodies of the methods (in fact, it is the purpose of this lab to help you develop these bodies).

Experiment J4.2: Simple `boolean` methods

Required files:

- `DateTester.java`
- `SimpleDate.java`
- `SimpleInput.java`
- `SimpleOutput.java`

Step 1. Make copies of `SimpleDate.java` and `DateTester.java`. Compile both files and execute `DateTester`. Record the results.

Step 2. Add the `inJanuary` method to the `SimpleDate` class. Here is the code for that method.

```
/**
 * Determine whether the current date falls in January.
 */
public boolean inJanuary() {
  return this.month == 1;
} // inJanuary()
```

Update `DateTester` to print out whether each day is in January with

```
out.println("Is " + day_one.toString() + " in January? " +
            day_one.inJanuary());
```

Recompile both files and execute `DateTester`. Record the new results.

Step 3. Add an `isAugust` method to the `SimpleDate` class. You will need to write this method yourself. Update `DateTester` to print out whether each day is in August. Enter the code for your new method here.

Step 4. Add an `inFirstHalf` method to the `SimpleDate` class. This method should test whether a date falls in the first half of the year (in any month through June). You can assume that the `month` field contains a number between 1 and 12. Recompile and test your method until you are confident that it works. Enter the method, the test code, and the output here.

Experiment J4.3: More boolean methods

Step 1. Add the isFirstDay method to the SimpleDate class. Update DateTester to use that method. Add a few more dates to DateTester to make sure that your testing is more comprehensive. Recompile the files and execute DateTester. Record the results here.

Step 2. Add the isWinter method to the SimpleDate class. Update DateTester to test that method (perhaps adding more dates if appropriate). Recompile the files and execute DateTester. Record the results here.

Step 3. Update the isWinter method so that it correctly (rather than approximately) answers the question "Is it winter?" In particular, your method should only claim that days on or after the winter solstice but before the vernal equinox are in winter. Record your code for isWinter here.

Step 4. Run DateTester. Note that you should not need to make any changes to DateTester. Record your results here.

Step 5. Finish the `equals` method begun below. This method should return <u>true</u> if the parameter is equal to the current date and <u>false</u> otherwise.

```
/**
 * Determine whether the parameter is the same as this date.
 */
public boolean equals(SimpleDate d) {



} // equals(SimpleDate)
```

Experiment J4.4: Improved output

Step 1. Update `DateTester` so that for each sample date it prints

```
Brr ... the date falls in winter.
```

for dates that fall in winter and

```
Fortunately, the date does not fall in winter.
```

for those dates that do not fall in winter. Summarize your code here.

Step 2. Update `DateTester` so that for each sample date it prints

```
It seems that the date falls in the first half of the year.
```

for dates that do just that. It should not print anything for other dates. Summarize your code here.

Experiment J4.5: More fun with conditionals

Step 1. Add the `precedes` method to the `SimpleDate` class. Update `DateTester` to check at least three interesting pairs of dates and print appropriate messages concerning their relative appearance in the year. Record your output here.

Step 2. Write a `daysInMonth` method that returns the number of days in the current month. For now, your method need only work for dates in January, February, and March (return some default value for every other date). Summarize your code here.

Step 3. Update `DateTester` to test the `daysInMonth` method. Summarize the test and enter the output here.

Step 4. Write a new constructor

```
public SimpleDate(int y, String m, int d)
```

that allows one to create a new date by using an appropriate string for the month (e.g., `March`). Note that to compare two strings, you need to use the `equals` method, as in

```
if (s1.equals(s2)) {
  out.println("'" + s1 + "' is the same as '" + s2 + "'");
}
```

Your constructor need only work with the months January, February, and March, although it should support both the full names of the months and the abbreviated versions. Summarize your code here.

**Experiment J4.6:
Using the `switch`
statement**

Step 1. Using a `switch` statement, write a `daysInMonth` method that returns the number of days in the current month. Summarize the code for the method here.

Step 2. Update `DateTester` to test the `daysInMonth` method. Enter the output here.

Step 3. Using your `daysInMonth` method from Step 1 above, write a `days-LeftInMonth` method. Update `DateTester` to test this new method. Enter the output here.

Step 4. Using a `switch` statement, write a new constructor

```
public SimpleDate(int y, String m, int d)
```

that allows one to create a new date by using an appropriate string for the month (e.g., `March`). Test your constructor. Does it seem to do what you expect? Why or why not?

When you have answered this question, you may wish to read the notes on this step.

Experiment J4.7: Applet parameters

Required files:

- `ConfigurableGreeting.java`
- `greeting.html`

Step 1. Make copies of <u>ConfigurableGreeting.java</u> and <u>greeting.html</u>. Consider the code for `ConfigurableGreeting.java`. Explain, in your own words, what each part of the `paint` method does.

Step 2. Look at `greeting.html`. What message do you expect this page will display?

Step 3. Compile `ConfigurableGreeting` and load the applet with `greeting.html`. Describe the output.

Step 4. Change the line in `greeting.html` that reads

```
<param name="message" value="A Configurable Applet">
```

to instead read

```
<param name="message" value="Reconfigured">
```

What do you expect to happen if you load the applet using the modified `greeting.html`? Note that you have not recompiled `ConfigurableGreeting`.

Load the applet using `greeting.html` to confirm your answer.

Step 5. Change the line in `greeting.html` that reads

```
<param name="message" value="Reconfigured">
```

to read

```
<param name="MESSage" value="Reconfigured">
```

That is, change the capitalization of `message`. What effect do you expect this change to have?

Step 6. Load the applet using `greeting.html` to confirm your answer. You may also wish to consult the notes on this step.

Change the line in `ConfigurableGreeting.java` that reads

```
message = getParameter("message");
```

to instead read

```
message = getParameter("MESSAGE");
```

That is, change the capitalization of `message`. What effect do you expect this change to have?

Recompile `ConfigurableGreeting` and then load the applet using `greeting.html` to confirm your answer. You may also wish to consult the notes on this step.

Step 7. Change the line in `greeting.html` that reads

```
<param name="MESSage" value="Reconfigured">
```

to read

```
<param name="greeting" value="Reconfigured">
```

Change the line in `ConfigurableGreeting.java` that reads

```
message = getParameter("MESSAGE");
```

to read

```
message = getParameter("greeting");
```

What effect do you expect these changes to have?

Recompile `ConfigurableGreeting` and then load the applet using `greeting.html` to confirm your answer. You may also wish to consult the notes on this step.

Step 8. Change the line in `greeting.html` that reads

```
<param name="greeting" value="Reconfigured">
```

to again read

```
<param name="message" value="Reconfigured">
```

Do not change `ReconfigurableGreeting`. What effect do you expect the change to `greeting.html` to have?

Load the applet using `greeting.html` to confirm your answer. You may also wish to consult the notes on this step.

Step 9. As you may have observed, the difficulty here is that the HTML file no longer contains a `greeting` parameter. Good programming style dictates that our applet have a default message. Change the line in `ReconfigurableGreeting` that reads

```
message = getParameter("greeting");
```

to read

```
message = getParameter("greeting");
if (message == null) {
  message = "No message specified.";
}
```

What effect do you expect this change to have?

Recompile `ConfigurableGreeting` and then load the applet using `greeting.html` to confirm your answer.

Step 10. What changes would we need to make to `ConfigurableGreeting` in order to support a `font` parameter? Do not make the changes, just summarize them.

Step 11. Add a line to `greeting.html` that reads

```
<param name="font" value="SansSerif">
```

What effect do you expect this line to have?

Step 12. Add the following line to the `paint` method of `ConfigurableGreeting`.

```
fontName = getParameter("font");
```

This should follow the steps used to get the message and precede the call to `setFont`. What effect do you expect this change to have?

Confirm your answer by recompiling `ConfigurableGreeting` and then loading the applet with the modified `greeting.html`.

Step 13. Replace the line in `greeting.html` that reads

```
<param name="font" value="SansSerif">
```

with

```
<param name="font" value="Monospaced">
```

What effect do you expect this change to have?

Step 14. Replace the line in `greeting.html` that reads

```
<param name="font" value="Monospaced">
```

with

```
<param name="font" value="NoSuchFont">
```

What effect do you expect this change to have?

Step 15. For a robust applet, the one line added in step 12 is not enough. Why not? What other lines should we also include?

Experiment J4.8: More applet parameters

Required files:

- `ConfigurableGreeting.java`
- `greeting.html`

Before you begin, if you have not already done so, make copies of `Config-urableGreeting.java` and `greeting.html`. Make sure that you understand the code in `ConfigurableGreeting.java`.

Step 1. Add the following lines to `greeting.html` within the `applet` tags.

```
<param name="size" value="24">
<param name="style" value="bold">
<param name="color" value="white">
<param name="shadow" value="black">
```

What effect do you expect these changes to have?

After recording your answer, you may wish to consult the notes on this step.

Step 2. Add the following lines to the `paint` method of `Config-urableGreeting`. They should fall after the other calls to `getParameter`, but before the calls to `setFont` and `setColor`.

```
String colorName = getParameter("color");
if ("black".equals(colorName)) { fontColor = Color.black; }
else if ("blue".equals(colorName)) { fontColor = Color.blue; }
else if ("green".equals(colorName)) { fontColor = Color.green; }
else if ("purple".equals(colorName)) { fontColor = new
Color(255,0,255); }
else if ("red".equals(colorName)) { fontColor = Color.red; }
else if ("white".equals(colorName)) { fontColor = Color.white; }
else if ("yellow".equals(colorName)) { fontColor = Color.yellow; }
```

What effect do you expect these new lines to have?

Confirm your answer by recompiling `ConfigurableGreeting` and loading the applet from `greeting.html`.

Step 3. Replace the line in `greeting.html` that reads

```
<param name="color" value="white">
```

with one that reads

```
<param name="color" value="yellow">
```

Do not recompile `ConfigurableGreeting`. What effect do you expect this change to have?

Confirm your answer by loading the applet from `greeting.html`.

Step 4. Replace the line in `greeting.html` that reads

```
<param name="color" value="yellow">
```

with one that reads

```
<param name="color" value="WHITE">
```

Do not recompile `ConfigurableGreeting`. Load the applet from `greeting.html`. What color does the text appear in? Why?

After recording your answer, you may wish to consult the notes on this step.

Step 5. Update `ConfigurableGreeting` so that it also reads the color of the shadow from the HTML file. Summarize your changes here.

Step 6. Update `ConfigurableGreeting` so that it also reads the font style from the HTML file. Summarize your changes here.

Step 7. Add the following lines to the `paint` method of `ConfigurableGreeting`. They should fall after the other calls to `getParameter`, but before the calls to `setFont` and `setColor`.

```
String sizeParam = getParameter("Size");
try {
  fontSize = Integer.parseInt(sizeParam);
}
catch (Exception e) {
  fontSize = 12;
}
```

Recompile `ConfigurableGreeting` and load the applet from `greeting.html`. What effect did this new code have?

Step 8. Replace the lines added in Step 7 with the following two lines.

```
String sizeParam = getParameter("size");
fontSize = Integer.parseInt(sizeParam);
```

Recompile `ConfigurableGreeting` and load the applet from `greeting.html`. What effect did this new code have?

Step 9. It seems that it's just as easy to use the shorter code from Step 8 rather than the longer code from Step 7. However, this isn't always so. Try replacing the line in `greeting.html` that sets the font size with

```
<param name="size" value="twenty">
```

Load the applet from `greeting.html`. What happens?

Step 10. Replace the two lines inserted in Step 8 with the longer code from Step 7. Recompile `ConfigurableGreeting`. Load the applet from `greeting.html`. What happens? What does that suggest about the `try`/`catch` clause?

After recording your answer, you may wish to consult the notes on this step.

Step 11. Replace the line in `greeting.html` that reads

```
<param name="size" value="twenty">
```

with one that reads

```
<param name="size" value="32">
```

What effect does this have?

Post-Laboratory Problems

**Problem J4-A:
Rethinking
`precedes`**

It is possible to write `precedes` without any `if` statements. How? By using a complex <u>boolean</u> expression. Write `precedes` so that it has only one line, a <u>return</u> of an appropriate boolean expression. Make sure to test your method.

Which version of `precedes` do you prefer? Why?

**Problem J4-B:
Incrementing a
date**

Write and test a method, `SimpleDate tomorrow()`, that returns the day after the current date. For example, if `d` is August 29, 1987, then `d.tomorrow()` should be August 30, 1987. If `d` is July 31, 1995, then `d.tomorrow()` should be August 1, 1995.

**Problem J4-C: Is
the date valid?**

Write and test a method, `isValid`, that returns true if the current date is legal and false otherwise. A date is legal if the month is legal and the day is at least one and no more than the number of days in that month.

**Problem J4-D:
Correcting dates**

Write and test a method, <u>void</u> `correct`, that corrects an invalid date by advancing or backing up the appropriate amount. For example, the 14th month of 1964 should be the second month of 1965, the 0th month of 1931 should be the 12th month of 1930, the 32nd day of June should be the 2nd day of July, the 62nd day of June should be the 1st day of August, and the −4th day of December should be the 26th day of November.

**Problem J4-E:
Printing dates,
revisited**

Write and test a method, `String toLongString`, that returns the string corresponding to the longer version of the date. For example, for the date 12/3/1964 (in U.S. format), it might return *December 3, 1964*.

**Problem J4-F:
Printing dates,
revisited again**

Add a method, `setPrintFormat`, to `SimpleDate`. This new method should allow the user to select which date format (U.S. short, U.S. long, European short, etc.) to use. Update `toString` to check which format it should use.

**Problem J4-G:
`isWinter`,
revisited**

Rewrite `isWinter` so that it uses `precedes` appropriately.

**Problem J4-H:
Selecting colors,
revisited**

In Experiment J4.8, you found that Java's string comparison is case-sensitive, so "white" and "WHITE" are treated as different strings. Update the `ConfigurableGreeting` applet so that it is case-insensitive.

Hint: Look at the documentation for the methods provided by `java.lang.String`.

**Problem J4-I:
Selecting colors,
revisited again**

Update `ConfigurableGreeting` to support another dozen or so colors (of your choice). These colors should be available for both the message and the shadow.

Note: You may find it helpful to create a method that converts strings to colors.

**Problem J4-J:
Multiple
greetings**

Update `ConfigurableGreeting` so that it prints up to three messages, one per line. The applet parameters should be named `firstMessage`, `secondMessage`, and `thirdMessage`. Each will appear in the same font and color. If any of the three messages is missing, you should skip it.

Note: you'll need to take the font size into account when displaying one message per line.

**Problem J4-K:
Parameterized
drawings**

Create an applet that draws shapes (squares, circles, etc.) and that permits the HTML page to customize at least three aspects of the drawing.

**Problem J4-L:
Stick figures**

Create a `StickFigure` applet that permits the HTML page to customize at least three aspects of the stick figure (arm length, shirt color, hat size, etc.).

Notes

Experiment J4.6, Step 4. It is likely that you failed in your attempt. Java only lets you switch on selected primitive types, and not on strings and other objects.

Experiment J4.7, Step 5. Hopefully, you've observed that the capitalization used within the `param` tag does not affect the passing of the parameter to the applet. In fact, the Java specification says that parameters are case-insensitive.

Experiment J4.7, Step 6. Hopefully, you've observed that the capitalization of the string used with `getParameter` tag does not affect the passing of the parameter to the applet. In both cases (`param` tag and `getParameter`), the Java specification says that parameters are case-insensitive.

Experiment J4.7, Step 7. It may seem confusing that the parameter is called `greeting` in the HTML file, but is stored in the variable `message` within the applet. However, Java does not require you to use the same name for the variable that stores a parameter that you've used for naming the parameter. We'll take advantage of this ability to choose a different internal name in the next experiment.

Experiment J4.7, Step 8. As you may have surmised, there is no longer a parameter tag for the `greeting` parameter that the applet expects. Hence, the call `getParameter("greeting")` returns null. The `drawString` method is unhappy with the null string and gives an error.

Experiment J4.8, Step 1. Since the applet does not yet read these new parameters, they have no effect.

Experiment J4.8, Step 4. While the name of the parameter is case-insensitive, the value of the parameter is case-sensitive. Java treats "`white`" and "`WHITE`" as different strings. Hence, none of the strings match the applet and never changes `fontColor` from `Color.red` (which it was set to at the start of the `paint` method).

Experiment J4.8, Step 10. As suggested earlier, the try/catch permits us to specify a default value. More importantly, it stops the program from reporting an error when we use values that Java does not know how to convert.

Session J5: Control Structures for Repetition

In this laboratory session, you will learn about control structures for repetition, which permit your Java programs to perform actions repeatedly. You will learn about these control structures as we further extend the `Date` object that represents dates. The goals of this laboratory are to

- motivate the need for repetition;
- digress temporarily into *function overloading;*
- introduce the primary Java structures for repetition: <u>while</u> and <u>for</u>;
- consider a few mathematical expressions typically used in looping; and
- consider further extensions to the `SimpleDate` class.

Your instructor will tell you which of the proposed experiments you are to perform.

Prerequisite skills:

- Basic Java programming, up to and including objects and classes
- Boolean variables and conditional control structures
- Understanding of the `SimpleDate` class created in the previous laboratory session

Required code files:

- `DateTester.java`
- `ForExamples.java`
- `SimpleDate.java` (as extended in the previous laboratory session)
- `SimpleInput.java`
- `SimpleOutput.java`
- `WhileExamples.java`

Optional applet files:

- `Bounce.java`
- `ConfigurableGreeting.java`
- `GridApplet.java`
- `Rainbow.java`
- `bounce.html`
- `grid.html`
- `rainbow.html`

Discussion

In the previous laboratory session, we developed a number of methods for the `SimpleDate` class, progressing from simple methods to more advanced methods. In this laboratory, we will continue with our exploration of the `SimpleDate` class. We will begin by looking at a `dayOfYear` method which determines which day of the year it is. From that method, we will develop a `daysUntil` method that determines the number of days until a particular date. Using that method in the experiments, you will develop a `dayOfWeek` method that determines the day of the week a date falls on.

Repetition

How do we determine what day of the year a particular date is? We can determine the number of days between the first day of the year and the first day of the month, and then add which day of the month it is. For example, consider February 3. The zeroth day of February is 31 days from the beginning of the year. February 3 comes three days later, so February 3 is 34 days from the beginning of the year.

Unfortunately, the computation for later months is not so easy. For example, how many days is August 1 from the beginning of the year? It may be possible to precompute all of those numbers, as in

```
/**
 * Compute the position of this day within the current year.
 */
public int dayOfYear() {
  int to_start_of_month;
  switch (this.month) {
    case 1:  // January
      to_start_of_month = 0;
      break;
    case 2:  // February
      to_start_of_month = 31;
      break;
    case 3:  // March
      to_start_of_month = 59;  // We'll deal with leap years later in
                               // this function.
      break;
    ...
  } // switch(this.month)
  // Handle leap years
  if (this.isLeapYear() && this.month > 2) {
      to_start_of_month = to_start_of_month + 1;
  } // After February in a leap year
  // Add the days in this month
  return to_start_of_month + this.day;
} // dayOfYear()
```

However, the work precomputing the position of the beginning of each month from the beginning of the year is painful and prone to simple errors in calculation if done by hand. Hence, we'd prefer to have the computer do such computation. How do we compute the number of days until the first of month `m`? We sum the number of days in each of the previous months. Algorithmically, we might write

```
// Compute the number of days until the start of month m
daysUntilStartOfMonth(m)
   sum the number of days in each month, p, that precedes m
   if it's a leap year and after February, add 1
   return the result
```

The `sum` command in that algorithm is vague and is not included in most programming languages. Hence, we must expand it to work out the details. How do we compute the sum? By explicitly adding the days in each prior month.

```
// Compute the number of days until the start of month m
daysUntilStartOfMonth(m)
   days = 0
   for each month, p, that precedes m
     add the number of days in month p to days
   end for
   if it's a leap year and after February, add 1 to days
   return days
```

The "for each month" is also vague. It may be better to make it explicit by using a counter.

```
// Compute the number of days until the start of month m
daysUntilStartOfMonth(m)
   days = 0
   p = 1
   while p < m
     add the number of days in month p to days
     add 1 to p
   end for
   if it's a leap year and after February, add 1 to days
   return days
```

Rewriting this in Java-like syntax, we get

```
//**
 * Compute the number of days until the start of the month.
 */
public int daysUntilStartOfMonth(int m) {
   int prev = 1; // A previous month
   int days = 0; // Total number of days

   // Sum the days in the previous months.  We assume that the
   // daysInMonth method handles leap years
   // correctly.
   while (prev < m) {
     days = days + this.daysInMonth(prev);
     prev = prev + 1;
   } // while
   // And that's it.
   return days;
} // daysUntilStartOfMonth(int)
```

`while` loops

In fact, this is legal Java. Java provides a <u>while</u> statement with the following form.

```
while (test) {
  body
} // while
```

The test is executed. If it fails, the `while` loop terminates and control passes to the subsequent statement. If the test holds, then the statements in the body are executed. After the body is executed, the test is done again. The test and body are repeatedly executed until the test no longer holds.

Note that the test is done once per repetition, which means that the test need hold only at the beginning of the body. If, during the body, the test would no longer hold, execution of the body still continues until the end.

In Experiment J5.1 you will experiment with some basic looping examples.

**Detour:
Overloading
revisited**

Wait! Something seems wrong with the code above. It uses a `daysInMonth(int)` method, and you may recall that we designed `daysInMonth` to take no parameters. What do we do? Once again, this is an instance of *overloading* method names: providing multiple methods with the same name, but different types of parameters.

Using overloading, we might extend our old `SimpleDate` class with the new, parameterized `daysInMonth`. We can also have the old `daysInMonth` use the new one, as in

```
/**
 * Compute the number of days in the current month.
 */
public int daysInMonth() {
  return this.daysInMonth(this.month);
} daysInMonth()

/**
 * Compute the number of days in month m.
 */
public int daysInMonth(int m) {
  switch (m) {
    case 1:
    case 3:
    ...
      return 31;
      break;
    case 2:
      if (this.isLeapYear()) {
        return 29;
      } // February in a leap year
      else {
        return 28;
      } // February, but not a leap year
      break;
    ...
```

```
    } // switch
} // daysInMonth(int)
```

In Experiment J5.2 you will consider how to use loops to count days in the year.

for loops

Is the `while` loop the only looping mechanism that Java provides? No. Because so many algorithms naturally include a section that reads *for every value of* n *between* a *and* b *do ...* that Java includes a `for` control structure to make it more convenient to express such algorithms.

The `for` loop has the following form

```
for (initialization; test; increment) {
  body
} // for
```

In effect, this is a shorthand for the following `while` loop.

```
initialization;
while (test) {
  body;
  increment;
} // while
```

That is, a `for` loop begins by executing the initialization portion. Traditionally, this sets the initial value for a counter variable. Next, it executes the test. If the test fails, the loop terminates and control moves on to the next statement. If the test succeeds, the body is executed. After the body is done, the increment is executed. The test is done again, and the cyclic process continues.

For example, we might rewrite our `daysUntilStartOfMonth` method as

```
//**
 * Compute the number of days until the start of the month.
 */
public int daysUntilStartOfMonth(int m) {
  int prev = 1; // A previous month
  int days = 0; // Total number of days
  // Sum the days in the previous months
  for (prev = 1; prev < m; prev = prev + 1) {
    days = days + this.daysInMonth(prev);
  } // for
  // Deal with leap years
  if (this.isLeapYear() && m > 2) {
    days = days + 1;
  } // After February in a leap year
  // And that's it.
  return days;
} // daysUntilStartOfMonth(int)
```

In Experiment J5.3 you will consider some simple examples of `for` loops.

**Detour:
Arithmetic
shorthand**

As you read other people's Java code (or C code or C++ code or ...), you will find many *shorthand* expressions for common arithmetic expressions. For example, it is so typical to add one to a variable that Java includes a `++` operator that does just that. In particular,

```
++i;
```

is the same as

```
i = i + 1;
```

Hence, you will often see `for` loops that look like

```
for (i = 0; i < n; ++i)
```

The prefix `++` (also called *preincrement*) differs from the longer form in that it can be more easily used as part of larger expressions. For example,

```
j = ++i + 3;
```

represents "Add 1 to `i`. Add 3 to the updated `i`, and store the result in `j`."

There is also a postfix `++` (also called *postincrement*) that adds 1 to the argument, but returns the old value. For example,

```
j = i++ + 3;
```

represents "Add 1 to `i`; add 3 to the old value of `i`; store the result in `j`".

As you might guess, there are also prefix and postfix `--` operators (predecrement and postdecrement), with the intended meaning of decrementing the corresponding variable.

Finally, Java also provides a `+=` assignment which has the affect of adding the right-hand-side to the left-hand-side. For example,

```
k += 5;
```

represents "Add 5 to `k`".

In Experiment J5.4 you will consider Java's various arithmetic shorthands.

**Loops and
applets**

This section is optional and is intended for classes emphasizing applets or pursuing a simultaneous discussion of applications and applets.

Loops have many applications for applets, particularly with regards to drawing regular and repetitious figures, such as sequences of images. In Experiment J5.5, you will use `for` loops to create a rainbow text effect. In Experiment J5.6, you will track down errors in an applet designed to draw a regular grid using a `for` loop.

In Experiment J5.7, you will attempt a more complicated task: showing the positions of a bouncing ball. In order to make the ball bounce, you need to be able to determine the area available to the applet.

You may have noted that the dimensions (width and height) of the area reserved for an applet are set within the HTML files that loads the applet and not within the applet itself. Clearly, it is possible to load the same applet with different dimensions and different pages may therefore choose different dimensions for the same applet. For many applets, it becomes important for the applet designer to be able to determine these dimensions. This is particularly true of our bouncing ball applet, in which the ball must change direction.

Fortunately, Java provides a mechanism for the applet author to determine the dimensions given for the applet. You can call `this`.getSize() to obtain a `java.awt.Dimension` object. You can then get the width of that object by referring to its `width` and `height` fields.

For example, you might write the following to set the right and bottom edges of the area allocated to the applet. Note that since the area begins at (0,0), the width of the applet gives the horizontal offset of the right edge, and the height of the applet gives the vertical offset of the bottom edge.

```
int right;  // The right edge of the area allocated to the applet.
int bottom; // The bottom edge of the area allocated to the applet.
Dimension dim = this.getSize();
right = dim.width;
bottom = dim.height;
```

Now, how do you make the ball bounce? We'll explore that issue in Experiment J5.7.

Experiments

Name: _____

ID: _____

Experiment J5.1:
Simple loops

Required files:

- `SimpleInput.java`
- `SimpleOutput.java`
- `WhileExamples.java`

```
/**
 * A collection of methods that use Java's looping mechanisms.
 *
 * @author Samuel A. Rebelsky
 * @version 1.0 of August 1998
 */
public class WhileExamples {
  /**
   * Print the numbers from 1 to n
   */
  public void countTo(int n, SimpleOutput out) {
    int i = 1;
    while (i < n) {
      out.println(i);
      i = i + 1;
    } // while
  } // countTo(int n, SimpleOutput out)

  /**
   * Keep reading passwords until you read the supplied password.
   */
  public void readPass(SimpleInput in,
                       SimpleOutput out,
                       String pass) {
    String name = "";
    while (!name.equals(pass)) {
      out.print("Enter the password: ");
      name = in.readString();
      // If the password was entered correctly, the loop
      // should terminate.
      out.println("'" + name + "' was not a valid password.");
    } // while
  } // readPass(SimpleInput, SimpleOutput, pass)
} // class WhileExamples
```

Step 1. Make a copy of `WhileExamples.java`. That class includes a `countTo` method. What should this method do (in general)? What should the method do if called with a value of `10` for n? Do you think that `countTo` will work correctly? Why or why not?

Step 2. Write a class, TestLoops, that includes a main method that calls countTo with 10 as the value for n. Record the results. Were these what you expected?

Step 3. If countTo did not have the correct results, explain why not. If countTo did have the correct results, can you envision any simple errors one might have made?

Step 4. Add a count(<u>int</u> from, <u>int</u> to, SimpleOutput out) method to WhileExamples. This method should count all the numbers beginning with from and ending with to. Test your method. Enter the code for your method here.

Step 5. Read the code for the readPass method from WhileExamples.java. This code has a small logical problem. What do you think the problem is?

Step 6. Update your `main` method to call `readPass` with a password of `Hello`. Run your program using passwords of `hi`, `hello`, and `Hello`. Record the results.

Step 7. Based on those results, what is the logical problem in `readPass`?

Step 8. Update `readPass` so that it gives the correct output. Summarize the changes.

Experiment J5.2: Counting the day of the year

Required files:

- `SimpleDate.java`, as updated in the previous lab.

Step 1. Add a `daysInMonth(int m)` method to `SimpleDate`. Test your code. Enter your code for the method here.

Step 2. You may have observed that both of the versions of `daysInMonth` assume that you want to use the current year. Add a `daysInMonth` method that takes both month and year as parameters. Test your code. Enter your code for the method here.

Step 3. Update the original `daysInMonth` and the `daysInMonth` you created in Step 1 to use the `daysInMonth` you created in Step 2. Enter the revised code for your methods here.

Step 4. Using the ideas from above, add a `daysUntilStartOfMonth` method for the `SimpleDate` class. This method should compute the number of days until the beginning of the current month. Test your code. Enter your code here.

Step 5. Write a program that computes how many days there are before the start of December in a non-leap year. You should use the `SimpleDate` class and the corresponding methods you developed earlier.

Step 6. Using the `daysUntilStartOfMonth`, add a `dayOfYear` method to the `SimpleDate` class. This method should compute the number of days from the beginning of the year until the current date. Test your code and enter it here.

Step 7. Using the updated `SimpleDate` class, determine on which day of the year the following dates fall:

- January 1
- March 17, 1996
- March 17, 2000
- March 17, 1900
- August 29, 1987
- December 3, 1964
- Your birthday

Experiment J5.3:
Simple for loops

Required code files:

- `ForExamples.java`

```java
/**
 * Simple examples of Java's for loops.
 *
 * @author Samuel A. Rebelsky
 * @version 1.0 of September 1998
 */
public class ForExamples {

  /**
   * Sum the squares of the numbers from 1 to n.
   */
  public int sumSquares(int n) {
    int sum = 0;   // The sum of the numbers
    int i;         // A counter for the loop
    for (i = 0; i <= n; ++i) {
      sum = sum + i*i;
    }

    return sum;
  } // sumSquares(int)
} // class ForExamples
```

Step 1. Read the code for sumSquares from the class ForExamples. What does the method do? Do you expect that it will work correctly? Why or why not?

Step 2. Using ForExamples, write a program that reads in an integer, n, and prints the sum of squares from 1 to n. For example, if you enter 3, it should compute 1*1 + 2*2 + 3*3 = 14 and print out 14. Enter your code for the program here.

Step 3. Run your program on inputs of 1, 3, 5, 10, 20, 0, and −3. Record your results.

Step 4. Add a `sumCubes` method to `ForExamples`. This method should compute the sum of cubes of integers from 1 to `n`. Enter your code for the method here.

Step 5. Run your program on inputs of 1, 3, 5, 10, 20, 0, and −3. Record your results.

Step 6. Add a `sumTo` method to `ForExamples`. This method should compute the sum of the integers from 1 to n. Enter your code for the method here.

Step 7. Did you use a <u>for</u> loop for Step 6? If so, see if you can rewrite it without using a <u>for</u> loop, <u>while</u> loop, or recursive function calls. (The sum of 1+2+...+*N* is a well-known formula; you should already know it. If not, you should find it.)

Experiment J5.4: Arithmetic shorthand

Step 1. Write a program that includes the following two lines. Print out the values of i and j after the two statements. (Note that i and j must be integer variables.) Record the values.

```
i = 2;
j = ++i + 3;
```

Step 2. Write a program that includes the following two lines. Print out the values of i and j after the two statements. Record the values.

```
i = 2;
j = i++ + 3;
```

Step 3. Did you get the same values in Steps 1 and 2? Why or why not?

Step 4. Write a program that includes the following two lines. Print out the values of i and j after the two statements. Record the values.

```
i = 2;
j = i-- + 3;
```

Step 5. Write a program that includes the following two lines. Print out the values of i and j after the two statements. Record the values.

```
i = 2;
j = i-- + 3;
```

Step 6. What do you think the value of i and j will be after the following lines are executed. Why?

```
i = 2;
j = i++ - i++;
```

Step 7. Execute the lines from the previous step and record the results. What do they suggest?

Experiment J5.5: Rainbow text

Optional applet experiment

Required files:

- `ConfigurableGreeting.java`
- `Rainbow.java`
- `rainbow.html`

Step 1. Make copies of `ConfigurableGreeting.java`, `Rainbow.java`, and `rainbow.html`. Compare `ConfigurableGreeting.java` (which you've used in previous experiments) and `Rainbow.java`. How are they similar? How are they different?

Step 2. Why do you think `Rainbow.java` includes the variables `changeRed`, `changeBlue`, and `changeGreen`?

Step 3. Why do you think `Rainbow.java` includes the variables `horiz` and `vert`?

Step 4. Compile `Rainbow.java` and load the applet from `rainbow.html`. Describe the output from the applet.

Step 5. The stated goal of `Rainbow` is to draw text in a rainbow. `Rainbow`, however, does not appear to do so. Rather, it draws the text in a single color. To draw the text in a rainbow of colors, we'll need to draw the text multiple times, changing the color and position each time. We'll start by adding a `for` loop. Replace the lines that read

```
paintBrush.setColor(new Color(redPart, greenPart, bluePart));
paintBrush.drawString(message, horiz, vert);
```

with the following `for` loop.

```
// Repeatedly draw the message in different colors and positions.
for (int step = 1; step <= steps; step = step + 1) {
    // Draw the message in the current color at the current position.
    paintBrush.setColor(new Color(redPart, greenPart, bluePart));
    paintBrush.drawString(message, horiz, vert);
} // for(step)
```

What effect do you expect the change to have?

Confirm your answer by recompiling `Rainbow` and loading the applet from `rainbow.html`. You may also want to consult the notes on this step.

Step 6. We will now update the applet so that the message is printed in a different space each time. Add the following lines to the end of the `for` loop that you added in the previous step.

```
// Update the position.
horiz = horiz + 1;
vert = vert + 2;
```

What effect do you expect the change to have?

Confirm your answer by recompiling `Rainbow` and loading the applet from `rainbow.html`.

Step 7. As you may have noted, the result of the previous step is a somewhat smudged version of the message, which makes it hard to read. We can make it somewhat clearer by writing the message in black at the end. Add the following lines after the `for` loop.

```
// Draw the message a final time.
paintBrush.setColor(Color.black);
paintBrush.drawString(message, horiz, vert);
```

Test the appearance using both white and black. Which do you prefer?

Step 8. We are now ready to start changing the color (something we would hope to happen in a rainbow). In Step 6, we changed `horiz` and `vert`. In this step, we'll change `redPart`, `greenPart`, and `bluePart`. Choose an appropriate way to change each of the three (hint: use `changeRed`, `changeBlue`, and `changeGreen`). Verify that your change works by recompiling `Rainbow` and loading the applet from `rainbow.html`. Summarize your changes here.

After you have recorded your answer, you may wish to consult the notes on this step for the recommended changes.

Step 9. Currently, we have the <u>for</u> loop draw the message twenty times. What do you expect to happen if we draw the message forty times?

Confirm your answer by updating `rainbow.html` and then loading the applet from `rainbow.html`. You may also wish to consult the notes on this step.

Step 10. As you may have noted, the difficulty with taking too many steps is that the color components eventually fall outside of the acceptable range (values between 0 and 255). We can account for this problem by checking the value and, if it's outside the range, either (1) stopping at the maximum/minimum value or (2) changing the way we change the color. We'll use the second technique.

Add the following lines to the <u>for</u> loop, after the change to the color. (Also add corresponding lines for blue and green.)

```
// Handle colors out of the range 0..255.
if (redPart < 0) {
  redPart = 0;
  changeRed = Math.abs(changeRed);
}
```

```
if (redPart > 255) {
  redPart = 255;
  changeRed = -(Math.abs(changeRed));
}
```

Recompile `Rainbow` and load the applet from `rainbow.html`. In your own words, explain what these new lines do.

Step 11. At present, our rainbow appears as a diagonal line. We might prefer it to appear as a curve (perhaps even in something resembling a rainbow shape). How might we make the rainbow curve?

Step 12. Delete the lines that read

```
horiz = horiz + 1;
vert = vert + 2;
```

Insert the following lines before the call to `drawString` in the `for` loop in the `paint` method in `Rainbow`.

```
// Determine the position.
horiz = 2*step;
int tmp = step-steps/2;
vert = 20+100*4*(tmp*tmp)/(steps*steps);
```

What do you think these lines do?

Confirm your answer by updating `rainbow.html` and then loading the applet from `rainbow.html`. You may wish to use 100 steps. You may also wish to consult the notes on this step.

Experiment J5.6:
A grid applet

Optional applet experiment

Required files:

- `GridApplet.java`
- `grid.html`

Step 1. In many graphics applications, it is useful to be able to create a regularly spaced grid of points. The applet given by `GridApplet.java` is intended to do just that. Make copies of `GridApplet.java` and `grid.html`. Compile `GridApplet` and load the applet from `grid.html`. Describe the output.

Step 2. Describe, in your own words, how you might write an applet to create that grid. *Do not read the code for* `GridApplet`.

After recording your answer, you may wish to consult the notes on this step.

Step 3. Consider the code for `GridApplet`. That code contains a number of logical errors. Identify as many as you can. List them here.

Step 4. Update `grid.html` so that it uses eight rows and eight columns. Do not change `GridApplet`. Reload the applet using the modified `grid.html`. Does the grid change? Why or why not?

Step 5. One reason you may have speculated that the grid doesn't change is that the applet never consults the HTML file. Add appropriate Java code so that `GridApplet` reads the number of columns and rows from the HTML file. You should be able to develop that code on your own. However, if you need help, you may consult the notes on this step. Summarize the new code here.

Step 6. Recompile `GridApplet` and load the applet using `grid.html`. Do you get the appropriate number of rows and columns? Why or why not?

After recording your answer, you may wish to consult the notes on this step.

Step 7. Update the `for` loops to use the appropriate variables. More particularly, replace the line that reads

```
for (int row = 1; row < 4; row=row+1) {
```

with

```
for (int row = 1; row < rows; row=row+1) {
```

Replace the line that reads

```
for (int col = 1; col < 5; col=col+1) {
```

with

```
for (int col = 1; col < cols; col=col+1) {
```

Recompile `GridApplet` and load the applet using `grid.html`. Do you get the appropriate number of rows and columns? Why or why not?

After recording your answer, you may wish to consult the notes on this step.

Step 8. Update the `for` loops to use appropriate termination conditions. More particularly, replace the line that reads

```
for (int row = 1; row < rows; row=row+1) {
```

with

```
for (int row = 1; row <= rows; row=row+1) {
```

Replace the line that reads

```
for (int col = 1; col < cols; col=col+1) {
```

with

```
for (int col = 1; col <= cols; col=col+1) {
```

Recompile `GridApplet` and load the applet using `grid.html`. Do you get the appropriate number of rows and columns? Why or why not?

Step 9. Update `grid.html` so that it draws ten rows and five columns. Reload the applet using the modified `grid.html`. Do you get the appropriate number of rows and columns? Why or why not?

After recording your answer, you may wish to consult the notes on this step.

Step 10. As you may have noted, rows and columns seem to be reversed. Often problems like this happen because programmers nest their loops incorrectly. Update your code so that the columns loop is the outer loop and the rows loop is the inner loop. For example, you might write

```
// For each column ...
for (int col = 1; col <= cols; col=col+1) {
  // Step through the rows, drawing the grid point at
  // the current row/column.
  for (int row = 1; row <= rows; row=row+1) {
    ...
  } // for each row
} // for each column
```

Do you think this will fix the problem? Why or why not?

Confirm your answer by recompiling `GridApplet` and reloading the applet with `grid.html`.

Step 11. It seems that the problem does not have to do with the nesting of the loops. What is the problem? If we look closely, we may notice that it has to do with the `fillOval` command. That command makes the vertical position (the first coordinate) dependent on the row, and the horizontal position (the second coordinate) dependent on the column. However, all points in the same row should have the same vertical position, and all points in the same column should have the same horizontal position. Replace the line that reads

```
paintBrush.fillOval(row*spacing, col*spacing, 3, 3);
```

with one that reads

```
paintBrush.fillOval(col*spacing, row*spacing, 3, 3);
```

Confirm that the applet now works correctly.

Step 12. After all that hard work, it's time for a little bit of fun. Add the following line before the line you just changed.

```
paintBrush.setColor(new Color(row*255/rows,128,col*255/cols));
```

What effect do you expect this new line to have?

Confirm your answer by recompiling `GridApplet` and reloading the applet with `grid.html`.

Experiment J5.7: A bouncing ball

Required files:

- `Bounce.java`
- `bounce.html`

Step 1. Make copies of `Bounce.java` and `bounce.html`. Compile `Bounce` and load the applet from `bounce.html`. Describe the output of the applet.

Step 2. Update `bounce.html` to change the horizontal velocity to 9 and the acceleration to 2. Reload the applet from the modified `bounce.html`. What effect do the changes have?

Step 3. Update `bounce.html` to change the number of repetitions to 10. Reload the applet from the modified `bounce.html`. What effect does the change have?

When you are done, restore the number of repetitions to 100.

Step 4. Read the code for `Bounce.java`. In your own words, describe what it does.

Step 5. Add the following lines to the `paint` method of `Bounce`, just before the call to `fillOval`.

```
int tmp = 200-200*step/repetitions;
paintBrush.setColor(new Color(tmp,tmp,tmp));
```

What effect do you expect these new lines to have?

Confirm your answer by recompiling `Bounce` and loading the applet from `bounce.html`.

Step 6. As you may have noted, the ball does not yet bounce. In your own words, suggest how we might make the ball bounce.

Step 7. If you ask a physicist, you may learn that when a ball bounces, its velocity changes from downward to upward. You can simulate this change by reversing the sign on `horizVelocity`. When do you do what? When the ball reaches the bottom of the screen, replace the lines that read

```
// Update the speed.
vertVelocity = vertVelocity + acceleration;
```

with the following

```
// Update the speed.
if (vert > bottom) {
  vertVelocity = -Math.abs(vertVelocity);
}
vertVelocity = vertVelocity + acceleration;
```

What effect do you expect these new lines to have?

Confirm your answer by recompiling `Bounce` and loading the applet from `bounce.html`.

Step 8. Explain why we used

```
vertVelocity = -Math.abs(vertVelocity);
```

instead of

```
vertVelocity = -vertVelocity;
```

After recording your answer, you may wish to consult the notes on this step.

Step 9. As you may have observed, it is now possible for the ball to exit the right edge of the screen. Update your applet so that the ball bounces at both the right and left edges of the screen. Summarize your changes here.

After recording your answer, you may wish to consult the notes on this step.

Post-Laboratory Problems

Problem J5-A:
`daysUntil`

Using Java's two primary looping mechanisms, we can investigate a more complicated issue: How do we determine the number of days between two dates? More precisely, how do we write the following method?

```
/**
 * Determine the number of days from the current day until
 * the event.  Note that the event must occur after the
 * current day.
 */
public int daysUntil(Date event) {
  ...
} // daysUntil(Date)
```

We might employ a number of strategies to answer this question. We might determine the number of days each date falls from a set date (e.g., January 1, 1970) and then subtract the two. We might also use a strategy like the one we used for determining the number of days until the start of the month. That is, rather than counting up days in each month, we might count up the days in each year, starting with the first year and ending with the final year.

We recommend that you try both.

Add a `daysSinceDayZero` method to the `SimpleDate` class. This method should compute the number of days since some designated day zero (you can determine what that date is) until the current date (i.e., the one represented by `this`).

Write a `daysUntil` method that uses `daysSinceDayZero` to compute the number of days until another day.

Problem J5-B:
`daysSince`

Write a `daysSince` method that computes the number of days since another date. Don't use `daysSinceDayZero` or `daysUntil`. You will probably need to count up the days in each year, as described earlier.

Problem J5-C:
Reflection

Having done Problems J5-A and J5-B, which one seems the more elegant way to solve the problem?

Problem J5-D:
Loop mechanisms

What looping mechanisms did you use in problems J5-A and J5-B? Why?

Problem J5-E:
Grade averaging

Write a program that reads in a sequence of grades, terminated by `-1` and prints out the average of the grades.

Problem J5-F: Maximum grade

Write a program that reads in a sequence of grades, terminated by `-1` and prints out largest of the grades.

Problem J5-G: Revising the rainbow's shape

In Experiment J5.5, we created a simple rainbow from a message. We saw how to make that rainbow appear as a diagonal line, and as a simple curve. Find a few other interesting curves for the rainbow. Make it possible for the HTML page to select what curve to use.

Problem J5-H: Revising the rainbow

One of the difficulties of the rainbow from Experiment J5.5 is that the progression of colors was not particularly sophisticated. This is because it's difficult to switch between our normal sense of a rainbow (which is based on wavelengths) and the RGB color model. Java's `java.awt.Color` class also supports the hue, saturation, and brightness (HSB) model. Read the documentation on `java.awt.Color` and the corresponding `getHSBColor` method, and use this method to improve the appearance of the rainbow.

Problem J5-I: A complete grid

In Experiment J5.6, we created a grid of points whose spacing and number of columns and rows were specified by the corresponding HTML page. However, one might instead prefer to have the number of columns and rows determined by the area given to the applet, along with the spacing. Write a new grid applet that fills the applet's area with a regularly spaced grid of points.

Problem J5-J: Improving the bouncing simulation

You may have observed that there are some problems with the bouncing simulation from Experiment J5.7. In particular, even though the bouncing is supposed to be 100 percent elastic, the ball seems to bounce lower and lower at each step. Why is this? Because our code does not appropriately account for the part of the "step" in which the ball bounces. In particular, it effectively treats a ball that bounces early in the step (i.e., if it started quite near the floor) the same as one that bounces later in the step (i.e., that fell most of the way before bouncing). *Improve the simulation to handle that issue.* While doing so, make sure that the ball does not fall below the bottom of the screen.

After making that improvement, consider how you might take elasticity more explicitly into account.

Notes

Experiment J5.5, Step 5. The applet now draws the given message twenty times. However, since we don't change the value of any of the variables, the message appears twenty times in the same place. Hence, the output of the applet will be the same.

Experiment J5.5, Step 8. To support more variation in the applet, use something like the following when updating the colors

```
// Update the colors.
redPart = redPart + changeRed;
greenPart = greenPart + changeGreen;
bluePart = bluePart + changeBlue;
```

These lines belong within the `for` loop.

Experiment J5.5, Step 9. Eventually, one or more of the components (`red-Part`, `greenPart`, or `bluePart`) will exceed 255 (or fall below 0). The `java.awt.Color` class does not permit this, and will report an error to the browser or applet viewer. Think about how you might deal with this problem.

Experiment J5.5, Step 12. The seemingly complicated math is not that complicated. Basically, we're drawing part of a parabola. As you may recall, a parabola is given by a quadratic equation. In this case, we make the vertical component depend on the square of the step number (`tmp*tmp`) and the horizontal component linear in the step number. We make the peak of the parabola at the middle by subtracting `steps/2` from the `step` before squaring. (Hence, that value will be zero when we are at the middle of our steps.) We divide by `steps*steps` and multiply by 4 to scale the value (the largest value should be approximately `(steps/2)*(steps/2)`, so we divide by that value). We multiply by 100 so that we end up with a value between 0 and 100 (more or less).

You may wish to try variants of these values to see what effects they have.

Experiment J5.6, Step 2. A typical strategy will involve nested `for` loops. We step through the rows (using a `for` loop). Within each row, we step through the columns (again, using a `for` loop). For example,

```
// For each row ...
for (int row = 1; row <= rows; row = row + 1) {
  // Draw all the grid points on this row.
  // For each column ...
  for (int col = 1; col <= cols; col = col + 1) {
    // Draw the grid point for the given row/column.
    ...
  } // for each column
} // for each row
```

Experiment J5.6, Step 5. Your new code should resemble the following.

```
// Read the parameters from the HTML page.
String rowString = getParameter("rows");
String colString = getParameter("columns");
String spacingString = getParameter("spacing");
try { rows = Integer.parseInt(rowString); }
catch (Exception e) { rows = 1; }
try { cols = Integer.parseInt(colString); }
catch (Exception e) { cols = 1; }
try { spacing = Integer.parseInt(spacingString); }
catch (Exception e) { spacing = 10; }
```

Experiment J5.6, Step 6. Although we are reading the number of rows and columns, we are not using them within our code. More precisely, the `for` loops use specified ending values, rather than the variables `rows` and `cols`.

Experiment J5.6, Step 7. As you may have noted if you looked closely, we have seven rows and seven columns. What might be wrong? It could be that the first row and the first column fall outside the applet's window. It could be that we're counting wrong. You might verify that the first is not the problem by using a drawing command that you are sure will place the points within the screen (e.g., by adding 10 to horizontal and vertical positions). In fact, because our `for` loops use `<` rather than `<=`, they stop one step too soon.

Experiment J5.6, Step 9. It appears that we've drawn five rows and ten columns, rather than ten rows and five columns. Obviously, we've gotten something backwards.

Experiment J5.7, Step 8. Because our simulation currently allows the ball to go below the bottom of the area, it is possible that it remains below the bottom, even after it starts upward. We want to make sure that the velocity is always negative (upwards) when the ball is below the bottom. In a post-laboratory problem, you will have the opportunity to consider how to prevent the ball from going below the bottom.

Experiment J5.7, Step 9. When the ball reaches the right edge, it should start moving towards the left (a negative horizontal velocity). Hence, we use

```
if (horiz > right) {
  horizVelocity = -Math.abs(horizVelocity);
}
```

When the ball reaches the left edge, it should start moving toward the right (a positive horizontal velocity). Hence, we use

```
if (horiz < left) {
  horizVelocity = Math.abs(horizVelocity);
}
```

Your answer may differ slightly.

Session J6: Arrays and Hash Tables

In this laboratory session, you will learn about two of Java's key built-in objects for managing groups of data: arrays and hash tables. The goals of this laboratory are to:

- motivate grouping of objects;
- consider design issues pertaining to size of groups and indexing of objects within groups;
- introduce two key grouping mechanisms in Java: arrays and hash tables;
- compare and contrast these mechanisms; and
- apply these mechanisms to a variety of problems.

Your instructor will tell you which of the proposed experiments you are to perform.

Prerequisite skills:

- Familiarity with objects in Java
- Java's looping mechanisms: `while` and `for` loops
- Java's conditional execution statements: `if` and `switch`

Required files:

- `CountWords.java`
- `NewScoreCounter.java`
- `ScoreCounter.java`
- `SimpleInput.java`
- `SimpleOutput.java`

Discussion

In this laboratory session, we will move on from dates into other issues. In particular, we will consider how one might *count* a variety of things.

Counting scores

The CoolStuff company has recently done a survey on the usefulness of their CoolStuff brand thingamabobs. Each participant in the survey gave the thingamabobs an integer score between one and three. The company would like you to write a program to read in all the scores and print out the count for each score.

How might we approach this problem? We could possibly create a `Score` object for each score. However, since scores are integers, it is likely to be sufficient to use an integer variable for each one. Then, we could step through the input until we reach the end of input. For each number read, we increment the appropriate counter.

How do we know when we've reached the end of the input? We'll require that a value of 0 be entered to mark the end of input. How do we select which counter to update? A `switch` statement is an appropriate solution.

Putting it all together,

```java
import SimpleInput;
import SimpleOutput;

/**
 * Count the number of scores assigned to something.
 *
 * @author Samuel A. Rebelsky
 * @version 1.0 of September 1998
 */
public class ScoreCounter {
  /**
   * Read in a sequence of scores, count them, and print out
   * the results.
   */
  public static void main(String[] args) {
    SimpleInput in = new SimpleInput();
    SimpleOutput out = new SimpleOutput();
    int count1 = 0;   // Count of scores with value 1
    int count2 = 0;   // Count of scores with value 2
    int count3 = 0;   // Count of scores with value 3
    int score;        // The next score to be read.

    // Prompt the user
    out.println("Enter the sequence of scores terminated by a 0.");

    // Read the first score.
    score = in.readInt();

    // Keep reading scores until we hit the "end of scores" mark (0).
    while (score != 0) {
```

```
// Process the score
switch (score) {
  case 1:
    count1 = count1 + 1;
    break;
  case 2:
    count2 = count2 + 1;
    break;
  case 3:
    count3 = count3 + 1;
    break;
  default:
    out.println("Invalid entry: " + score);
    break;
} // switch
// Read the next score
score = in.readInt();
} // while

// Print out the results
out.println(count1 + " people entered a score of 1.");
out.println(count2 + " people entered a score of 2.");
out.println(count3 + " people entered a score of 3.");
} // main(String[])
} // class ScoreCounter
```

In Experiment J6.1 you will use this class to count scores.

Arrays

While this solution works relatively well for a few counters, it does not work as well for more counters. For example, it would be tedious (and, therefore, error prone) to support one hundred different counters. At the same time, there seems to be a gap between the comment we write (e.g., "update the counter corresponding to score") and the corresponding code (e.g., a switch statement).

In fact, this program has places where it would be natural and appropriate to apply our newly formed skills with loops. In particular, when printing out the counts of the individual scores, we would like to be able to write

```
for (score = 1; score < 3; ++score) {
   out.println(countscore + "  people entered " + score);
}
```

Unfortunately, Java will treat countscore as a new variable and not as count1 (when score is 1), count2, and count3.

Fortunately, Java provides structures for creating groups of variables that can be indexed by numbers. These structures are called *arrays* and have a special syntax.

You declare an array of integers with

```
int[] array-name;
```

For example, to declare an array of integers called `scores`, you would write

```
int[] scores;
```

Once you have declared an array, you can refer to an element of the array by writing the array name, a left brace, an index into the array (the number of the element you want to use), and a right brace. For example, to add 5 to the third element of `scores`, I might write

```
scores[3] += 5;
```

Because arrays are objects, you need to create them with `new` (or more precisely, a variant of `new`).

```
name = new int[size];
```

This says to create a new array that will hold up to *size* integers. So if we wanted to have scores hold three integers, we would write

```
scores = new int[3];
```

What are the valid indices for this array? You might assume they are 1, 2, and 3. However, Java starts numbering at 0. Hence, if `scores` holds three integers, then they are numbered 0, 1, and 2. Similarly, if `scores` holds five integers, then they are numbered 0, 1, 2, 3, and 4.

We can use arrays to simplify our counter program as follows

```java
import SimpleInput;
import SimpleOutput;

/**
 * Count the number of scores assigned to something.
 *
 * @author Samuel A. Rebelsky
 * @version 1.2 of February 1998
 */
public class NewScoreCounter {
  /**
   * Read in a sequence of scores, count them, and print out
   * the results.
   */
  public static void main(String[] args) {
    // Prepare for input and output.
    SimpleInput in = new SimpleInput();
    SimpleOutput out = new SimpleOutput();
    // A count of scores with values 1,2,3.  A score with value i
    // is stored in counts[i-1].
    int[] counts = new int[3];
    // Keep track of the next score read.
    int score;

    // Prompt the user.
    out.println("Enter the sequence of scores terminated by a 0.");

    // Read the first score.
    score = in.readInt();
```

```
    // Keep reading scores until we hit the "end of scores" mark (0).
    while (score != 0) {
      // Process the score.
      if ((score < 0) || (score > 3)) {
        out.println("Invalid entry: " + score);
      } // if it's an invalid score
      else { // it's a valid score
        counts[score-1] += 1;
      } // a valid score
      // Read the next score.
      score = in.readInt();
    } // while

    // Print out the results.
    for (score = 1; score <= 3; ++score) {
      out.println(counts[score-1] +
                  " people entered a score of " +
                  score + ".");
    } // for each score
  } // main(String[])
} // class NewScoreCounter
```

Note that arrays work particularly well with for loops. If we want to do something to every element of an array, then we can use a for loop to do so.

In Experiment J6.2, you will use NewScoreCounter to begin your investigation of arrays.

Some important details

As you may have noticed, arrays are *objects* in Java. That means that the variables that store arrays really store *references* to those arrays. Why is this important? For the same reason that it's important with objects. Often, when you change one array, you end up changing another array (which is, in fact, a reference to the same array).

What can you do about this? Be careful and copy arrays when necessary.

Are there other problems you are likely to encounter? Because arrays are objects, they must be created with new. If you fail to do so, you are likely to receive serious error messages.

In addition, you should be careful to ensure that the indices you use for your arrays fall within the appropriate range. Your program will crash with an error message if you do not. (However, in a subsequent lab we will learn how to deal with such errors.)

A final note: It is often useful to determine the number of elements in an array. (Believe it or not, you may forget. More precisely, you may pass the array to another method that needs to determine how many elements are in the array.) You can determine the number of elements in an array, A, with A.length.

In Experiment J6.3, you will consider what happens when you assign the same array to different variables.

Counting words

Let us now turn our attention to a more complicated counting problem: counting the number of times each word appears in an essay. How might we approach this problem? This is a complicated enough problem that it is appropriate to use multiple objects. In particular, we will create a `Word-Counter` object that provides two methods, `count(String word)` and `getCount(String word)`. The first method increments the count for a particular word. The second method retrieves the count.

For example, the code

```
SimpleOutput out = new SimpleOutput();
WordCounter words = new WordCounter();
words.count("Hello");
words.count("Hello");
words.count("Hi");
words.count("Hello");
out.println("Hello appears " + words.getCount("Hello") + " times.");
out.println("Hi appears " + words.getCount("Hi") + " times.");
out.println("Goodbye appears " + words.getCount("Goodbye") + " times.");
```

will print

```
Hello appears 3 times.
Hi appears 1 times.
Goodbye appears 0 times.
```

Given a `WordCounter` class, it is fairly easy to count the number of words in a text. Simply read each word and count it. Note that this does not give us any output (yet), but should give us correct counts if we can get to them.

```
import SimpleInput;
import SimpleOutput;
import WordCounter;

/**
 * Count the occurrences of each of the words given on input.
 * Print out the number of appearances of "The" and "A".
 *
 * @author Samuel A. Rebelsky
 * @version 1.0 of September 1998
 */
public class CountWords {
  /**
   * Read all the words in standard input, count them, and print
   * out some interesting statistics.
   */
  public static void main(String[] args) {
    SimpleInput in = new SimpleInput();
    SimpleOutput out = new SimpleOutput();
    WordCounter words = new WordCounter();
    String word;
    // Count all the input words.
    // Stop when you hit the last word.
    word = in.readString();
```

```
while (!word.equals("")) {
  words.count(word);
  word = in.readString();
} //while

// Print out selected results
out.println("'The' appears " + words.getCount("The") +
            " times.");
out.println("'A' appears " + words.getCount("A") + " times.");
} // main
} // class CountWords
```

Now, how can we build `WordCounter`? One simple way is to work with two parallel arrays. One array, `words`, will contain all the words being counted. The other array, `counts`, will have the corresponding counts. For example, if `words[1]` is `hello`, then `counts[1]` will count the number of times `hello` occurs.

Given those arrays, it is reasonably easy to count words already entered in the `words` array.

```
for(i = 0; i < words.length; ++i) {
  if (words[i].equals(word)) {
    ++counts[i];
  } // if
} // for
```

How do we declare an array of strings? The same way we declare an array of integers, except that we change the type slightly.

```
String[] words;
```

How do we add a new word to be counted? We find an empty element of `words` and set it to the word to be counted.

In Experiment J6.4, you will use arrays and `CountWords` to count words.

Hash tables

Obviously, this solution to the problem is not very elegant. In particular, the `for` loops may seem a little bit excessive. It would be much more convenient to have a structure, like an array, but indexed by words. Such structures are typically called *dictionaries*. In Java, `java.util.Hashtable` provides a particular implementation of dictionaries.

In particular, hash tables are structures that store groups of objects and index those objects by objects (usually strings).

How does that differ from arrays? Arrays are structures that store groups of objects and index those objects by integers.

The big difference appears to be in the indexing mechanism. However, other differences include the following:

- Hash tables use the syntax of standard objects, rather than the brackets that arrays use.
- Hash tables do not have a specified size, while arrays do.
- It is difficult (at least at this stage of your learning) to step through hash tables, while it is very easy to step through arrays.

What methods do hash tables provide? Given a hash table, `ht`, you can add an index/value pair to the hash table with `ht.put(index,value)`. You can look up an element in the hash table with `ht.get(index)`. You can determine whether there is an element corresponding to a particular index with `containsKey(index)`.

For example, suppose that Professors Smith and Jones are writing a program to store class grades. They may create a hash table, `grades`, that associates a letter grade with each student. To print out the grade for John Doe, they might write

```
if (grades.containsKey("John Doe")) {
  out.println("John Doe's current grade is " +
              grades.get("John Doe"));
}
else {
  out.println("John Doe does not seem to be enrolled.");
}
```

Similarly, to set Jane Doe's grade to A minus, they might write

```
grades.set("Jane Doe", "A-");
```

In Experiment J6.5, you will use hash tables to do grading.

Experiments

Name: _____

ID: _____

Experiment J6.1: Counting scores

Required file:

- ScoreCounter.java

Step 1. Make a copy of ScoreCounter.java. Compile and execute it. Enter the sequence 1 1 2 22 3 2 1 0. (Here, and in the subsequent steps, you should enter only one value per line.) Record the results.

Step 2. Execute ScoreCounter. Enter the sequence 0 1 1 1. Record the results. Explain the results.

Step 3. Execute ScoreCounter. Enter the sequence 1 2 3 01 012 03 1 01 0. Explain the results.

Step 4. Update ScoreCounter so that it indicates which score was most frequently entered (1, 2, or 3). Summarize your changes to the code. (If more than one score was entered the most number of times, you can print all top scores, or just one such score.)

After entering an answer, you may wish to look at the notes on this problem.

Step 5. Update `ScoreCounter` so that it counts the number of invalid entries that were given. Summarize your changes to the code.

Step 6. Run your modified version on input `1 3 2 1 22 -5 012 01 0`. Record and explain your output.

Step 7. Update `ScoreCounter` so that it counts scores between 1 and 5 (inclusive). You need no longer print out the most frequently entered score. Summarize your changes to the code.

Step 8. How might you update `ScoreCounter` to handle scores between 1 and 10? How long would it take you to make those changes? (Don't make the changes; just speculate on what they would be.)

Experiment J6.2: Introducing arrays

Required file:

- `NewScoreCounter.java`

Step 1. Make a copy of `NewScoreCounter.java`. Compile and execute it. Enter the sequence `1 1 2 22 3 2 1 0`. (In this, and the subsequent steps, enter one score per line.) Record the results.

Step 2. Update `NewScoreCounter` so that it reports on the score most frequently entered. Summarize your changes.

Step 3. Was it easier to update `ScoreCounter` or `NewScoreCounter` to report this count? Why?

Step 4. Update `NewScoreCounter` so that it reports on the number of invalid scores entered. Summarize your changes.

Step 5. Was it easier to update `ScoreCounter` or `NewScoreCounter` to report this count? Why?

Step 6. Update `NewScoreCounter` so that it counts scores between 1 and 5 inclusive. You should still print out the score that appears most frequently. Summarize your changes.

Step 7. Was it easier to update `ScoreCounter` or `NewScoreCounter` to handle the greater range of scores? Why?

Step 8. What changes would you need to make to support scores between 1 and 100? How long would it take you to make those changes?

Step 9. Is there an overall change we can make to `NewScoreCounter` so that it's even easier to change the number of scores?

Step 10. What changes would you need to make to have `NewScoreCounter` handle scores between −5 and 5?

After recording your answer, you may wish to look at the notes on this problem.

Experiment J6.3: Arrays and references

Step 1. Write a class, `ArrayTester`, with a `main` method that includes the following two lines

```
int[] A;
A[1] = 2;
```

What happens when you try to compile that program?

Step 2. Update that program so that `A` is an array containing one integer. What happens when you try to compile the program? If you successfully compile the program, what happens when you try to execute the program?

Step 3. What do you expect to happen when you try to compile or execute a program that includes the following code?

```
SimpleOutput out = new SimpleOutput();
int[] stuff = new int[10];
out.println(stuff[1]);
```

Step 4. Add the lines from Step 3 to the `main` method of your `ArrayTester` class. What happens when you try to compile the program? If it successfully compiles, what happens when you try to execute the program?

Step 5. Add the following lines to your `main` method. Compile and execute the program. Record your results.

```
int[] alpha = new int[10];
int[] beta = alpha;
int i;
for (i = 0; i < 10; ++i) {
  alpha[i] = i;
  beta[i] = 2*i;
} // for
for (i = 0; i < 10; ++i) {
  out.print(alpha[i] + " ");
} // for
out.println();
for (i = 0; i < 10; ++i) {
  out.print(beta[i] + " ");
} // for
out.println();
```

Experiment J6.4: Counting words

Required files:

- `CountWords.java`

Step 1. Make a copy of `CountWords.java`. Create a new class, `Word-Counter` (stored in `WordCounter.java`), with two methods, `void count(String word)` and `int getCount(String word)`. For now, the methods should be empty. That is, `count` need not count words, and `get-Count` can return 0. Compile your classes. Execute `CountWords`. Type in a phrase of your choice.

Step 2. Add two fields, `words` and `counts` to `WordCounter`. Add a constructor that initializes those fields. *You must initialize array fields in a constructor! You cannot simply assign to them.* Recompile `WordCounter` and execute `CountWords`.

Step 3. Add the following lines to `count`

```
int i;
for(i = 0; i < words.length; ++i) {
  if (words[i].equals(word)) {
    ++counts[i];
  } // if
} // for
```

Replace the body of `getCount` with

```
int i;
// Try all the words we know
for(i = 0; i < words.length; ++i) {
  if (words[i].equals(word)) {
    return counts[i];
  } // if
} // for
// We don't know the word, assume the count is 0
return 0;
```

Recompile `WordCounter` and execute `CountWords`. Type in "The The The A The". Record your results. Are they what you expected? Why or why not?

Step 4. Add the following lines to your constructor

```
words[0] = "The";
```

Recompile `WordCounter` and execute `CountWords`. Type in "The The The A The". Record and explain your results.

Step 5. Update `WordCounter` to add new words when they appear. Recompile `WordCounter` and execute `CountWords`. Type in "The The The A The". Record and explain your results.

Step 6. Rerun `CountWords` using "the The the a A A" as input. Record your results. What do your results suggest?

Experiment J6.5: Hash tables

Step 1. Create a new class, `GradeReporter`, with a `main` method that includes the following lines.

```
Hashtable grades = new Hashtable();
SimpleOutput out = new SimpleOutput();
grades.put("Fred", "B+");
grades.put("Amy", "B");
grades.put("Elaine", "A");
out.println("Elaine's grade is " + grades.get("Elaine"));
```

Note that you will need to import `java.util.Hashtable` in order to use hash tables. Compile and execute your program. Record the output.

Step 2. Add the following lines to your program. Recompile and execute. Record the output.

```
if (grades.containsKey("Bennett")) {
  out.println("Bennett's grade is " + grades.get("Bennett"));
}
else {
  out.println("Bennett has no recorded grade.");
}
```

Step 3. Add the following lines to your program. *Do not recompile the program.* What do you think the new output will be?

```
if (grades.containsKey("fred")) {
  out.println("Fred's grade is " + grades.get("fred"));
}
else {
  out.println("Fred has no recorded grade.");
}
```

Step 4. Recompile and run your program. Record the output. Is that what you expected? Explain why the given output was produced.

Step 5. Add the following lines to your program. *Do not recompile the program.* What do you think the new output will be?

```
out.println("Michelle's grade is " + grades.get("Michelle"));
```

Step 6. Recompile and run your program. Record the output. Is that what you expected? Explain why the given output was produced.

Step 7. Add the following lines to the end of your program. *Do not recompile the program.* What do you think the new output will be?

```
grades.put("Lloyd", "C");
out.println("Lloyd's grade is currently " + grades.get("Lloyd"));
grades.put("Lloyd", "A");
out.println("Lloyd's grade is currently " + grades.get("Lloyd"));
grades.put("lloyd", "F");
out.println("Lloyd's grade is currently " + grades.get("Lloyd"));
```

Step 8. Recompile and run your program. Record the output. Is that what you expected? Explain why the given output was produced.

Post-Laboratory Problems

**Problem J6-A:
Improving
`daysUntilStart-
OfMonth`**

In an earlier lab, we developed a `daysUntilStartOfMonth` method for the `SimpleDate` class that computed the number of days until the start of a month. Our solution was relatively elegant; rather than computing this value by hand, we computed the sum of the days in the previous months. Unfortunately, this comes at some computational cost. For example, if we need to compute the days until the start of November again and again and again, we are clearly doing extra work. We can do less work by precomputing an array that contains the number of days until the beginning of each month.

Update your `SimpleDate` class to do just that. That is, add an array to your class that, for each month, stores the number of days until the start of that month (perhaps for a normal year). Update the constructors for the class to initialize that array. Finally, update `daysUntilStartOfMonth` to use that array.

**Problem J6-B:
Counting grades**

Often, when instructors look at trends in classes, they do not count individual grades, but rather ranges of grades. For example, one might count the number of 90s, 80s, 70s, and so on down the line. Write a Java program that reads in a sequence of grades terminated by a -1 and prints out the number of entries in each range.

**Problem J6-C:
Counting
different scores**

Update `NewScoreCounter` so that it counts scores between -5 and 5, inclusive.

**Problem J6-D:
Copying arrays**

Create a class, `ArrayUtils`, that will contain a number of utility functions for dealing with arrays. Write the following method and add it to the class.

```
/**
 * Make a real copy of an integer array (as opposed to
 * just a copy of the reference).
 */
public int[] copyIntegerArray(int[] copyme) {
  ...
} // copyIntegerArray(int[])
```

Test your method with the following (which you will need to place within a `main` routine).

```
SimpleOutput out = new SimpleOutput();
ArrayUtils helper = new ArrayUtils();
int[] A = new int[3];
A[1] = 2;
int[] B = helper.copyIntegerArray(A);
B[1] = 1;
if (B[1] == A[1]) {
```

```
    out.println("You failed to make a real copy!");
}
else {
  out.println("You successfully made a real copy.");
}
```

Problem J6-E:
Hashing words

Rewrite your `WordCounter` class to use a hash table. You will likely need to create a `Counter` class and store a `Counter` for each word in the hash table.

Problem J6-F:
Game boards

Java permits you to create multidimensional arrays. For example, you can create a 4x4 matrix of integers with

```
int[][] fourbyfour = new int[4][4];
```

Using multidimensional arrays, create a `GameBoard` class that supports 8x8 game boards. You can assume that pieces on the board are represented by integers, and that a square with a value of 0 is empty. Include a `print` method that prints out the board and a `set(int row, int col, int val)` method that sets the value of a particular position on the board.

Notes

Experiment J6.1, Step 4. The simplest way (without loops) to print the most frequently occurring score is something like the following.

```
if ((count1 >= count2) && (count1 >= count3)) {
  out.println("1 was among the most frequently occurring scores");
}
if ((count2 >= count1) && (count2 >= count3)) {
  out.println("2 was among the most frequently occurring scores");
}
if ((count3 >= count1) && (count3 >= count2)) {
  out.println("3 was among the most frequently occurring scores");
}
```

One disadvantage of this is that it may do extra work. It also prints all of the most frequently occurring scores.

As an alternative, you might consider nesting tests, as in the following code.

```
if (count1 > count2) {
  // We know that count2 cannot be one of the top scores, so
  // it must be 1 or 3.
  if (count1 > count3) {
    out.println("Score 1 occurred most frequently.");
  }
  else {
    out.println("Score 3 occurred most frequently.");
  }
} // (count1 > count2)
else {
  // We know that count1 cannot be one of the top scores, so
  // it must be 2 or 3.
  if (count2 > count3) {
    out.println("Score 2 occurred most frequently.");
  }
  else {
    out.println("Score 3 occurred most frequently.");
  }
} // (count1 <= count2)
```

This code only prints one of the most frequently occurring scores. Can you tell which one in each case? It may also be more difficult to extend than the previous solution.

Experiment J6.2, Step 10. One significant problem with using such a range is that 0 can no longer serve as the input terminator.

Session A1: Recursion

In this laboratory session, you will investigate an alternate control mechanism for repetition: recursion. The goals of this session are to

- motivate the uses of recursion;
- compare recursion and iteration; and
- introduce a few key important functions.

Your instructor will tell you which of the proposed experiments you are to perform.

Prerequisite skills:

- Java methods
- Java's looping mechanisms: `while` and `for` loops
- Java's conditional execution statements: `if` and `switch`

Required files:

- `DateTester.java`, as created in prior laboratory sessions.
- `RecursiveExamples.java`
- `RecursiveExperiments.java`
- `SimpleDate.java`, as modified in prior laboratory sessions.
- `SimpleInput.java`
- `SimpleOutput.java`
- `SplitDown.java`

Discussion

As you may have noted by now, methods provide an elegant and usable mechanism for encapsulating code. By putting collections of statements in a method, we can clarify our code (a method call, in effect, gives a short summary of what the body does), simplify reuse (in that we can easily reuse methods rather than copy code), and ease updating (in that when we need to change or fix a problem in a common action, we need only update one method, rather than a large number of copies of identical or near-identical code). As methods become more and more common in your programs, you will find that you will often write methods that call other methods (that call other methods that call other methods that ...).

If a method can call other methods, can it call itself? Would we ever want a method to call itself? In some programming languages, the answer is no. In Java, it is perfectly acceptable to have a method call itself. A method that calls itself is called a *recursive* method.

Why recurse?

You may ask yourself, "Why would I ever write a recursive function?" Surprisingly (or perhaps not so surprisingly), many algorithms are naturally expressed recursively. For example, let us once again consider the problem of determining the number of days before the start of the current month. You may recall that we developed a program to answer that question when we first encountered Java's looping mechanisms. Here is another way to look at the solution:

- There are 0 days before January 1.
- Suppose we knew the number of days before the first day of month m. Then the number of days before the first of month $(m + 1)$ is the number of days before the first day of m plus the number of days in m.

The "suppose we knew" in that solution is somewhat misleading. Even if we didn't know the number of days before the first day of month m, it is still the case that the number of days before the first day of month $(m + 1)$ is the number of days before the first day of month m plus the number of days in month m. Alternately, the number of days before the first day of month m is the number of days before the first day of month $m - 1$ plus the number of days in month $m - 1$.

That is, to determine the number of days before the first day of some month, we need to determine the number of days before the first day of the prior month. We might use the daysUntilStartOfMonth that we developed in a prior lab. However, the new method we are developing, which we will call daysBeforeFirstOfMonth, should also be able to solve that problem.

Putting it all into Java code, we get the following.

```
/**
 * Determine the number of days before the start of month m.
 * Returns -1 for invalid months.
 */
```

```
public int daysBeforeFirstOfMonth(int m) {
  // Is the month invalid?
  if ((m < 1) || (m > 12)) {
    return -1;
  } // Invalid month
  // Base case: it's January.  There are no days before January 1.
  else if (m == 1) {
    return 0;
  } // January
  // Every other month
  else {
    return daysBeforeFirstOfMonth(m-1) + daysInMonth(m-1);
  }
} // daysBeforeFirstOfMonth(int)
```

As this method suggests, most recursive methods have two parts. First, there are one or more base cases that do not involve any recursion. In `daysBeforeFirstOfMonth`, the base cases are the test for an invalid month and the test for January. Next, there are one or more *recursive cases* in which the function calls itself. In `daysBeforeFirstOfMonth`, the recursive call is done for every valid month except January.

In Experiment A1.1, you will explore some simple recursion functions.

Mathematics and recursion

It turns out that recursion is a natural mechanism for expressing many mathematical functions. Consider the factorial function, which we may define informally as

The factorial of *N*, written *N!*, is the product of all the numbers from 1 to *N*.

However, this definition is somewhat vague. First of all, it is unclear what we mean by "the numbers from 1 to *N*". Is 1.5 one of the numbers between 1 and 2? In addition, it is unclear what the domain of factorial is. Can we compute the factorial of −2? Of 0? Of 1.5? It is also conceivable that "product" could be misunderstood.

Let's try again.

The factorial of a positive whole number *N*, written *N!*, is the product 1 * 2 * 3 * ... * *N*.

This definition is also vague, although in somewhat different ways than the previous definition. In particular, what the sequence is may not be obvious. It could be a sequence of positive whole numbers. It could be a sequence of positive whole numbers divisible only by themselves and 1. In addition, this definition may make us question whether it is possible to compute 2! or 1!.

Hence, most mathematicians tend to define factorial recursively. In addition, they define the factorial of 0 as 1. A definition might read

The factorial of 0, written 0!, is 1. The factorial of a positive whole number *N*, written *N!*, is *N* multiplied by the factorial of *N* − 1.

Note that it is relatively easy to turn this into Java code.

```java
/**
 * Compute n!.
 */
public int factorial(int n) {
  // Base case: The factorial of 0 is 1.
  if (n == 0) {
    return 1;
  } // base case
  // Recursive case: The factorial of n is n*n-1.
  else {
    return n * factorial(n-1);
  } // recursive case
} // factorial(int)
```

Do we need to express factorial recursively? Certainly not. It is also possible to express factorial iteratively, using a while or for loop.

```java
/**
 * Compute n! iteratively.
 */
public int fact(int n) {
  int result = 0; // The value of the factorial
  int i;          // A counter variable
  for(i = 1; i <= n; ++i) {
    result *= i;
  } // for
  return result;
} // fact(int)
```

Is one method better than the other? It depends on the criteria used to define better. For example, writing clear code is important. Which method is clearer? Different people will give different answers. Some find the recursive version much clearer and the iterative version muddled. Others find the iterative version clearer and are confused by the recursive version. When comparing the two, you might also look at the use of variables and note that while fact uses two variables, factorial uses none. On the other hand, fact will work (although perhaps not correctly) even when given an invalid input (such as a negative number), while factorial will run forever on negative inputs.

In Experiment A1.2, you will investigate the factorial function.

Fibonacci numbers

Another mathematical object commonly described recursively is the *Fibonacci sequence*. The Fibonacci numbers (i.e., the elements of the sequence) are defined as follows:

- The first two elements of the sequence are 1 and 1.
- Every subsequent element is the sum of the previous two elements.

For example, the third element of the sequence is 2 (1 + 1 = 2), the fourth element of the sequence is 3 (1 + 2 = 3), the fifth element of the sequence is 5 (2 + 3 = 5), and the sixth element of the sequence is 8 (3 + 5 = 8).

The following is a recursive method that computes the Nth Fibonacci number.

```
/**
 * Compute the nth Fibonacci number.
 */
public int fib(int n) {
  // Base case: n is 1 or 2
  if ((n == 1) || (n == 2)) {
    return 1;
  } // base case
  // Recursive case
  else {
    return fib(n-1) + fib(n-2);
  } // recursive case
} // fib(int)
```

Unfortunately, it turns out that this method is relatively slow (we will explore why in the experiments). Hence, it may be more efficient to rewrite the method iteratively. How? We could use an array of the Fibonacci numbers and fill it in left to right.

```
/**
 * Compute the nth Fibonacci number iteratively.
 */
public int fibit(int n) {
  // The array of Fibonacci numbers.  fibs[i] is the ith
  // Fibonacci number.
  int[] fibs = new int[n];
  // A counter to be used in loops.
  int i;
  // Fill in the first two elements
  fibs[0] = 1;
  fibs[1] = 1;
  // Fill in the remaining elements
  for (i = 2; i < n; ++i) {
    fibs[i] = fibs[i-1] + fibs[i-2];
  } // for
  // We're done.  Return the answer.
  return fibs[n-1];
} // fibit
```

In Experiment A1.3, you will investigate Fibonacci numbers.

A guessing game   Suppose we want to play the game of "I'm thinking of a number. Can you guess which one?" Is there a strategy that makes it easier to find the number? It depends on what kind of answers you get when you guess. If the answers are only "No" or "Yes", then you might as well guess each number in sequence. However, if the answers are "Too small", "Too large", or

"Correct", then there is a better strategy, expressed by the following Java-like pseudocode.

```
/**
 * Try to guess a number in the range [small ... large].  Only the
 * oracle knows the correct answer.
 */
void guessNumber(int small, int large, SimpleOutput out, Oracle
oracle) {
  // Make sure there are possibilities.
  if (large < small) {
    out.println("No possible answers!");
    return;
  }

  // Make a guess directly between the two.
  int guess = (small+large) / 2;
  out.println("I guess: " + guess);
  // Is it correct?
  if (oracle.isCorrect(guess)) {
    out.println("Wa hoo!  The answer is " + guess);
  }
  // Is it too small?  If so, we know it has to be in the range
  // [guess+1 ... large].
  else if (oracle.isSmall(guess)) {
    guessNumber(guess+1,large,out,oracle);
  }
  // It's not correct.  It's not too small.  It must be too large.
  // Hence, the number must be in the range [small ... guess-1].
  else {
    guessNumber(small,guess-1,out,oracle);
  }
} // guessNumber(int,int)
```

Is this a good strategy? Yes, it's surprisingly good. Note that each time, we throw away about half of the numbers left to consider (we may throw away half or we may throw away one more than half). If we had to guess a number between 1 and 100, after one step we'd be left with no more than fifty numbers (from now on, we won't write "no more than"). After two steps we'd be left with twenty-five numbers. After three steps we'd be left with twelve numbers. After four steps we'd be left with six numbers. After five steps we'd be left with three numbers. After six steps, we'd be left with one number. In this step, we'd get the answer (unless we'd guessed the answer in an earlier step). Seven steps to find an answer in one hundred numbers is fairly good.

Suppose we had 1,000,000 numbers? How many steps would it take? 1,000,000; 500,000; 250,000; 125,000; 62,500; 31,125; 15,625; 7,812; 3,906; 1,953; 976; 488; 244; 122; 61; 30; 15; 7; 3; 1. Less than twenty steps. Not too shabby, given that we've gone from one hundred numbers to one million.

This technique is called *divide and conquer*. If you can split your problem in half in one step (as we were able to eliminate half the range in one step), you can often get much better solutions.

If you'd like to see how many steps it would take to guess a number in other ranges, you can use `SplitDown.java`. We will return to this problem in a subsequent lab on searching.

Exponentiation

Let us turn to another interesting mathematical problem, that of exponentiation, computing the value of a number raised to a power. We will limit ourselves to powers that are nonnegative whole numbers.

Here is a simple iterative method that does the necessary computation. Basically, we multiply 1.0 by x the appropriate number of times (n times when computing x to the n power).

```
/**
 * Iteratively compute x^n, for n >= 0.
 */
public double itExp(double x, double n) {
  double result = 1.0;
  int i;                    // A counter
  for (i = 1; i <= n; ++i) {
    result = result * x;
  } // for
  return result;
} // itExp(double,int)
```

However, if we rewrite this recursively, we can use the divide-and-conquer technique to improve the running time. In particular, we can take advantage of the fact that $x^{2k} = (x^k) * (x^k)$.

```
/**
 * Recursively compute x^n, for n >= 0.
 */
public double recExp(double x, double n) {
  // Base case: n is 0, x^n is 1.
  if (n == 0) {
    return 1.0;
  } // base case
  // Recursive case: n is 2k.  Compute x^k.
  else if (n is even) {
    double tmp = recExp(x, n/2);
    return tmp*tmp;
  } // n is even
  // Recursive case: n is odd.  Compute x*x^(n-1).
  else {
    return x * recExp(x, n-1);
  } //n is odd
} // recExp(double,int)
```

How do we determine if a number is even or odd? We use the modulus or remainder operator, `%`. `a%b` gives the remainder after dividing `a` by `b`. For example, `10%3` is 1 (since 10 is 3 * 3 + 1), `20%7` is 6 (since 20 is 2 * 7 + 6), and `20%6` is 2 (since 20 is 3 * 6 + 2).

How does the modulus operator help us? Well, we know that a number is even if its remainder when dividing by two is 0. Hence, we can change

```
else if (n is even) {
```

to

```
else if (n%2 == 0) {
```

Again, this provides a relatively efficient mechanism for computation. If we use the iterative exponentiation method, computing 2^{32} takes 32 steps. If we use the recursive method, computing 2^{32} takes about eight steps.

In Experiment A1.4, you will investigate the various mechanisms for exponentiation.

Experiments

Name: _____

ID: _____

Experiment A1.1: Simple recursive functions

Required code files:

- `SimpleDate.java`, as modified in the prior laboratory sessions.
- `DateTester.java`, as created in prior laboratory sessions.

Step 1. Add the following method to your `SimpleDate` class.

```
/**
 * Determine the number of days before the start of month m.
 */
public int daysBeforeFirstOfMonth(int m) {
  // Base case: it's January.  There are no days before January 1.
  if (m == 1) {
    return 0;
  } // January
  // Every other month
  else {
      return daysUntilStartOfMonth(m-1) + daysInMonth(m-1);
    } // A month that's not January
} // daysBeforeFirstOfMonth(int)
```

Note that this is slightly different from the method we developed in the discussion. In particular, it doesn't include the test for errors and it uses `days-UntilStartOfMonth` to compute the number of days before the start of the prior month.

Add the following lines to the `main` method of `DateTester`. If you do not already have a `DateTester` class, create one that includes a `main` method that creates a `SimpleOutput` object called `out`.

```
SimpleDate helper = new SimpleDate(7, 31, 1930);
out.print("The number of days before June is ");
out.println(helper.daysBeforeFirstOfMonth(6));
```

Recompile the two classes and execute `DateTester`. What output do you get? Is that output correct?

Step 2. If you are confident that your `daysUntilStartOfMonth` method written in the laboratory session on loops is correct, add the following lines to `DateTester` to test our new `daysBeforeFirstOfMonth` method.

```
int m;
int days1;
int days2;
for (m = 1; m <= 12; ++m) {
  days1 = helper.daysUntilStartOfMonth(m);
  days2 = helper.daysBeforeFirstOfMonth(m);
  if (days1 != days2) {
    out.println("Error on month " + m);
    out.println("  The old algorithm computed: " + days1);
    out.println("  The new algorithm computed: " + days2);
  } // if
} // for
```

Recompile the two classes and execute `DateTester`. What output do you get? What does that suggest?

After writing your answer, you may want to look at the notes on this step.

Step 3. Hopefully, your work in the previous step indicated that the two methods are identical. This should mean that `daysBeforeFirstOfMonth` can be used wherever `daysUntilStartOfMonth` is used. (There is a well understood adage that if two methods behave identically on all significant inputs, then one can be used in place of the other.)

In particular, we can replace the call to `daysUntilStartOfMonth` with a call to `daysBeforeFirstOfMonth` within the body of `daysBeforeFirstOfMonth`. Do that. Your new method body should be

```
// Base case: it's January.  There are no days before January 1.
if (m == 1) {
  return 0;
} // January
// Every other month
else {
    return daysBeforeFirstOfMonth(m-1) + daysInMonth(m-1);
} // A month that's not January
```

Recompile `SimpleDate`. Execute `DateTester`. Record the output. What does this output suggest?

After writing your answer, you may want to look at the notes on this step.

Step 4. We are now ready to consider cases in which the two competing methods might fail. In particular, since there are only twelve months in the year, what do they do about month 13? Update the <u>for</u> loop to use 13 as an upper bound. Recompile and execute `DateTester`. Record the output. What does this output suggest?

Step 5. It may also be instructive to see what value the two methods generate for month 13. Add the following lines to your `main` method. Recompile and execute `DateTester`. Record the output. What does this output suggest?

```
days1 = helper.daysUntilStartOfMonth(13);
days2 = helper.daysBeforeFirstOfMonth(13);
out.println(days1 + "," + days2);
```

Step 6. Extend the loop to test months up to month 20. You may find it convenient to print out the number of days in the month for each iteration of the loop. Recompile and execute `DateTester`. Record the output. What does this output suggest?

Step 7. Remove the loop from your `main` method. If you'd like to keep it around but not execute it, you may find it easiest to comment out the code.

Put an opening slash-star comment before the loop and a closing star-slash comment after the loop. For example,

```
/*
    // The following lines are no longer being used,
    // since we've verified that the two methods are identical
    // on the given values.
    for (m = 1; m <= 20; ++m) {
      days1 = helper.daysUntilStartOfMonth(m);
      days2 = helper.daysBeforeFirstOfMonth(m);
      if (days1 != days2) {
        out.println("Error on month " + m);
        out.println("  The old algorithm computed: " + days1);
        out.println("  The new algorithm computed: " + days2);
      } // if
    } // for
*/
```

Recompile and execute `DateTester` to ensure that we haven't introduced any errors.

Step 8. Create a variant of `daysBeforeFirstOfMonth` that also takes a `SimpleOutput` object as a parameter. Have that method print out information about the method. Here is an example

```
/**
 * Determine the number of days before the start of month m.
 * Print out information on the computation.
 */
public int daysBeforeFirstOfMonth(int m, SimpleOutput out) {
  int days = 0;
  out.println("Computing the number of days in month " + m);
  // Base case: it's January.  There are no days before January 1.
  if (m == 1) {
    days = 0;
  } // January
  // Every other month
  else {
    days = daysBeforeFirstOfMonth(m-1,out) +
           daysInMonth(m-1);
  } // A month that's not January
  out.println("There are " + days + " days in month " + m);
  return days;
} // daysBeforeFirstOfMonth(int,SimpleOutput)
```

Update `DateTester` to compute the number of days in June using `daysBeforeFirstOfMonth`. Recompile the two classes and execute `DateTester`. Record your output. What does this output suggest?

Step 9. We've tested month values that are too large. What about month values that are too small? Add the following line to `DateTester`.

```
out.println(daysBeforeFirstOfMonth(0, out));
```

Recompile and execute `DateTester`. What happens? What does this suggest?

After you've answered the question, you may want to look at the notes on this step.

Step 10. As the previous step suggests, when you write recursive methods, testing special cases is particularly important. In `daysBeforeFirstOf-Month`, we should test the special cases of months that fall before month 1 and months that fall after month 12. What value should we return in those cases? We could return a special value, such as -1. We could also throw an exception. (Exceptions are discussed in an optional lab.)

Add the following code to the beginning of both versions of `daysBefore-FirstOfMonth`.

```
// Check for valid month.  Return -1 for invalid months.
if ((m < 1) || (m > 12)) {
  return -1;
} // invalid month
```

Recompile `SimpleDate` and execute `DateTester`. What happens when the month is 6? What happens when the month is 0?

Step 11. Which of the two methods (`daysBeforeFirstOfMonth` and `day-sUntilStartOfMonth`) do you prefer? Why?

Experiment A1.2: Factorial

Required file:

- `RecursiveExamples.java`

Step 1. Make a copy of `RecursiveExamples.java`. Create a new program, `RecursiveExperiments.java` with a `main` method that contains the following lines.

```
SimpleOutput out = new SimpleOutput();
RecursiveExamples helper = new RecursiveExamples();
out.println("5! = " + helper.factorial(5));
```

Compile the classes and execute `RecursiveExamples`. Record the output. Is the output correct?

Step 2. Update the `main` method of `RecursiveExperiments` to compute the factorial of 0. Recompile and execute `RecursiveExperiments`. Record the output. Is the output correct?

Step 3. Update the `main` method of `RecursiveExperiments` to compute the factorial of −1. Recompile and execute `RecursiveExperiments`. What happens? Explain.

Step 4. Here is a new version of `factorial` that gives an indication of what is happening.

```
/**
 * Compute n!.
 */
public int factorial(int n, SimpleOutput out) {
  int result;
  out.println("Computing the factorial of " + n);
  // Base case: The factorial of 0 is 1.
  if (n == 0) {
    result = 1;
```

```
  } // base case
  // Recursive case: The factorial of n is n*n-1.
  else {
    result = n * factorial(n-1);
  } // recursive case
  out.println("The factorial of " + n + " is " + result);
  return result;
} // factorial(int)
```

Add this method to `RecursiveExamples` and update `RecursiveExperiments` to use this method. Recompile the two classes and execute `RecursiveExperiments`. What happens? Explain.

Step 5. Update the two versions of `factorial` so that they return negative one when given a negative parameter. Summarize the changes you've made here.

Experiment A1.3: Fibonacci numbers

Required files:

- `RecursiveExamples.java`
- `RecursiveExperiments.java`

Before you begin, if you have not already done so, make a copy of `RecursiveExamples.java`. If you have not already created `RecursiveExperiments.java`, make a copy of a sample version.

Step 1. Reread the code for `fib` and `fibit`, both of which can be found in `RecursiveExamples.java`. Which do you prefer? Why?

Step 2. Update `RecursiveExperiments` to use `fib` and `fibit` to determine the values of the sixth, tenth, twentieth, and fortieth Fibonacci numbers. Enter those values here.

Step 3. It is useful to compare the two methods of computing Fibonacci numbers by counting the number of steps they execute. In the recursive method, we will count the number of recursive calls. In the iterative method, we will count the number of times the loop repeats. How do we do this? By adding a `steps` field to the `RecursiveExamples` class and updating it appropriately.

Update `RecursiveExamples` to include the following lines

```
/**
 * A count of the number of steps used by some algorithms.
 */
protected int steps;
/**
 * Reset the count of steps to 0.
 */
public void resetSteps() {
  steps = 0;    } // resetSteps()
/**
 * Determine the number of steps used since the last call to
 * resetSteps().
 */
public int getSteps() {
  return steps;
} // getSteps()
```

Next, add the following lines to the beginning of `fib` and to the beginning of the loop in `fibit`.

```
// Update the count of steps
++steps;
```

Finally, add the following lines to the `main` method of `RecursiveExperiments`.

```
helper.resetSteps();
out.println("fib(3) = " + helper.fib(3));
out.println("  that computation took " +
            helper.getSteps() + " steps.");
helper.resetSteps();
out.println("fibit(3) = " + helper.fibit(3));
out.println("  that computation took " +
            helper.getSteps() + " steps.");
```

Recompile the two classes and execute `RecursiveExperiments`. Record the output.

Step 4. How many steps do you think it will take `fib` to compute the sixth Fibonacci number? How many steps do you think it will take `fibit` to compute the sixth Fibonacci number?

Step 5. Update, recompile, and execute `RecursiveExperiments` so that you can get precise answers to the questions of the previous step. Record the answers. What do these numbers suggest?

Step 6. Make a copy of `fib` and extend it to print information on the computation. Your new version should resemble

```java
/**
 * Compute the nth Fibonacci number.
 * Print notes on the computation.
 */
public int fib(int n,
               SimpleOutput out) {
  int result; // The value we compute
  out.println("Computing fib of " + n);
  // Base case: n is 1 or 2
  if ((n == 1) || (n == 2)) {
    result = 1;
  } // base case
  // Recursive case
  else {
    result = fib(n-1,out) + fib(n-2,out);
  } // recursive case
  out.println("Fibonacci number " + n + " is " + result);
  return result;
} // fib(int,SimpleOutput)
```

Update the `main` method of `RecursiveExperiments` to compute the sixth Fibonacci number using this new version of `fib`. Summarize the output. What does this output suggest?

Step 7. How many times is the first Fibonacci number computed during the recursive computation of the sixth Fibonacci number?

Step 8. How many times do you think the first Fibonacci number will be computed during the recursive computation of the tenth Fibonacci number?

Step 9. Update the `main` method of `RecursiveExperiments` to answer the previous question. What answer did you get?

Step 10. In this and the next step, you'll consider a different issue relating to the two computations. You should use the original version of `fib`. Add the following code to the `main` method of `RecursiveExperiments`.

```
out.println("fib(1) = " +
            helper.fib(1));
out.println("fibit(1) = " +
            helper.fibit(1));
```

Recompile and execute `RecursiveExperiments`. Record and explain what happens.

Step 11. Add the following code to the `main` method of `RecursiveExperiments`.

```
out.println("fib(0) = " +
            helper.fib(0));
out.println("fibit(0) = " +
            helper.fibit(0));
```

Recompile and execute `RecursiveExperiments`. Record what happens.

After recording the results, you may want to refer to the notes on this subject.

Experiment A1.4: Exponentiation

Required files:

- `RecursiveExamples.java`
- `RecursiveExperiments.java`

Before you begin, if you have not already done so, make a copy of `RecursiveExamples.java`. If you have not already created `RecursiveExperiments.java`, make a copy of a sample version.

Step 1. Using both `recExp` and `itExp` determine the value of 2^{10} and 1.05^{20}. Are the answers the same or different?

Step 2. Which version of the exponentiation function do you prefer, and why?

Post-Laboratory Problems

Problem A1-A: Printing information on recursive calls, revisited

In Experiment A1.1, you created a method that printed out information on each recursive call. Unfortunately, the information was somewhat hard to read as it was all left justified. Write a recursive version of `factorial` that indents before recursive calls. For example, if we asked for the factorial of 5, this function would print something like

```
Computing the factorial of 5
  Computing the factorial of 4
    Computing the factorial of 3
      Computing the factorial of 2
        Computing the factorial of 1
          Computing the factorial of 0
          The factorial of 0 is 1
        The factorial of 1 is 1
      The factorial of 2 is 2
    The factorial of 3 is 6
  The factorial of 4 is 24
The factorial of 5 is 120
```

Problem A1-B: How large can a factorial be?

You may have noticed that the factorial function grows surprisingly fast. Because of this, if you try to compute the factorial of larger numbers, you may generate a number larger than the computer can represent. Determine the largest factorial our method can correctly compute.

Update `factorial` so that it returns negative one when one attempts to compute a factorial larger than it can compute.

Problem A1-C: Large Fibonacci numbers

You may have noticed that the Fibonacci sequence also grows surprisingly fast. Because of this, if you try to compute the nth Fibonacci number for larger values of n, you may generate a number larger than the computer can represent. Determine the largest n for which our methods correctly compute the nth Fibonacci number.

Problem A1-D: More efficient iterative computation of Fibonacci numbers

One problem with the iterative Fibonacci method is that it uses an array. If we are computing a large Fibonacci number, we may use a significant amount of memory for the array. It turns out that we don't need to use all that memory. Since each Fibonacci number is only based on the previous two Fibonacci numbers, we only need to keep track of three numbers.

Rewrite the iterative Fibonacci method so that it does not use an array. The following is some code to get you started.

```
/**
 * Compute the nth Fibonacci number iteratively.
 */
public int newfibit(int n) {
    int i;        // A counter
```

```
int current; // The ith Fibonacci number
int prevnum; // The (i-1)st Fibonacci number
int nextnum; // The (i+1)st Fibonacci number
// Initialize
i = 1;
current = 1; // The 1st Fibonacci number is 1
prevnum = 0; // If fib(2) is 1, fib(1) is 1, and
             //   fib(2) is fib(1) + fib(0), then fib(0) is 0.
...
nextnum = prevnum + current;
...
} // newfibit(int)
```

Problem A1-E: More efficient recursive computation of the Fibonacci numbers

It is also possible to efficiently compute the nth Fibonacci number recursively. Rather than counting down from n, we will count up from 2. In each recursive call, we can pass in the two previous Fibonacci numbers. Here are a pair of methods to do just that.

```
/**
 * Compute the nth Fibonacci number recursively.  Return
 * -1 for n <= 0.
 */
public int fibrec(int n) {
  // Check for invalid input
  if (n <= 0) {
    return -1;
  } // invalid input
  else {
    return fibrec(n,1,1,0);
  } // normal input
} // fibrec(int)
/**
 * Compute the nth Fibonacci number, given the ith and (i-1)st
 * Fibonacci numbers.
 *
 * This does not do the validity testing that fibrec(int) does
 * because it should only be called from fibrec(int).
 */
protected int fibrec(int n, int i, int ith, int prev) {
  // Base case: we already have the nth Fibonacci number.
  if (n == i) {
    return ith;
  } // base case
  // Recursive case: move on to the (i+1)st Fibonacci number.
  else {
    return fibrec(n, i+1, ith+prev, ith);
  } // recursive case
} // fibrec(int,int,int,int)
```

Add those methods to `RecursiveExamples` and confirm that they work correctly. Update them to count the number of steps (method calls) used to compute the nth Fibonacci number. How many steps are required to compute the sixth Fibonacci number? The tenth?

In your own words, explain how this method works.

Problem A1-F: Understanding the Fibonacci numbers

Believe it or not, there are reasons why we study the Fibonacci numbers other than their use in illustrating recursion. By doing research in the library or elsewhere, determine other reasons that the Fibonacci numbers are valuable.

Problem A1-G: Counting steps during exponentiation

In Experiment A1.3, we counted the number of steps in two methods that computed the Fibonacci numbers. Using a similar strategy, count the number of steps in two versions of the exponentiation function. Try computing 1.05 to the tenth power, to the twentieth power, and to the fiftieth.

Problem A1-H: From recursion to iteration

We have seen that it is sometimes possible to turn recursive methods into iterative methods. (In fact, it should always be possible to turn a recursive method into an equivalent iterative method and an iterative method into an equivalent recursive method.) Rewrite the efficient recursive exponentiation method iteratively.

Notes

Experiment A1.1, Step 2. If the logic was correct for both of our methods, there should be no new output from the loop. If there is, then there is either a serious logical problem in our design or a small typo in the program (or both). Look for the latter.

Experiment A1.1, Step 3. There should be no output. If our logic was correct, the two methods should still produce identical results.

Experiment A1.1, Step 9. When we call the method with 0 as a parameter, it checks whether the month is 1. It isn't, so it calls itself with $0 - 1 = -1$ as a parameter. Negative one isn't 1, so it calls itself with $-1 - 1 = -2$ as a parameter. This isn't 0 so ... the method keeps calling itself again and again and again. Since you should never reach 1 by repeatedly subtracting 1 from 0, the method will run forever.

Experiment A1.3, Step 4. You may have noted that `fib` takes significantly more steps and also more time than `fibit`. Why is this? Because the recursive version repeats a lot of work. For example, to compute the fifth Fibonacci number, it must compute the fourth Fibonacci number and the third Fibonacci number. To compute the fourth Fibonacci number, it must compute the third Fibonacci number and the second Fibonacci number. Hence, the third Fibonacci number is computed at least twice. The second computation should be unnecessary.

Experiment A1.3, Step 11. It is likely that the program ran forever when you tried to compute the zeroth Fibonacci number recursively. Why? Because the base case was for values of 1 and 2. If we start with a number less than 1, we will keep subtracting 1 or 2, never reaching the base cases.

Session A2: Searching

In this laboratory session, you will investigate a number of algorithms for *searching;* that is, finding an element in a collection. Search is one of the most basic and most instructive introductory problems in computer science. The goals of this laboratory session are to:

- introduce the problem of searching;
- consider a more general sequence class as an alternative to arrays;
- learn about random sequence generation;
- investigate variations on the problem of searching;
- consider sequential search, one of the most basic searching algorithms;
- consider binary search, an improved algorithm that only works on lists in which the elements are sorted.

Prerequisite skills:

- Objects, classes, and methods
- Arrays
- Loops
- Recursion

Required files:

- `NumberGame.java`
- `NumberGameOracle.java`
- `NumberGameGuesser.java`
- `IntSeq.java`
- `IntSeqTester.java`
- `SimpleInput.java`
- `SimpleOutput.java`

Discussion

In previous experiments, we've worked with a variety of collections of elements. Why? Because a wide variety of problems in life (and therefore in computing) have to do with collections. For example, the phone book is a collection of name/number entries; most people have file cabinets that collect papers; many people collect other objects, such as books, records, beer cans, and autographs.

One of the most common problems relating to collections is that of searching. Given a collection, determine whether the collection contains a particular object. For example,

- Does John Smith or Jane Doe have a phone number?
- Do I have a record by the Modern Lovers?
- Do you have any jacks (as in the card game "Go Fish")?

Since arrays provide one of the simplest and most universal mechanisms for collecting elements, we will primarily consider search algorithms as they pertain to arrays. In particular, we build search algorithms that determine the position of an integer in an array of integers. (You should be able to generalize these algorithms for other cases.)

Sequences

Rather than working directly with arrays, we will build a new class `IntSeq` for "sequences" of integers. How do these sequences differ from arrays?

- `IntSeq`s will be objects (arrays are also objects, but we'll be able to use the syntax of objects with sequences).
- `IntSeq`s will support a number of algorithms pertaining to sequences and arrays, particularly searching algorithms.
- `IntSeq`s will expand when needed.
- `IntSeq`s will provide a number of mechanisms for filling in a number of elements.
- `IntSeq`s will support a `toString` method.

In Experiment A2.1, you will consider the `IntSeq` class.

Detour: Random sequences

If we are going to search through arrays of numbers, generating "random" sequences of numbers will be useful. What do we mean by "random"? Typically, random means that each sequence of a particular size is equally likely or that at each point in the sequence, each number is equally likely as the next element. How can we generate such sequences? Fortunately, Java provides a standard utility class, `java.util.Random`. This class includes a `nextInt` method that gives that next "random" number in the sequence. In truth, this number is not random, in that it is generated by an algorithm. However, it is close enough to random for our purposes.

Hence, to fill the array `elements` with a random sequence of 100 integers, we might write

```
import java.util.Random;
   ...
     int i;
     Random generator = new Random();
     elements = new int[100];
     for (i = 0; i < 100; ++i) {
       elements[i] = generator.nextInt();
} // for
```

However, when we're comparing two algorithms, to have the same input to both algorithms is helpful. Fortunately, Java's random number generator can take a seed that uniquely determines the random sequence. You can think of a seed as being a number for the sequence. If you use the same seed, you end up with the same sequence. For example, to get the first sequence, you would write

```
Random generator = new Random(1);
```

Note that random sequences are not always the best test cases for your algorithms. For example, when testing an algorithm on sequences, you should also test sequences of varying lengths, sequences that contain all the same value, sorted sequences, and backwards-sorted sequences (in which the numbers are organized largest to smallest). Nonetheless, random sequences still serve many purposes and are often a good starting point.

In Experiment A2.2, you will investigate random number generators.

Sequential search

Sequential search is a straightforward attempt to solve the problem. In sequential search, we look at the elements of the array, one by one, until we find the element or run off of the array. In the former case, we return the index of the matching item. In the latter case, we return an error value (negative one is a good choice).

Here is a simple sequential search method written in Java. It is one of the methods supplied by `IntSeq`, which uses `this.elements` as the array to search through.

```
/**
 * Search through the sequence of integers for a particular value.
 * Return the index of the value if it is found.
 * Return -1 otherwise.
 */
public int sequentialSearch(int val) {
  // An index into the sequence.
  int i;
  // Check each position of the array
  for (i = 0; i < this.elements.length; ++i) {
    // If the value is at position i, we're done.
    return i;
  } // if
```

```
  } // for
  // Unable to find the element.  Return -1.
  return -1;
} // sequentialSearch(int)
```

Sequential search is useful and correct. However, it may also be slow. In particular, sequential search looks at all of the elements in the array. For example, if the array has one million elements, it may be necessary to look at one million elements. Even if each look takes 1/1000 of a second, this will take 1000 seconds or sixteen minutes. Can we do better? As we'll soon see, the answer is yes, but only in certain cases.

In Experiment A2.3, you will investigate sequential search.

Detour: The number game, revisited

In the session on recursion, you encountered a simple game (guess a number) and a simple but fast strategy for guessing the number. This game illustrates one type of search: We are searching for a matching number in the set of numbers; we just don't know what number we're matching. The strategy is

```
guess the midpoint of the range of valid answers
if it's correct, we're done
if it's too small, shrink the range and try again
if it's too large, shrink the range and try again
```

The following class implements the guessing strategy and reports on the steps it uses.

```
/**
 * An "intelligent" number guesser that can guess numbers within a
 * particular range, provided an oracle can tell it a little about
 * its guesses.
 *
 * @author Samuel A. Rebelsky
 * @version 1.0 of January 1999
 */
public class NumberGameGuesser {
  // +---------+------------------------------------------------------
  // | Methods |
  // +---------+

/**
 * Try to guess a number in the range [lower ... upper].  Only the
 * oracle knows the correct answer.  The upper end of the range
 * cannot be larger than Long.MAX_VALUE/2, and the lower end of the
 * range cannot be smaller than Long.MAX_VALUE/2 (see if you can
 * figure out why).
 */
void guessNumber(long lower, long upper,
                 SimpleOutput out,
                 NumberGameOracle oracle) {
  // Make sure there are possibilities.
  if (upper < lower) {
```

```
      out.println("No possible answers!");
      return;
   } // if the range is empty.
   if (upper > Long.MAX_VALUE/2) {
      out.println("The upper bound of the range cannot be higher than "
                  + Long.MAX_VALUE/2);
      return;
   } // If the upper bound is too high.
   if (lower < Long.MIN_VALUE/2) {
      out.println("The lower bound of the range cannot be smaller
                  than " + Long.MIN_VALUE/2);
      return;
   }
   // Make a guess directly between the two.
   long guess = (lower+upper) / 2;
   out.println("I guess: " + guess);
   // Is it correct?
   if (oracle.isCorrect(guess)) {
      out.println("Wa hoo!  The answer is " + guess);
   }
   // Is it too small?  If so, we know it has to be in the range
   // [guess+1 ... upper].
   else if (oracle.isSmall(guess)) {
      out.println(" Oh well, that guess is too small.");
      guessNumber(guess+1,upper,out,oracle);
   }
   // It's not correct.  It's not too small.  It must be too large.
   // Hence, the number must be in the range [lower ... guess-1].
   else {
      out.println(" Hmmm.  That guess is too large.");
      guessNumber(lower,guess-1,out,oracle);
   }
   } // guessNumber(long,long,SimpleOutput,Oracle)
} // class NumberGameGuesser
```

What does the oracle that this class uses look like? Basically, it has a field that contains the answer. Each of the methods compares the guess to that answer. The following is the code for that class.

```
/**
 * An oracle for numeric guessing games.  You tell the oracle the
 * number, and the oracle can answer questions about guesses.
 *
 * @author Samuel A. Rebelsky
 * @version 1.0 of January 1999
 */
public class NumberGameOracle {
   // +--------+-----------------------------------------------------
   // | Fields |
   // +--------+

   /** The number we're trying to guess. */
   long solution;
```

```
// +-------------+-------------------------------------------------
// | Constructors |
// +-------------+
/**
 * Create a new oracle who knows that the solution is the given
 * value.
 */
public NumberGameOracle(long solution) {
  this.solution = solution;
} // NumberGameOracle

// +---------+-------------------------------------------------------
// | Methods |
// +---------+

/**
 * Check if a guess is correct.
 */
public boolean isCorrect(long guess) {
  return guess == solution;
} // isCorrect(long)

/**
 * Check if a guess is too small.
 */
public boolean isSmall(long guess) {
  return guess < solution;
} // isSmall(long)

/**
 * Check if a guess is too large.
 */
public boolean isLarge(long guess) {
  return guess > solution;
} // isLarge(long)
} // class NumberGameOracle
```

We can put these together into a game as follows.

```
import SimpleOutput;
import SimpleInput;
import NumberGameOracle;          // The oracle knows the answer.
import NumberGameGuesser;         // The guesser does not.

/**
 * Let the computer play the number game.  The user tells the
 * computer which number, and then the guesser tries to guess.
 *
 * @author Samuel A. Rebelsky
 * @version 1.0 of January 1999
 */
public class NumberGame {
  /**
   * Play the game.
   */
```

```java
public static void main(String[] args) {
  // A game with no output is fairly boring.
  SimpleOutput out = new SimpleOutput();
  // We'll need to read a number to guess.
  SimpleInput in = new SimpleInput();
  // Our intelligent guesser.
  NumberGameGuesser guesser = new NumberGameGuesser();
  // And our even more intelligent oracle.  We'll create the oracle
  // once we know the solution.
  NumberGameOracle oracle;
  // The number to guess.
  long solution;
  // The lower bound of the range.
  long lower;
  // The upper bound of the range.
  long upper;
  // The minimum lower and maximum upper bounds (required by the
  // guesser).
  long min_lower = Long.MIN_VALUE/2;
  long max_upper = Long.MAX_VALUE/2;
  // Describe the game.
  out.println("Welcome to the amazing number game.  You will give
              me");
  out.println("a range of numbers and a number to guess.  I will
              tell");
  out.println("my friend to guess the number, and we'll see how it
              does.");
  out.println();
  // Ask for the range.
  out.print("Enter the smallest possible answer " +
            "(at least " + min_lower + "): ");
  lower = in.readLong();
  if (in.hadError()) { lower = min_lower; }
  out.print("Enter the largest possible answer " +
            "(at most " + max_upper + "): ");
  upper = in.readLong();
  if (in.hadError()) { upper = max_upper; }
  // Validate the range.
  if (lower < min_lower) {
    out.println("Your smallest number is too small.");
    return;
  }
  if (upper > max_upper) {
    out.println("Your largest number is too large.");
    return;
  }
  if (upper < lower) {
    out.println("The smallest number is larger than the largest
                number.");
    return;
  }
```

```
      // Ask for input.
      out.print("Please enter the number to guess: " +
                "(between " + lower + " and " + upper + "): ");
      solution = in.readLong();
      // Validate the solution.
      if (solution < lower) {
        out.println("Your solution is less than the smallest number.");
        return;
      }
      if (solution > upper) {
        out.println("Your solution is larger than the largest
                    number.");
        return;
      }
      // Create the oracle.
      oracle = new NumberGameOracle(solution);
      // Okay, let's play the game.
      guesser.guessNumber(lower,upper,out,oracle);
      // We're done.
    } // main(String[])
} // class NumberGame
```

Why do we limit the lower and upper bounds? You'll learn why in our discussion of binary search below. You will investigate the problem further in the post-laboratory problems.

In Experiment A2.4, you will play with this game.

Binary search

We can turn this strategy into a searching algorithm, as long as the list we are searching is sorted. How could you take advantage of it being sorted? If the sequence is sorted, then you learn a lot about where the name belongs by comparing the name you're looking for to the middle element. For example, if the name you are looking for is smaller than the middle element, then you can throw away everything after the middle element. In effect, you have eliminated half the sequence in one step!

What do we do with the remaining half of the sequence? We search through it again, using the same technique. (Yes, that's recursion in action.) We keep splitting the sequence, again and again, until we find the element we are searching for or end up with no remaining elements.

Expressed in approximate Java, we have

```
/**
 * Determine whether a name appears in a sequence.
 */
public boolean search(String name, Sequence names) {
  // A name cannot appear in the empty sequence
  if (names.length() == 0) {
    return false;
  }
  // empty sequence
  // Nonempty sequences: check the middle and recurse
```

```
    else {
      // Is the element at the middle?
      if (name.equals(names.middle())) {
        return true;
      } // at the middle
      // Is the element before the middle?
      else if (name.precedes(names.middle())) {
      return search(name, names.firstHalf());
    } // In the first half
    // Otherwise, look in the second half
    else {
      return search(name, names.secondHalf());
    } // In the first half
} // search(String,Sequence)
```

Note that this is not a working method. In particular, there is no `precedes` method for strings, nor a built-in `Sequence` class. In addition, binary search requires some care at the extremes (e.g., single-element lists) to ensure that it does not recurse indefinitely. However, this code should give you a sense that recursion provides an elegant way to solve a variety of problems. In fact, the problem-solving technique used in binary search is so common that it has its own name, *divide-and-conquer*.

Working code for the preceding method follows. The code is part of the `IntSeq` class, which uses `this.elements` as the array it searches through. This implementation of the method also returns the index of the element, rather than a boolean value indicating whether or not it is found.

```
/**
 * Search through the elements for a particular value.
 * Return the index of the value if it is found.
 * Return -1 otherwise.
 */
public int binarySearch(int val) {
  return binarySearch(val, arr, 0, this.elements.length-1);
} // binarySearch(int)

/**
 * Search for a value in a subrange of the array.
 * The subarray is given by lb .. ub.
 * Return the index of the value if it is found.
 * Return -1 otherwise.
 */
protected int binarySearch(int val, int lb, int ub) {
  // The index of the middle value
  int mid = (lb + ub) / 2;
  // Is the subarray empty?
  if (lb > ub) {
    return -1;
  } // empty subarray
  // Is the value at the middle?
  else if (val == this.elements[mid]) {
    return mid;
  } // Found it!
```

```
// Should the value be in the left half?
else if (val < this.elements[mid]) {
  return binarySearch(val, lb, mid-1);
} // left half
// The value must be in the right half.
  return binarySearch(val, mid+1, ub);
} // left half
} // binarySearch(int,int,int)
```

Problems with binary search

Although binary search is a popular and useful algorithm, many programmers end up making mistakes when they implement it, even if they've been warned that they are likely to make mistakes. What kinds of mistakes? Most are relatively subtle, but almost all can lead to significant problems in practice.

Some programmers forget to ensure that the array they're searching is nonempty. This means that when they look at the "middle" element, they are looking at a nonexistent element. In Java, this oversight will lead to an error at the time the attempt to access the element happens. In other languages, no error may be noticed until later.

Some programmers include the midpoint in the recursive call (using [small .. midpoint] or [midpoint .. large] rather than [small .. midpoint−1] or [midpoint+1 .. large]. While this usually works, in some cases it can lead to problems. For example, consider the case in which the element is at position 3, small is 2, and large is 3. The midpoint is 2 (Java rounds down when dividing integers). The element at position 2 is too small, so we try again, using small=middle and large=large. So, small is 2 and large is 3. The midpoint is 2. The element at position 2 is too small, so we try again. And so on and so forth.

Some programmers try to reduce the number of tests so that, for example, there are not separate tests for less-than and equals. While this can be done successfully, it may have the problem mentioned with including the midpoint in the recursive call.

A more subtle problem comes in the computation of the midpoint. Recall that the computation uses `(lb+ub)/2`. Since Java limits the size of integers, it is possible that `lb+ub` will be greater than the largest integer. In fact, this is why `NumberGameGuesser` limits the range to half of the two bounds. This problem is rarely encountered in practice, but is worth considering as data sets get larger and larger.

In Experiment A2.6, you will investigate some of these problems.

Finding the smaller elements of a sequence

In the previous examples, we've known what we were searching for (e.g., Is this number in this sequence?). There are related problems in which we have less information about what we are searching for. For example, consider the problem of searching for the smallest element of a sequence. How might you find such an element? A first guess might be the first element, but that's often an incorrect guess. You might then refine your guess by then stepping through the remaining elements, updating your estimate of the smallest whenever you found a smaller element. In pseudocode,

```
guess = the first element of the sequence
for each remaining element of the sequence, e
  if (e < guess) then
    guess = e;
  end if end for
```

Using arrays in Java, we might express this as follows.

```
/**
 * Compute the smallest element in the sequence.
 */
public int smallest() {
  // Our guess as to the smallest element
  int guess = this.elements[0];
  // A counter variable
  int i;
  // Look through all subsequent elements
  for (i = 1; i < this.elements.length; ++i) {
    // If the element is smaller than our guess, then
    //    update the guess
    if (this.elements[i] < guess) {
      guess = this.elements[i];
    } // if
  } // for
  // That's it, we're done
  return guess;
} // smallest()
```

As a variation, we might write an indexOfSmallest that returns the index of the smallest element in a subsequence. Why would we want such a method? As you've seen, whenever you write a method for a sequence, it is helpful to write a similar method for a subsequence. Why return an index rather than the actual value? Because it will be helpful for the subsequent experiments. The following is the method as it appears in the IntSeq class.

```
/**
 * Compute the index of the smallest element in the subsequence
 * given by lower bound lb and upper bound ub.
 */
public int indexOfSmallest(int lb, int ub) {
  // Make sure the upper bound and lower bound are reasonable.
  if (lb < 0) {
    lb = 0;
  }
  if (ub >= this.elements.length) {
    ub = this.elements.length - 1;
  }
  // Our guess as to the index of the smallest element
  int guess = lb;
  // A counter variable
```

```
  int i;
  // Look through all subsequent elements
  for (i = lb + 1; i <= ub; ++i) {
     // If the element is smaller than our guess, then
     //   update the guess
     if (this.elements[i] < this.elements[guess]) {
       guess = i;
     } // if
  } // for
  // That's it, we're done
  return guess;
} // indexOfSmallest()
```

Experiments

Experiment A2.1:
Integer
sequences

Required files:

- `IntSeq.java`
- `IntSeqTester.java`

Step 1. Make copies of `IntSeq.java` and `IntSeqTester.java`. Write a summary of the methods provided by `IntSeq`. You need not read the code for the methods; simply read the introductory comments (and perhaps the internal comments) to gain an understanding of what they might do.

Step 2. Compile `IntSeq` and `IntSeqTester`. Execute `IntSeqTester`. Ask the tester to fill the elements between 0 and 10 with the sequence starting with 1 and stepping by 2. Print out that sequence. Record the results.

Step 3. Execute `IntSeqTester`. Ask the tester to fill the elements between 5 and 10 with the sequence starting with 1 and stepping by −2. Print out that sequence. Record the results.

Step 4. Execute `IntSeqTester`. Ask the tester to fill the elements between 0 and 10 with the sequence starting with 5 and stepping by 0. Print out that sequence. Record the results.

Step 5. What command(s) might you use to create the sequence [1, 3, 5, 7, 9,...,301]? What command(s) might you use to create the sequence [301, 299, 297,...,5, 3, 1]?

Step 6. At times, you need to set elements individually, rather than en masse. Using `IntSeqTester`, build and print the sequence [2,1,5,4,−1,6]. (You do not need to record anything for this step.)

Step 7. Although programs like `IntSeqTester` provide a simple and useful mechanism for testing other classes, it is also helpful to be able to write small programs that do more explicit tests. Write a small program, `SampleSeq` that builds and prints the sequence [2,1,5,4,−1,6]. Summarize your code here.

Experiment A2.2: Random sequences

Required files:

- `IntSeq.java`
- `IntSeqTester.java`

Step 1. Make copies of `IntSeq.java` and `IntSeqTester.java`. Compare the two files. Using `SortTester`, make five lists of ten random numbers. Record those lists.

Step 2. Using `IntSeqTester`, make three lists of ten random numbers, using the same seed each time (do not use zero as your seed). Record your results.

Step 3. Using `IntSeqTester`, make the following lists of random numbers using the same seed each time. Note that the r entries stand for "some random number".

```
r,r,r,r,r
0,r,r,r,r
0,0,r,r,r
0,0,0,r,r
0,0,0,0,r
```

Record the results.

Step 4. Based on those results, what can you say about seeds?

**Experiment A2.3:
Sequential
search**

Required files:

- IntSeq.java
- IntSeqTester.java

Step 1. Make a copy of IntSeq.java and IntSeqTester. Compile the two classes and execute IntSeqTester. Create the list [1,2,3,4,5]. Using sequential search, determine the index of 1, the index of 5, and the index of 20.

Step 2. Execute IntSeqTester. Create the list [1,1,1,2,2,2,3,3,3]. Using sequential search, determine the index of 1, 2, and 3.

Step 3. What, if anything, do you observe from the previous step?

Step 4. Execute IntSeqTester. Create a sequence of 1000 elements. Does 0 appear in that sequence? How likely do you think it is that 0 will appear in the sequence?

Experiment A2.4: The guessing game

Required files:

- `NumberGame.java`
- `NumberGameOracle.java`
- `NumberGameGuesser.java`

Before you begin, make copies of `NumberGame.java`, `NumberGameOracle.java`, and `NumberGameGuesser.java`. Compile the three classes.

Step 1. Execute `NumberGame`. What numbers does the guesser guess when searching for 6 in the range [0...100]?

Step 2. Execute `NumberGame`. What numbers does the guesser guess when searching for −6 in the range [−100...0]?

Step 3. Execute `NumberGame`. What numbers does the guesser guess when searching for 101 in the range [−100...100]?

Step 4. Execute `NumberGame`. What numbers does the guesser guess when searching for 100 in the range [−100...100]?

Step 5. Update `NumberGameGuesser` so that it reports on the number of guesses that it takes to find a solution. Summarize your changes here.

Step 6. Execute `NumberGame`. How many guesses does it take to look for 511231 when searching in the range [0...1000000]?

Step 7. How many guesses does it take to find 0 in the full range? Note that you can just type a carriage return when prompted for lower and upper bounds to get the specified bounds. How many guesses does it take to find 1? How many guesses to find 1000000?

Step 8. What is the largest number of guesses that it takes to find a number in the full range? What number requires that many guesses?

Step 9. How did you determine your answer to the previous step?

Experiment A2.5: Binary search

Step 1. Consider the array of the first sixteen integers, [2,4,...,32]. What elements would binary search look at in determining whether 16 is in the array? Note that Java rounds down when dividing integers.

Step 2. Create a new class, `SearchTester`, with a `main` method that contains the following lines.

```
// Prepare for reading input and generating output.
SimpleInput in = new SimpleInput();
SimpleOutput out = new SimpleOutput();
// Prepare our sequence.
IntSeq seq = new IntSeq();
// The value we're looking for
int val;
// The position of that value
int pos;

// Fill the sequence with the even numbers from 2 to 32.
seq.fill(0,15,2,2);
// Read a value and determine its position.
out.print("Search for what value? ");
val = in.readInt();
// Search for the value.
pos = seq.binarySearch(val);
if (pos == -1) {
  out.println(val + " is not in the first sixteen even numbers");
} // invalid position
else {
  out.println(val + " falls at position " + pos);
} // valid position
```

Compile and execute `SearchTester`. How many steps does it take to determine whether 16 is in the array? 12? 1? 15? 0? Do the answers correspond to your answers from the previous step? If not, can you guess why not?

Step 3. What happens when binary search is used on an unsorted list? Update `SearchTester` to build the sequence [5,1,3,7,2,8,0]. Search for 8, 1, 5, and 2. Which does it get correct? How many steps does it take in each case? Explain.

Step 4. Suppose we were interested in more details on the steps used in binary search. Add methods to `IntSeq` that do binary search and also print the steps involved in binary search. The two methods should be

- `binarySearch(SimpleOutput out, int val)` and
- `binarySearch(SimpleOutput out, int val, int lb, int ub)`

For example, in searching for 4 in [1,3,5,7,9,11,13], the output might be

```
Looking for 4 in positions 0 to 6
  The middle element (position 3) is 7.
  4 < 7: Throwing away elements at positions 3 to 6
Looking for 4 in positions 0 to 2
  The middle element (position 1) is 3.
  4 > 3: Throwing away elements at position 0 to 1
Looking for 4 in positions 1 to 2.
  The middle element (position 2) is 5.
  4 < 5: Throwing away elements at position 2
  There are no elements remaining.
4 is not in the array.
```

You need not record anything for this step.

Step 5. Using your modified `IntSeq`, redo Step 3 and explain the results.

Step 6. We have not considered what binary search does when the same element appears multiple times in a list. Update `SearchTester` to determine which version of each number is found in [1,1,1,2,2,2,3,3,3]. Summarize your results.

Experiment A2.6: Problems with binary search

Required files:

- `IntSeq.java`, as modified in the previous experiment to report on positions in binary search.
- `SearchTester.java`, created in the previous experiment.

Before you begin, if you have not modified `IntSeq.java` to print the steps used in binary search, here are the appropriate methods to add.

```java
/**
 * Search through a sorted array of integers for a particular value.
 * Print the steps as you go.
 * Return the index of the value if it is found.
 * Return -1 otherwise.
 */
public int binarySearch(SimpleOutput out, int val) {
  return binarySearch(out, val, 0, this.elements.length-1);
} // binarySearch(int)

/**
 * Search for a value in a subarray of a sorted array of integers.
 * The subarray is given by lb .. ub.
 * Return the index of the value if it is found.
 * Return -1 otherwise.
 */
protected int binarySearch(SimpleOutput out, int val, int lb, int ub)
{
  // Compute the index of the middle value.
  int mid = (lb + ub) / 2;
  // Print some feedback.
  out.println("Looking for " + val + " in positions " + lb + " to " +
              ub);
  if (mid > 0) {
    out.println("  The middle element (position " + mid + ") is " +
                this.elements[mid]);
  }
  // Is the subarray empty?
  if (lb > ub) {
    out.println("  There are no elements remaining.");
    out.println(val + " is not in the array");
    return -1;
  } // empty subarray
  // Is the value at the middle?
  else if (val == this.elements[mid]) {
    return mid;
  } // Found it!
  // Should the value be in the left half?
  else if (val < this.elements[mid]) {
    // Give feedback.
    out.println("  " + val + " < " + this.elements[mid] +
                ": Throwing away elements at positions " +
                mid + " to " + ub);
    // And recurse.
    return binarySearch(out, val, lb, mid-1);
  } // left half
  // The value must be in the right half.
  else {
    // Give feedback.
    out.println("  " + val + " > " + this.elements[mid] +
                ": Throwing away elements at positions " +
                lb + " to " + mid);
```

```
    // And recurse
    return binarySearch(out, val, mid+1, ub);
  } // right half
} // binarySearch(SimpleOutput, int, int, int)
```

Step 1. Using `SearchTester`, record the steps used to search for 1,2,3, and 4 in the array [2,4,6,8] using binary search.

Step 2. Using `SearchTester`, record the steps used to search for 1,2,3, and 4 in the array [2,4] using binary search.

Step 3. Modify `binarySearch` so that it includes the midpoint in the recursive calls. These new recursive calls should resemble

```
        return binarySearch(out, val, lb, mid);
...
        return binarySearch(out, val, mid, ub);
```

(Note that the extra parameter was included when you added support for printing the steps.)

Step 4. Using `SearchTester`, record the steps used to search for 1,2,3, and 4 in the array [2,4,6,8] using the modified binary search.

Step 5. Using `SearchTester`, record the steps used to search for 1,2,3, and 4 in the array [2,4] using the modified binary search.

Step 6. What do these results suggest?

Post-Laboratory Problems

**Problem A2-A:
An iterative
binary search**

Rewrite the binary search given in `IntSeq.java` iteratively; that is, use loops rather than recursive calls.

**Problem A2-B:
Evaluating
binary search**

Build an ordered array of the first sixteen positive even integers (2, 4, ..., 32). For each integer N between 1 and 33, find the number of steps required to determine whether or not N is in the array.

**Problem A2-C:
Searching
through names**

Build a `StringSeq` class that provides many of the same facilities as `IntSeq`, but that uses arrays of strings rather than arrays of integers. You need not include the various `fill` methods.

**Problem A2-D:
Finding the first
element**

As we saw in Experiment A2.5, binary search does not always find the first instance of an element in the array. Rewrite binary search so that it finds the first instance of each element. For example, in searching through [1,1,1,2,2,2,3,3,3], your algorithm should give 0 as the position of 1, 3 as the position of 2, and 6 as the position of 3.

**Problem A2-E:
Extending the
number game**

As you may recall, the `NumberGameGuesser` restricted the possible range to values between `Long.MIN_VALUE/2` and `Long.MAX_VALUE/2`. Remove that restriction and see what happens when you try using values outside those ranges.

The problem you will encounter has to do with the computation `(lower+upper)/2`. While the result of that computation will always be between `Long.MAX_VALUE` and `Long.MIN_VALUE`, the intermediate value `(lower+upper)` may be too large or too small.

Rewrite `(lower+upper)/2` so that it never gets too large or too small.

**Problem A2-F:
Variations on
search**

At the end of the discussion, we considered an alternate searching problem: searching for the smallest element in a list of elements. Are there other related searching problems you can think of?

**Problem A2-G:
Smallest,
revisited**

It seems somewhat odd that we have a different search method for finding the smallest element and for finding a particular element. Consider how you might write one method that could be used to solve both problems. For example, you might pass an `Evaluator` object (one that you design and construct) to the `Search` method, and that object will determine what to do at each step.

Problem A2-H:
Further readings
In the books *Programming Pearls* (Addison-Wesley, 1986) and *More Programming Pearls* (Addison-Wesley, 1988), Jon Bentley reports on a number of aspects of binary search. Find the books, read the appropriate sections, and write a short report on them.

Session A3: Analyzing Algorithms

In this laboratory session, you will analyze the running time of algorithms by using two strategies for timing algorithms: wall clock timing and instruction counting. The purposes of this laboratory session are to

- introduce algorithm measurement;
- describe Java's built-in mechanism for timing programs;
- consider a variety of algorithms in more depth; and
- prepare you for more in-depth analysis of algorithms.

Prerequisite skills:

- Knowledge of recursion and recursive algorithms

Required files:

- IntSeq.java
- IntSeqTester.java
- MeasuredExponentiation.java
- MeasuredFibonacci.java
- RecursiveExamples.java
- SimpleInput.java
- SimpleOutput.java

Discussion

You may have noted that it is possible to develop a number of algorithms to solve the same problem. For example, in a previous laboratory session we developed a number of different methods to compute Fibonacci numbers and to do exponentiation. How do we choose between a number of competing algorithms for the same problem? One way is to compare the efficiency of the algorithms. How do we quantify the efficiency of an algorithm or program? We might consider their use of memory, their running time, or their use of other resources. In this laboratory session, you will consider concrete ways of determining the running time of functions.

Timing algorithms

How do you determine the running time of an algorithm? You might try to measure the time it takes using a clock. Unfortunately, many algorithms run so quickly that they will finish before the second hand ticks. Humans are also notoriously inaccurate at noticing when programs start and stop. Fortunately, Java includes methods for determining the current time to a high precision.

In particular, the method `System.currentTimeMillis()` returns the current time in milliseconds since 00:00:00 January 1, 1970. Hence, to time an algorithm, you can simply determine the time immediately before the algorithm begins and the time immediately after the algorithm completes. By comparing the two times, you can determine how long the algorithm took. For example,

```
long start_time; // The time the algorithm started
long end_time;   // The time the algorithm ended
start_time = System.currentTimeMillis();
algorithm();
end_time = System.currentTimeMillis();
out.println("The algorithm took " +
            (end_time-start_time) +
            " milliseconds.");
```

(Note that `long` is a form of `int` that permits a larger range of integers.)

In Experiment A3.1, you will use wall-clock timing to consider the amount of time it takes to compute Fibonacci numbers. In Experiment A3.2, you will use wall-clock timing to investigate the exponentiation algorithms.

Problems with wall-clock timing

A number of disadvantages to using wall-clock timing exist, some of which you will explore in Experiment A3.1. First, timing is highly dependent on the machine being used. The same program can run much faster or much slower depending on the machine it is running on. In fact, the same program may run at different speeds on the same computer. In particular, a program is likely to run much more slowly on a computer that is doing a number of other tasks than on a computer that is just running that program.

It is often the case that programmers who time their programs end up timing things that they don't intend. For example, if you are timing an algorithm and doing input and output, you should time only the algorithm and not the input and output. This is particularly important because input and output can take significantly longer than many algorithms. In addition, things are often going on behind the scenes that you have no control over. For example, Java often spends longer on the first invocation of a method than on subsequent invocations.

Does this mean that you shouldn't use wall-clock timing? Certainly not. It is a valuable tool in your toolbox. If you are careful about your timing (e.g., you do your best to time only what you want to time, and you run all of your timing tests on the same computer with the same load), then it can give you useful results. As you develop larger programs, you may find it useful to use wall-clock timing to identify parts of your program that need to be improved.

Counting steps

Instead of measuring wall-clock time, we can augment our methods to count the number of steps they do. Obviously, counting every line executed in a program is difficult. Therefore, you will typically count one step for each function call and one step for each repetition of a loop. How do you do that counting? You may recall from the lab on recursion that we should

- add an appropriate counter field to the class that contains the method we wish to measure;
- add a method to reset the counter to 0;
- add a method to get the value of the counter; and
- add appropriate lines to the algorithm.

For example, the following class provides a Fibonacci method whose steps are counted.

```
/**
 * A measured Fibonacci function.
 *
 * @author Samuel A. Rebelsky
 * @version 1.0 of September 1998
 */
public class MeasuredFibonacci {

  // +--------+------------------------------------------------
  // | Fields |
  // +--------+
  /** The number of steps used to compute the nth Fibonacci number. */
  protected int steps;

  // +--------+------------------------------------------------
  // | Methods |
  // +--------+
  /**
   * Reset the count of steps to 0.
   */
```

```
      public void resetCounter() {
        steps = 0;
      } // resetCounter()

      /**
       * Determine the number of steps used since the last call to
       * resetCounter().
       */
      public int getSteps() {
        return steps;
      } // getSteps()

      /**
       * Compute the nth Fibonacci number.
       */
      public int fib(int n) {
        ++steps;
        // Base case: n is 1 or 2
        if ((n == 1) || (n == 2)) {
          return 1;
        } // base case
        // Recursive case
        else {
          return fib(n-1) + fib(n-2);
        } // recursive case
      } // fib(int)
    } // class MeasuredFibonacci
```

In Experiment A3.3, you will count the steps to compute Fibonacci numbers. In Experiment A3.4, you will count the steps used in the two exponentiation algorithms.

Problems with counting

Are there also problems with measuring the execution time of algorithms by counting steps? Certainly. First of all, this mechanism requires you to augment your code with lines that increment the counter. This is often much more difficult than simply using a timer. It also requires you to have access to the source code of the methods you wish to measure.

This mechanism can also lead to problems if we use the same counter for different methods in that we may end up counting steps that we do not intend to count or if we fail to use the same counter. For an example of the latter, consider a method that has one step, a call to another method. If we don't count the steps used in the sub-method, our analysis will be quite inaccurate.

In addition, this type of measurement is easily affected by slight variations in the input. For example, consider what happens if we call the recursive exponentiation function with exponents of 16 and 15. Recall that we developed an efficient recursive exponentiation function in which the exponent in the recursive call is either one less than the exponent (if the exponent is odd) or half of the exponent (if the exponent is even). The number 16 is even, so we divide by two, leaving 8 (one steps). The number 8 is even, so we divide by two, leaving 3 (two steps). 4 is even, so we divide by two, leaving 2 (three steps). The number 2 is even, so we divide by two, leaving 1 (four steps). The number 1 is odd, so we subtract 1 from 1, leaving 0 (five steps). 0 is the base case (six steps). The number 15 is odd, so we subtract 1, leaving 14 (one step). The number 14 is even, so we divide by two, leaving 7 (two steps). The number 7 is odd, so we subtract 1, leaving 6 (three steps). The number 6 is even, so we divide by two, leaving 3 (four steps). The number 3 is odd so we subtract 1, leaving 2 (five steps). The number 2 is even, so we divide by two, leaving 1 (six steps). The number 1 is odd, so we subtract 1 from 1, leaving 0 (seven steps). 0 is the base case (eight steps). *We did more steps for a smaller exponent!*

Once again, this is an imperfect method. Nonetheless, it is a useful one, provided you understand its drawbacks.

Is there a better method for analyzing algorithms? Yes, you can measure them abstractly. However, we will not consider such analysis in depth in this session.

Binary search, revisited

We will conclude our study of algorithm analysis by returning to two key searching methods: sequential search and binary search. For our purposes, a search algorithm will determine the position of an integer in an array or inform us if the integer is not in the array. As you may recall, we've included such methods as part of the `IntSeq` class.

You may recall that our sequential search algorithm looked at the elements of the array, one-by-one, until it found the element or exhausted the elements in the array. In the former case, it returned the index of the matching item. In the latter case, it returned -1 to indicate an error. In the worst case, sequential search looks at every element of the array.

Can we do better? Certainly, if we know particular facts about the array. For example, if we know the smallest element in the array and we discover that the value we're looking for is smaller than that element, then we can report that the value is not there in one step. However, this is clearly an uncommon case.

We can also do better if the array is sorted. Then we can use the divide-and-conquer technique of binary search. In binary search, we look at the middle element. If the value we're looking for is less than the middle element, we throw away the upper half of the array. If the value we're looking for is greater than the middle element, we "throw away" the lower half of the array. You should be able to figure out what to do if the value we're looking for is equal to the middle element.

In Experiment A3.5, you will consider the number of steps the various searching algorithms take.

Finding groups of smallest entries

Suppose you were instead asked to find the two smallest entries in a sequence. One question you might ask would be "How should I return two values?" So that we need not concern ourselves with that question, let us instead try to move the two smallest entries to the first two positions of the array.

One approach would be to look through the sequence to find the smallest entry and move it to the front of the sequence, then look through all but the first element of the modified sequence for the next smallest element. Using the `indexOfSmallest` method described above, we might phrase this as

```
/**
 * Put the two smallest elements of the sequence at the beginning
 * of the sequence.  The sequence must have at least two elements.
 */
public void twoSmallest() {
  // Swap the initial element with the smallest
  swap(0, indexOfSmallest(0, this.length()-1));
  // Swap the next element with the smallest remaining
  swap(1, indexOfSmallest(1, this.length()-1));
} // twoSmallest()
```

As you might guess, `swap(i,j)` swaps the elements at positions i and j in the sequence.

Now, how might we put the five smallest elements in a sequence of 50 elements at the front of that sequence? One approach would be to comb through the sequence to find the smallest entry and move it to the front of the sequence. Next, you could comb through the 49 entries following this newly positioned entry to find the next smallest entry and move it to the position following the smallest entry. By repeating this process three more times, each time finding the smallest entry remaining in the sequence and placing it just behind the entry found in the previous pass, you will have placed the five smallest entries at the beginning of the sequence in increasing order of size.

When turning this narrative into code, it is appropriate to use a loop (since the five pieces are quite similar). For example,

```
/**
 * Put the five smallest elements of the array at the beginning of
 * the array (naive method).  The sequence should have at least
 * five elements.
 */
public void fiveSmallest() {
  int i;
  // For each index i from 0 to 4,
  for (i = 0; i < 5; ++i) {
    // Swap the smallest element in [i .. last] with the ith element.
    swap(i, indexOfSmallest(i, this.length()-1));
  } // for
} // fiveSmallest()
```

What we have accomplished is a partial sorting of the sequence by *selecting* the smallest entries.

Our task now is to analyze the efficiency of this approach. This we do in terms of the number of times two entries in the sequence are compared. To find and position the smallest entry in the sequence requires 49 comparisons, to process the next smallest entry requires 48, and so on. Thus, the total number of comparisons to find the five smallest entries is

$$49 + 48 + 47 + 46 + 45 = 235$$

In general, applying this selection method to find the K smallest entries in a sequence of N entries requires

$$(1/2)(2 * N * K - K^2 - K)$$

comparisons. Can you derive this formula? Thus, to find the 10 smallest entries in a sequence of 10,000 entries requires 99,945 comparisons. We might also say that this is an $O(nk)$ algorithm.

Can we do better? Recall that when we found the smallest element in a sequence, we began with a guess of the smallest and then refined that guess by looking at the remaining elements. We can do the same thing to find the five smallest elements. Initially, we'll assume that the first five elements are the five smallest elements. Sort the first five entries in the sequence by any method. Then consider the sixth entry. Compare it to the fifth entry in the sequence, which is now the largest of the first five entries. If the sixth entry is larger, pass over it because it is not one of the five smallest entries. If, however, the sixth entry is smaller than the fifth, compare it with the fourth, third, and so on, inserting it among the first five entries so that the first five entries in the list remain the smallest entries found so far in increasing order. Repeat this process for the entries in positions 7, 8, ..., 50.

Note that this process creates a partially sorted list by inserting the smallest entries into the beginning of the list. To see why the insertion strategy is superior to the selection strategy, let us compare the two approaches when searching for the 10 smallest entries within a list of 1000 entries. We suppose that our insertion strategy has reached the halfway point. The 10 smallest items in the first 500 have been found and we are about to consider the entry in position 501. If the original list was randomly scrambled, it is unlikely that this entry will be less than the tenth entry, and only one comparison is required to discover this. The same is true for all the entries in positions 501 through 1000. However, if one of these entries does belong among the top 10, then this will be discovered with one comparison, and at most nine more comparisons will be required to position it properly. This is much more efficient than our selection strategy, in which each of the last 500 entries is involved in 10 comparisons.

In Experiment A3.6, you will revisit the problem of finding the smallest element in a sequence. In Experiment A3.7, you will investigate these two algorithms for computing collections of smaller elements.

Experiments

Name: _____

ID: _____

Note that different computers run at very different speeds. Your instructor may suggest that you use larger or smaller values in these experiments. (On faster computers, you may find that the times for these values are too short to measure well; on slower computers, you may spend too much time waiting for results based on these values.)

Experiment A3.1: Wall-clock timing

Required file:

- `RecursiveExamples.java`

Step 1. Create a new class, `Analyzer`, that includes a `main` method with the following lines.

```
SimpleOutput out = new SimpleOutput();
RecursiveExamples helper = new RecursiveExamples();
long start_time; // The time the algorithm started
long end_time;   // The time the algorithm ended
int tmp;         // The result of some algorithms
int n;           // The argument to some algorithms
n = 15;
start_time = System.currentTimeMillis();
tmp = helper.fib(n);
end_time = System.currentTimeMillis();
out.println("Fibonacci of " + n + " is " + tmp);
out.println("  That computation took " + (end_time-start_time) +
            " milliseconds.");
```

Compile and execute `Analyzer`. Record the output. Execute it three more times, recording the output each time. Are your times all the same? After writing your answer, you may want to read our notes on the subject.

Step 2. Compare your times with those of a few of your classmates. How much variation did you see? Why might you have seen such variation?

Step 3. Update the `main` method to time the twentieth Fibonacci number. Execute it four times, recording the output each time. How do these times relate to those in the previous step? Is that what you would expect?

Step 4. You may be wondering why we use `tmp` in the previous code. Let's try eliminating it. Update your `main` method with the following lines.

```
start_time = System.currentTimeMillis();
out.println("Fibonacci of " + n + " is " + helper.fib(n));
end_time = System.currentTimeMillis();
out.println("  That computation took " + (end_time-start_time) +
            " milliseconds.");
```

Recompile `Analyzer`. Execute it four times, recording the output each time. Are these times similar to those from the previous step? If not, why might they be different?

Step 5. Instead of rerunning `Analyzer` each time we want to compute the running time of Fibonacci on a different input, we might read in that input. First, we need to create a `SimpleInput` object.

```
SimpleInput in = new SimpleInput();
```

Then we add a line to read in the input. Here is one way to do it.

```
start_time = System.currentTimeMillis();
out.print("Enter n: ");
n = in.readInt();
out.println("Fibonacci of " + n + " is " + helper.fib(n));
end_time = System.currentTimeMillis();
out.println("  That computation took " + (end_time-start_time) +
            " milliseconds.");
```

What do you think about this idea?

Step 6. Recompile `Analyzer`. Execute it four times, entering 15 each time. Record the output. Do the times vary more or less than in the previous steps? Why?

After writing your answer, you may want to read the notes on this problem.

Step 7. Rather than executing `Analyzer` repeatedly, it might be better to use a loop to do the repetition. Replace the appropriate lines of the `main` method with

```
int repetitions;    // The number of times to time
int i;              // A counter
out.print("Enter n: ");
n = in.readInt();
out.print("Enter the number of repetitions: ");
repetitions = in.readInt();
for (i = 0; i < repetitions; ++i) {
  start_time = System.currentTimeMillis();
  tmp = helper.fib(n);
  end_time = System.currentTimeMillis();
  out.println("Fibonacci of " + n + " is " + tmp);
  out.println("   That computation took " + (end_time-start_time) +
              " milliseconds.");
} // for
```

Recompile and execute `Analyzer`, using an input of 15. Execute `Analyzer`. Record and explain the output.

After writing your answer, you may want to read the notes on the matter.

Experiment A3.2: Comparing wall-clock times

Required file:

- `RecursiveExamples.java` (preferably as modified in the lab on recursion).

Step 1. Using `Analyzer`, determine the wall clock time it takes to compute 2^N, for N equal to 0, 1, 2, 3, and 4, using the iterative exponentiation function provided by `RecursiveExamples`.

```
N  Time
-  ----
1
2
3
4
```

Step 2. Using `Analyzer`, determine the wall clock time it takes to compute 2^N, for N equal to 0, 1, 2, 3, and 4, using the recursive exponentiation function provided by `RecursiveExamples`.

```
N  Time
-  ----
1
2
3

4
```

Step 3. Based on those results, which do you expect to be the more efficient algorithm? Why?

Step 4. Using `Analyzer`, determine the wall clock time it takes to compute 2^N, for N equal to 10, 20, 30, 40, and 100, using the iterative exponentiation function provided by `RecursiveExamples`.

```
N    Time(R) Time(I)
---  ------- -------
 10
 20
 30
 40
100
```

Step 5. Using `Analyzer`, determine the wall clock time it takes to compute 2^N, for N equal to 10, 20, 30, 40, and 100, using the recursive exponentiation function provided by `RecursiveExamples`.

```
N    Time
---  ----
 10
 20
 30
 40
100
```

Step 6. Do these new results change your opinion? Why or why not?

Experiment A3.3: Counting steps

Required file:

- `MeasuredFibonacci.java`

Step 1. Update the `main` method of `Analyzer` with the following lines:
MeasuredFibonacci fibhelper = <u>new</u> MeasuredFibonacci();

```
out.print("Enter n: ");
n = in.readInt();
fibhelper.resetCounter();
out.println("Fibonacci of " + n + " is " +
            fibhelper.fib(n));
out.println("  That computation took " +
            fibhelper.getCounter() + " steps");
```

Compile and execute `Analyzer`. Record the output. Execute it three more times, recording the output each time. Are your outputs the same? Is this what you expected, based on your experience?

Step 2. Compare your times with those of a few of your classmates. How much variation did you see? Is this what you expected?

Step 3. Add a <u>for</u> loop that allows you to repeatedly test the number of steps.

```
int steps;
int i;
fibhelper.resetCounter();
for (i = 0; i < steps; ++i) {
  out.println("Fibonacci of " + n + " is " +
            fibhelper.fib(n));
  out.println(" That computation took " +
            fibhelper.getCounter() + " steps");
} // for
```

Recompile and execute `Analyzer`. Record and explain the output.

When you are done, read the notes on the subject.

Step 4. Determine the number of steps used in computing the Nth Fibonacci number, for each *N* from 1 to 10.

N	Nth Fib	Steps
1		
2		
3		
4		
5		
6		
7		
8		
9		
10		

What do you observe about these numbers?

Step 5. Update `MeasuredFibonacci` so that it only counts the number of times the base case (*N* is 1 or 2) is used. Determine the number of steps used in computing the Nth Fibonacci number, for each *N* from 1 to 10.

```
N       Nth Fib  Steps
--      -------  -----
 1
 2
 3
 4
 5
 6
 7
 8
 9
10
```

What do you observe about these numbers?

Experiment A3.4: Comparing steps

Required file:

- `MeasuredExponentiation.java`

Step 1. Create a new class, `ExpMeasurer` with a `main` method with the following lines.

```
// Prepare for reading input and writing output.
SimpleInput in = new SimpleInput();
SimpleOutput out = new SimpleOutput();
// Build something that can measure steps for exponentiation.
MeasuredExponentiation measurer = new MeasuredExponentiation()
// The values we will use.
int n;
double x;
// Get the values to use in computations.
out.println("This program computes x^n in two ways and reports on " +
            "the number of steps in each computation.");
out.println("Enter x: ");
x = in.readDouble();
out.println("Enter n: ");
n = in.readInt();
// Compute the exponent recursively, counting steps.
measurer.resetCounter();
out.println("Recursively: " +
            x + "^" + n + " = " + measurer.recExp(x,n));
out.println("   " + measurer.getCounter() + " steps");
measurer.resetCounter();
```

```
// Compute the exponent iteratively, counting steps.
out.println("Iteratively: " +
        x + "^" + n + " = " + measurer.itExp(x,n));
out.println("   " + measurer.getCounter() + " steps");
```

Using `ExpMeasurer`, determine the number of steps it takes to compute 2^N, for N equal to 0, 1, 2, 3, and 4, using the iterative and recursive exponentiation functions.

```
N  Time(R) Time(I)
-  ------- -------
1
2
3
4
```

Step 2. Based on those results, which do you expect to be the more efficient algorithm? Why?

Step 3. Using `Analyzer`, determine the number of steps it takes to compute 2^N, for N equal to 10, 20, 30, 40, and 100, using the iterative and recursive exponentiation functions provided by `MeasuredExponentiation`.

```
N    Time
---  ----
 10
 20
 30
 40
100
```

Step 4. Do these new results change your opinion? Why or why not?

Experiment A3.5:
Binary search

Required files:

- `IntSeq.java`

Step 1. Create a new class, `SearchTester`, with a `main` method that contains the following lines.

```
// Prepare for reading input and generating output.
SimpleInput in = new SimpleInput();
SimpleOutput out = new SimpleOutput();
// Prepare our sequence.
IntSeq seq = new IntSeq();
// The value we're looking for
int val;
// The position of that value
int pos;
// Fill the sequence with the even numbers from 2 to 32.
seq.fill(0,15,2,2);
// Read a value and determine its position.
out.print("Search for what value? ");
val = in.readInt();
// Search for the value, counting the steps.
seq.resetSteps();
pos = seq.binarySearch(val, evens);
if (pos == -1) {
  out.println(val + " is not in the first sixteen even numbers");
} // invalid position
else {
  out.println(val + " falls at position " + pos);
} // valid position
out.println("Searching took " + seq.getSteps() + " steps");
```

Compile and execute `SearchTester`. How many steps does it take to determine whether 16 is in the array? 12? 1? 15? 0? Can you explain why?

After recording your answer, you may wish to look at the notes on this problem.

**Experiment A3.6:
Finding the
smallest element**

Required files:

- `Counter.java`
- `IntSeq.java`
- `IntSeqTester.java`

Step 1. In the past, we've used internal fields to count the number of steps an algorithm takes. This introduces some overhead when we don't care about the number of steps. A more object-oriented solution would be to provide a separate `Counter` object that can be used for counting. Read the code for that class and explain what it does.

Step 2. Build a new version of the `smallest` method from `IntSeq` that takes a `Counter` as a parameter and uses that counter to count the steps it executes. Recompile `IntSeq` and correct any errors. Summarize your changes.

Step 3. Extend `IntSeqTester` so that it uses a `Counter` to count the steps in `IntSeq`'s `smallest` method. Recompile `IntSeqTester` and correct any errors. Summarize your changes.

Step 4. Execute `IntSeqTester` and record the number of steps required to find the smallest element in lists of size 10, 20, 100, and 1000.

10:

20:

100:

1000:

After recording your results, you may want to look at the notes on this step.

Experiment A3.7: Finding smaller elements

Required files:

- `IntSeq.java`
- `IntSeqTester.java`

Step 1. Make copies of `IntSeq.java` and `IntSeqTester.java`. Compile them and execute `IntSeqTester`. Find the five smallest elements in a list of size 50. Record the results.

Step 2. Update `IntSeq` so that `fiveSmallest`, `newFiveSmallest`, and any methods they use take `Counters` as parameters and count their steps. Update `IntSeqTester` to call those methods with a `Counter` and print out the number of steps executed. Recompile both files and correct any errors. Summarize your changes.

Step 3. Use your modified `IntSeqTester` to fill in the following table.

Steps to find the smallest five elements in a list of size N, *using the selection strategy and the better insertion strategy.*

N	steps (selection)	steps (insertion)
500		
1000		
2000		

Step 4. Update `IntSeq` and `IntSeqTester` to look for the seven smallest elements, rather than the five smallest elements. Fill in the table.

Steps to find the smallest seven elements in a list of size N, *using the selection strategy and the better insertion strategy.*

```
N          steps              steps
           (selection)        (insertion)
 500
1000
2000
```

Step 5. Add `kSmallest` and `newKSmallest` methods to `IntSeq`. These will behave like `fiveSmallest` and `newFiveSmallest` so that they take `k` (the number of small elements to find) as a parameter. Recompile `IntSeq` and correct any errors. Summarize your changes.

Step 6. Update `IntSeqTester` so that it reads in the number of elements to find in the cases in which we want *K* small elements. Recompile `IntSeq-Tester` and correct any errors. Summarize your changes.

Step 7. Using your augmented `IntSeqTester`, record the number of steps for each of the following

Steps to find the smallest K *elements in a list of size* N, *using the selection strategy and the better insertion strategy.*

```
K    N           steps              steps
                 (selection)        (insertion)
5    500
10   1000
15   2000
```

Step 8. Repeat Step 7 for the following table. In these cases you are selecting the top 10 percent of the list, while in Step 7 you selected the top 1 percent.

Steps to find the smallest K *elements in a list of size* N, *using the selection strategy and the better insertion strategy.*

```
K     N          steps              steps
                 (selection)        (insertion)
25    250
50    500
100   1000
```

200 2000

Step 9. Do those number match those theorized in the discussion? Why or why not?

Step 10. What do you conclude about the advantages of one strategy over the other?

Post-Laboratory Problems

Problem A3-A: Plotting exponentiation

Determine the wall-clock time it takes to compute 1.3^N recursively for every n between 0 and 100. (Note that you'll need to be careful to measure only the time of execution.) Plot the points. Is the curve smooth? If not, suggest why not.

Problem A3-B: Comparing exponentiation

Determine the wall-clock time it takes to compute 1.001^{1024} recursively. Determine the wall-clock time it takes to compute 1.001^{511} iteratively. Which is quicker? Why?

Problem A3-C: Plotting exponentiation, revisited

Determine the number of steps used to compute 1.3^N recursively for every N between 0 and 100. Plot the points. Is the curve smooth? If not, suggest why not.

Problem A3-D: Comparing exponentiation, revisited

Determine the number of steps it takes to compute 1.001^{1024} recursively. Determine the number of steps it takes to compute 1.001^{511}. Explain the difference.

Problem A3-E: Sorting

Note that we can use our modified `kSmallest` algorithm to sort arrays (i.e., put all of the elements in order). How? If there are n elements in the array, we ask to find the n smallest elements. Since the algorithm puts the n smallest elements in order, it has sorted the whole array.

Use this observation to add a `sort` method to `IntSeq` (and to `StringSeq`, if you developed it).

Problem A3-F: Sorting, revisited

Find a textbook or Web page that discusses sorting and determine the name of the sorting algorithm we developed in problem A3-E.

Notes

Experiment A3.1, Step 1. You will likely have seen a variety of different running times, but hopefully without much difference. Why? Because a number of external factors can influence the wall-clock time. Some of those factors are covered in the preceding discussion.

Experiment A3.1, Step 6. You will likely see much longer times and much more variation in times. Why? Because you are timing not just the algorithm, but also the time it took you to write the input. Humans are often much slower and much more variable than computers.

Experiment A3.1, Step 7. The first call to `fib` likely took significantly longer than the others. Why? Because Java needs to do a number of things the first time a method is invoked (e.g., on some machines a *just-in-time compiler* will convert the Java virtual machine code to local machine code). For subsequent calls to the method, that work does not need to be done.

Experiment A3.3, Step 3. You may have noted that the number of steps was different each time. Why? Because we neglected to reset the counter each time through the loop.

Experiment A3.6, Step 5. If you only count the number of times the body in the loop is executed, the number of steps in `smallest` is likely to be one less than the number of elements in the sequence.

Session G1: Graphics and Applets

In this laboratory session, you will develop a number of simple Java *applets* that are displayed in Web pages. The purposes of this lab session are to

- introduce graphics in Java;
- introduce Java's applets, an alternative model of programming; and
- have some fun.

Your instructor will tell you which of the proposed experiments you are to perform.

Note: As the introduction notes, this manual provides two mechanisms for learning about applets. One is this lab. The other is the applet problems that appear at the end of many experiments. If you've been doing the applet problems, you are likely to find this lab repetitious.

Prerequisite skills:

- Simple HTML (although this is not strictly required)
- Basic Java programming
- Classes and objects

Required HTML files:

- circle.html
- coloredtext.html

Required Java files:

- CircleApplet.java
- ColoredTextApplet.java
- FullCircleApplet.java
- MovingCircleApplet.java

Discussion

Applets

In addition to supporting the standard application model of programming, Java also supports a variant model, known as the *applet* model. Applets are programs that are designed to be run within other programs. Most often, applets are graphical programs that run within Web pages. In the first lab session, you may have experimented with applets that drew pictures on the screen or animated balls or balloons. In this session, we'll focus on the static applets.

Interestingly, the structure of an applet differs from that of an application. In particular, applets typically do not contain constructors or a `main` method. Rather, they use alternate methods to support the same concepts (of initialization and execution). These alternate methods are:

- `public void init()`, which specifies how to initialize your applet. In effect, `init` serves as the constructor and `main` for an applet.
- `public void paint(Graphics paintBrush)`, which paints a picture on the screen. Since most applets are graphical, the `paint` method is often the core of an applet. The parameter provides an object that you can use when painting.

(Note that some programmers write Java applets that are also applications, or vice versa. In this case, the classes are likely to include constructors, `init`, and `main`.)

In order for the Java interpreter or Web browser to run an applet successfully, you need to tell Java that your class describes applets as opposed to other things. You do this by including the phrase

`extends Applet`

in your class header.

For example, I might write

```
public class MyCoolApplet
  extends Applet {
```

In addition, you must tell Java that you will be using the various applet and graphics libraries. You do this with a series of `import` statements.

```
import java.applet.*;
import java.awt.*;
```

To include a Java applet within a Web page, you use the `applet` tag. Within the tag, you need to specify the code file for the applet and the width and height of the applet. For example, the following creates a 400 by 300 area for the applet `CircleApplet`.

```
<applet code="CircleApplet.class" width="400" height="300">
</applet>
```

Note that you do need an end tag for applets. Later, we will see things that can go between the two tags.

Painting pictures

You are almost ready to build your first applet. However, you will first need to learn how to paint. Java provides a class, `java.awt.Graphics`, that provides most of the core painting routines. If your instructor has provided you with a copy of the Java API (Application Programmer Interface), you may wish to refer to the section of the API that covers the `Graphics` class as we'll only cover a few of the many routines that class provides.

To draw anything in Java, you will first want to set the color of the pen that does the drawing. You do that with a call to `setColor`. What colors can you use? They are specified within `java.awt.Color`. For now, you should use `Color.red`, `Color.blue`, and `Color.green`. If your current graphics object is named `paintBrush`, you would indicate that the pen color should be set to green with

```
paintBrush.setColor(Color.green);
```

Java permits you to draw a number of different objects, including circles and ovals, squares and rectangles, lines, and pieces of text. You draw the outline of a circle or oval with

```
paintBrush.drawOval(int left, int top, int width, int height);
```

That is, you specify the farthest left side point on the oval, the top point on the oval, the width of the oval, and the height of the oval. You can fill in the oval with `paintBrush.fillOval`, which has the same parameters.

Other routines you may want to use include

- `paintBrush.drawRect(int left, int top, int width, int height)`
- `paintBrush.fillRect(int left, int top, int width, int height)`
- `paintBrush.drawLine(int x1, int x2, int y1, int y2)`
- `paintBrush.drawString(String str, int x, int y)`

Java uses an interesting coordinate system. The top-left corner of a drawing area is (0,0) and coordinates increase down and to the right.

A circle applet

Building applets that draw pictures is relatively easy. All such applets need to contain is a `paint` method. Here is a simple applet that draws a small circle on the screen. Note that all it contains is a `paint` method that sets the color and calls `paintBrush.fillOval`.

```java
import java.applet.*;

import java.awt.*;

/**
 * Draw a small blue circle on the screen.
 *
 * @author Samuel A. Rebelsky
 * @version 1.0 of March 1998
 */
public class CircleApplet extends Applet {
```

```
/**
 * Paint a blue circle on the screen.
 */
public void paint(Graphics paintBrush) {
    // Paint a circle of diameter 40
    paintBrush.setColor(Color.blue);
    paintBrush.fillOval(0,0,40,40);
} // paint(Graphics)
} // class CircleApplet
```

In Experiment G1.1, you will run this simple applet and make some basic modifications.

Colors

As you can tell from the previous experiment, Java supports a few different predefined colors, including `Color.red` and `Color.blue`. The available colors are `black`, `blue`, `cyan`, `darkGray`, `gray`, `green`, `lightGray`, `magenta`, `orange`, `pink`, `red`, `white`, and `yellow`. You can also create your own color using

```
new Color(int red, int green, int blue);
```

Each of the three color components is a number between 0 and 255. For example, you might set the pen to an interesting shade of green with

```
Color myColor = new Color(0, 200, 255);
paintBrush.setColor(myColor);
```

You might also use the more succinct

```
paintBrush.setColor(new Color(0, 200, 255));
```

In Experiment G1.2, you will experiment with different mechanisms for creating colors.

Pixels vs. coordinates

You have already noticed that Java's coordinate system is somewhat odd. In particular, while horizontal coordinates increase to the right, vertical coordinates increase as you move downward. Yet this is not the only way in which Java's drawing conventions defy many beginning programmers' initial assumptions.

Surprisingly, the coordinates on the grid are not where the ink appears. Rather, the ink appears between these points. For example, the top-left pixel is not at (0,0). Rather, it appears between the four points (0,0), (0,1), (1,0), and (1,1).

Why does this make a difference? Because `fillRect` and `fillOval` color only the pixels within the area described by the parameters, whereas `drawRect` and `drawOval` color the pixels to the left and down from the object described. For example, the lower-right pixel drawn by `fillRect(0,0,3,2)` is bounded by (2,1), (2,2), (3,1), and (3,2). However, the lower-right pixel drawn by `drawRect(0,0,3,2)` falls to the right of and below the lower-right corner (3,2) and therefore is bounded by (3,2), (3,3), (4,2), and (4,3). What is the moral? *Filled shapes are typically one pixel smaller horizontally and vertically than drawn shapes.* In Experiment G1.3, you will consider this difference.

Applet dimensions

You may have noted that the dimensions (width and height) of an applet are set within the HTML files that loads the applet and not within the applet itself. Clearly, it is possible to load the same applet with different dimensions and different pages may therefore choose different dimensions for the same applet. For many applets, it becomes important for the applet designer to be able to determine these dimensions.

Fortunately, Java provides a mechanism for the applet author to determine the dimensions given for the applet. You can call `this.getSize()` to obtain a `Dimension` object. You can then get the width of that object by referring to its `width` and `height` fields.

Here is a sample applet that uses the dimension to paint a blue oval that is the full width and height of the applet area.

```java
import java.applet.Applet;
import java.awt.Color;
import java.awt.Dimension;
import java.awt.Graphics;

/**
 * Draw a circle on the screen.
 *
 * @author Samuel A. Rebelsky
 * @version 1.1 of August 1999
 */
public class FullCircleApplet extends Applet {
  /**
   * Paint a blue circle on the screen.
   */
  public void paint(Graphics paintBrush) {
    // Get the dimensions of the applet
    Dimension dim = this.getSize();
    // Paint a circle
    paintBrush.setColor(Color.blue);
    paintBrush.fillOval(0,0,dim.width,dim.height);
  } // paint(Graphics)
} // class FullCircleApplet
```

In Experiment G1.4, you will work with applets that behave differently depending on the boundaries that they are given.

Repainting

Interestingly, Java repaints the screen every time the applet window is resized (or another window is moved over the window, etc.). Repainting the screen means that Java erases what is already there, or at least spreads some of the background color over what the applet has painted, and then calls the `paint` method again. You can use this to your advantage by changing the way you draw your picture each time.

For example, we might make an applet in which the circle moves down and to the right each time the picture is redrawn. Doing so requires us to add fields to our applet (e.g., the X and Y positions of the current circle). We will also need to initialize those fields (aha! a use for that init method we saw much earlier). Here is a sample applet that draws a circle in a slightly different position at each step.

```
import java.applet.*;
import java.awt.*;

/**
 * Draw a small blue circle on the screen.  Move it whenever the
 * window is repainted.
 *
 * @author Samuel A. Rebelsky
 * @version 1.0 of March 1998
 */
public class MovingCircleApplet extends Applet {

  // +--------+----------------------------------------------------
  // | Fields |
  // +--------+
  /** The position of the left edge of the circle.  */
  protected int left;
  /** The position of the top edge of the circle.  */
  protected int top;

  // +----------------+-------------------------------------------
  // | Applet Methods |
  // +----------------+

  /**
   * Initialize the applet (set the top-left of the circle to (0,0)).
   */
  public void init()
  {
    top = 0;
    left = 0;
  } // init()

  /**
   * Paint a blue circle on the screen.
   */
  public void paint(Graphics paintBrush) {
    // Paint a circle of diameter 40
    paintBrush.setColor(Color.blue);
    paintBrush.fillOval(top,left,40,40);
    // Increment top and left for the next repainting
    top = top + 15;
    left = left + 15;
  } // paint(Graphics)

} // class MovingCircleApplet
```

In a typical applet, we might choose to do a number of things at each redraw. We might move objects. We might change colors. We might add or delete objects. The sky's the limit, as it were. Note also that by updating our image we have begun to provide a form of animation.

In Experiment G1.5, you will investigate some capabilities of the `paint` method for redrawing.

Applet parameters

In addition to using the HTML document to set the dimensions of an applet, you can also use the document to set other attributes of the applet. These are often called the applet's parameters. What can the parameters be? Anything you think is appropriate. For our circle-drawing applications, they might be the position, size, or color of the circle. They might even specify which shape we use, although we only know a few right now.

You set a parameter with a `param` tag, which goes between your applet tags. The following tag indicates that the value of the `printMe` parameter is "Java Rocks!".

```
<param name="printMe" value="Java Rocks!">
```

How can you access that parameter? With the `getParameter` method. The `getParameter` method always returns a string even if you want a number. If the HTML code does not include a `param` tag with the appropriate name, `getParameter` returns the special `null` value.

What happens if you want some other type (e.g., an integer)? If you need to convert the parameter to another type, you'll need to use some slightly tricky Java. For now, rely on the function included in the sample code below.

The following simple applet displays a piece of text in a color selected by its red, green, and blue components.

```java
import java.applet.*;
import java.awt.*;

/**
 * Draw some colored text on the screen.  Intended as an illustration
 * of applet parameters.
 *
 * @author Samuel A. Rebelsky
 * @version 1.0 of March 1998
 */
public class ColoredTextApplet extends Applet {

  // +--------+----------------------------------------------------
  // | Fields |
  // +--------+
  /** The color of the text.  */
  protected Color color;
  /** The text to print.  */
  protected String text;

  // +----------------+--------------------------------------------
  // | Applet Methods |
  // +----------------+
```

```
/**
 * Initialize the color and text.
 */
public void init() {
   // The three components of the color
   int red;
   int green;
   int blue;
   // Get the text.
   text = getParameter("printMe");
   if (text == null) {
     text = "Jabberwocky";
   }
   // Get the color.
   red = getIntegerParameter("red");
   green = getIntegerParameter("green");
   blue = getIntegerParameter("blue");
   color = new Color(red, green, blue);
} // init()

/**
 * Paint the text on the screen.
 */
public void paint(Graphics paintBrush) {
   // Paint a circle of diameter 40
   paintBrush.setColor(color);
   paintBrush.drawString(text,10,40);
} // paint(Graphics)
// +----------+-------------------------------------------------------
// | Utilities |
// +----------+

/**
 * Get a parameter and convert it to an integer.  If the
 * parameter is unspecified or otherwise bad, use 0.
 */
protected int getIntegerParameter(String param_name)
{
   // Get the value of the parameter
   String param_value = getParameter(param_name);
   // If the parameter is unspecified, use 0
   if (param_value == null) return 0;
   // Attempt to convert to an Integer.
   try {
     return Integer.parseInt(param_value);
   }
   catch (Exception e) {
     return 0;
   }
} // getIntegerParameter(String)
} // class ColoredTextApplet
```

In Experiment G1.6, you will begin to consider the use of parameters in applets.

Experiments

Name: _____

ID: _____

Experiment G1.1: A colored circle applet

Required files:

- `circle.html`
- `CircleApplet.java`

Step 1. Make copies of <u>CircleApplet.java</u> and <u>circle.html</u>. Compile `CircleApplet`. Then run appletviewer on `circle.html`. Note what you see.

Step 2. Open `circle.html` from within your internet browser (e.g., Netscape) and note what you see. Is there a significant difference between the two versions?

Step 3. Modify `CircleApplet` so that it draws a second red circle whose center is ten spaces to the right and five spaces down from the center of the first circle. Recompile your code and then reload the applet. Were you able to successfully position the circle? Which one is on top? Why?

Experiment G1.2: Experimenting with colors

Required files:

- `circle.html`
- `CircleApplet.java`

Step 1. Using your `CircleApplet` class, try to figure out how much red, how much green, and how much blue you need to create a satisfactory purple. Presumably, it is better to create a large number of circles and fill each with a different color. Once you have determined the color, write it here.

Step 2. Using your `CircleApplet` class, try to make a sequence of shades of orange such as one might see in a custom paint shop. What color values did you use?

Experiment G1.3: Drawing vs. filling

Required files:

- `circle.html`
- `CircleApplet.java`

Before you begin, if you have not already done so, make copies of these two files.

Step 1. Update `CircleApplet` so that it fills two circles of different colors, but in the same size and at the same position. For example,

```
public void paint(Graphics paintBrush) {
paintBrush.setColor(Color.red);
paintBrush.fillOval(10,10,40,40);
paintBrush.setColor(Color.black);
paintBrush.fillOval(10,10,40,40);
} // paint(Graphics)
```

What do you expect to see?

After entering your answer, compile and view the applet. You may also wish to refer to the notes on this step.

Step 2. Change the first call to `fillOval` to `drawOval`. For example,

```
paintBrush.setColor(Color.red);
paintBrush.drawOval(10,10,40,40);
paintBrush.setColor(Color.black);
paintBrush.fillOval(10,10,40,40);
```

What do you expect to see?

After entering your answer, compile and view the applet. You may also wish to refer to the notes on this step.

Step 3. Change the calls to `drawOval` and `fillOval` to corresponding calls to `drawRect` and `fillRect`. For example,

```
paintBrush.setColor(Color.red);
paintBrush.drawRect(10,10,40,40);
paintBrush.setColor(Color.black);
paintBrush.fillRect(10,10,40,40);
```

In this example, do you expect to see any red drawn? If so, where?

Step 4. What Java commands might one use to draw a black circle with diameter 40 and a one-pixel red border all around the circle? You should draw the black portion with `fillOval` and the red portion with `drawOval`.

Confirm your answer by creating a corresponding applet and drawing the picture.

Step 5. Does it matter whether the red or black component in the previous drawing is drawn first?

Step 6. Can you draw a similar picture using only `fillOval` and no calls to `drawOval`? If so, how? If not, why not?

Experiment G1.4: Getting boundaries

Required files:

- `circle.html`
- `FullCircleApplet.java`

Step 1. Make a copy of `FullCircleApplet.java`. Compile `FullCircleApplet`. Modify `circle.html` to load this new applet instead of `CircleApplet`. Then load the applet with appletviewer. What do you see? Is that what you expected?

Step 2. Modify `circle.html` so that the width of the applet is 100 and the height is 10. Do not recompile `FullCircleApplet`. Load the applet with appletviewer. What do you see? Is that what you expected?

Step 3. Load `circle.html` with appletviewer. If you click on one of the edges of the applet window, you should be able to resize the window. Does the circle resize when the applet size changes? What, if anything, does this suggest?

Step 4. If we were to draw four circles of radius 10 in the four corners of the window, what would their positions and width and height be? Once you've determined (and written down) these positions, extend `FullCircleApplet.java` to draw these four small circles in the corners. If you miscomputed some positions or sizes indicate which ones and analyze why.

Experiment G1.5: Repainting

Required files:

- `circle.html`
- `MovingCircleApplet.java`

Step 1. Make a copy of `MovingCircleApplet.java`. Compile `MovingCircleApplet`. Modify `circle.html` to load this new applet instead of `CircleApplet`. Then load the applet with appletviewer. What do you see? Is that what you expected?

Step 2. Resize the window. What happens to the circle? Is that what you expected? Why or why not?

Step 3. Move another window over the circle. Then move it away. What happens to the circle? Is this what you expected? Why or why not?

Step 4. Move another window over the appletviewer window, but not over the circle. Then move it away. What happens to the circle? Is this what you expected? Why or why not?

Step 5. Shrink and then expand the window. What happens to the circle? Is this what you expected? Why or why not?

Step 6. See if you can determine other ways to make the circle move. List them here.

Experiment G1.6: Setting parameters

Required files:

- `coloredtext.html`
- `ColoredTextApplet.java`

Step 1. Make a copy of `ColoredTextApplet.java` and `coloredtext.html`. Compile `ColoredTextApplet` and run appletviewer on `ColoredText`. What do you see? Is that what you expected?

Step 2. Using your determination of the color purple from a previous experiment, modify `coloredtext.html` so that it displays your name in purple.

Step 3. Update `ColoredTextApplet.java` so that it changes the color each time it redraws. To support this, you will need to make fields for the red, green, and blue components of the current color. Each time you redraw, change the component fields and create a new color from those fields. Increment each component by ten at each redraw. What happens when one of the three component colors gets a value over 255? After noting any problems, fix your class so that none of the components gets a value outside of 0 to 255.

Step 4. Remove the `param` tag that sets the red value. What do you expect to happen? What does happen?

Step 5. Remove all of the `param` tags. What do you expect to happen? What does happen?

Post-Laboratory Problems

Problem G1-A.
A "real" drawing

Using Java's drawing operations, write an applet that draws a "real" picture (e.g., of a person, house, train, or whatever you think is appropriate). If you'd prefer to do abstract or modern art, that's okay, too.

Problem G1-B.
A parameterized face

Develop an applet that draws a face and that uses applet parameters to set the various aspects of the face (e.g., size of features, color of face).

Problem G1-C.
Rainbow text

Develop an applet that draws some text in a rainbow-like form, with the text repeated and moved in different colors.

Problem G1-D.
Repositioning the moving circle

You may have noted that the moving circle will eventually move off of the screen. Instead of moving off of the screen on the right or bottom edge, depending on the dimensions of the applet, it might be better to have the circle bounce back when it reaches an edge or wrap around to the other side. See if you can develop a mechanism for supporting either or both of these variations.

Problem G1-E.
Multiple circles

Update `MovingCircleApplet` so that it draws and moves multiple circles, rather than a single circle. See if you can find a way to prevent the two circles from overlapping.

Problem G1-F.
Looping circles

It is possible to use `for` loops to draw sequences of circles. For example,

```
public void paint(Graphics paintBrush) {
  int left = 0;
  int right = 0;
  for (int i = 0; i < 10; i = i + 1) {
    paintBrush.fillOval(left,right,10,10);
    left = left + 2;
    right = right + 3;
  } // for
} // paint()
```

Using a similar strategy, draw a sequence of 100 circles, changing color as you go and bouncing when you reach the edge.

Note that this is not an animation. Rather it is a still drawing that contains 100 different circles.

Problem G1-G.
Colors, revisited

We've seen two mechanisms for describing colors. We can use some built-in colors, like `Color.black`. We can provide red, green, and blue components. However, Java also provides other mechanisms for creating colors. Read the documentation for `java.awt.Color` and summarize the other possible techniques for creating colors.

Notes

Experiment G1.3, Step 1. Since Java draws both circles in exactly the same place, we might expect one of two things to happen: (1) the two colors could blend, yielding a third color or (2) the second color could obscure the underlying color. By <u>default</u>, Java uses opaque paints, so the second option occurs. That is, only the second circle is visible.

Experiment G1.3, Step 2. Although intuition would suggest that the first circle (red, in our example) would not appear, the differences between drawing and filling lead to a situation in which small pieces of blue should be visible.

Session G2: Java's Abstract Windowing Toolkit

In this laboratory session, you will begin investigations of Java's *Abstract Windowing Toolkit* (AWT), a collection of classes that support the creation of graphical user interfaces (GUIs), programs that interact with the user primarily through graphical components, such as windows, buttons, and fields. The goals of this laboratory are to

- introduce graphical user interfaces (GUIs);
- show how Java's abstract windowing toolkit can be used for creating simple interfaces; and
- investigate event-driven programming, the model of program control typically used by GUI programs.

Your instructor will tell you which of the proposed experiments you are to perform.

Prerequisite skills:

- Objects and classes in Java
- Applets and graphics (optional)
- Inheritance and interfaces

Note that many of these skills are optional if you are willing to accept "I'm not sure what this means, but I can just copy it" rather than a deeper understanding. At some point, you'll need to develop the deeper understanding in any case; however, you may find it best to delay such understanding until later.

Required files:

- HelloGUI.java
- HelpfulHelloGUI.java
- HelpListener.java
- ModularHelloGUI.java
- NewHelloGUI.java
- QuitListener.java

Discussion

As you've done the various labs, you may have been saying to yourself "Okay, I understand that this textual input and output is helpful as I'm just getting started with Java, but when am I going to start working on a *real* application?" For most people, modern computer applications require graphical user interfaces (GUIs) replete with windows, menus, buttons, fields, and other widgets.

In many languages, developing a GUI is a complicated and involved process. At times, the programmer may even be forced to work at the pixel level ("draw these pixels on the screen" rather than "create this window" or "build this button"). Fortunately, Java provides a useful and usable set of objects that you can use to quickly construct GUIs. The abstract windowing toolkit (AWT) is large enough that we will not be able to cover everything in a single laboratory session and would even have difficulty if we had half a dozen sessions. The purposes of today's laboratory are to get you started and to give you some of the tools to learn more on your own.

Because you will use so many different components of the AWT, it is useful to import them all into your programs with

```
import java.awt.*;
import java.awt.event.*;
```

Components

As you may have noted, most graphical programs are essentially a collection of components that are grouped together. A program may have windows, buttons, menus, pictures, and so on and so forth. Often, components are grouped within each other. For example, a window may contain menus and buttons, and a button might contain an image. In the AWT, many interface components can serve as containers that hold other elements.

Most of your interfaces will involve instances of `java.awt.Frame`. A frame is a window that also includes a title bar and optional menu bar, border, cursor, and icon. Frames are also containers, meaning that you can add buttons, pictures, and even other frames to your frames.

You create a frame with a `Frame` constructor. You can pass this constructor a string, which gives the name of the window. For example,

```
Frame myFrame = new Frame("Gooey");
```

You add things to a frame with the `add` method. For example,

```
myFrame.add(new Label("Greetings"))
```

Because of the wonders of polymorphism, you can add any AWT component.

Where does the object you've added go in the window? A layout manager controls the layout of objects within the frame. Experience shows that most programmers are better off providing general constraints and letting something else handle the particulars of layout. This way, if the window size changes (because you're working on a platform with a different screen size, because the user decides to change the size of the window, or for some other reason) you don't need to describe explicitly what to do to accommodate those changes. For our examples, we'll use the `java.awt.FlowLayout` that primarily puts the objects on the screen in the order that they are added to the frame. For example,

```
myFrame.setLayout(new FlowLayout());
```

In the post-laboratory problems, you are encouraged to explore other layouts.

What kinds of components will you put in your frames? For now, we'll stick to three basics: fields, buttons, and labels. A *field* provides space for the user to type. You will typically use fields to get input from the user. You may also use fields to give some feedback to the user, although other components may be more appropriate for output. A *button* allows the user to select actions for your program to perform. For example, a user might press a button to start a calculation or to quit the program. A *label* provides space for output. Labels differ from fields in that users cannot directly change the contents of a label.

Events and control flow

In writing Java programs, you may have already observed that there are different ways in which control passes through the program. Within a method, the statements are typically executed from top to bottom with some additional control provided by the control structures. Control can also pass to other objects through method calls. When you create some objects, such as our `SimpleDate` class, almost every method is reactive: i.e., when this method is called, do this. You do maintain some control, as your `main` method (or other method) is always responsible for calling other methods.

If you've created any applets, you've seen this reactive model taken to more of an extreme. For applets, you provide some basic methods, such as `paint`, but never explicitly call those methods. Instead, the application that displays the applet (appletviewer, a Web browser, or something else) is responsible for calling those methods when appropriate.

As you might expect, when building interactive graphical applications, such a reactive model is particularly appropriate. We might want to describe how our program works by saying, in effect, "when the user does this, my program does this". Such a programming model is typically called *event-driven programming*.

In Java's object-oriented event model, you attach listeners to the various components of your interface. A listener listens for events for a particular component and reacts when an event happens that pertains to the component. For example, you might listen for a click on a button or the close of a window. Since there are also different kinds of components, there are different kinds of listeners. Two of the basic ones are `WindowListeners`, which listen for events on windows, and `ActionListeners`, which listen for more generic action events. You will use `ActionListeners` for your buttons. The methods of listeners are typically called *event handlers* because they "handle" events.

How do you build a `WindowListener`? Officially, any `WindowListener` is expected to support seven different event handlers relating to opening, closing, being turned into an icon, and so on and so forth. Since it's painful to have to implement all of these when you only care about a particular event, Java provides a `WindowAdapter` class that defines all of these event handlers. When you only care about one event, you can simply extend `Window-Adapter`. In many cases, it makes sense for the object that creates a frame to serve as the listener for that frame.

```
public class Experiment
  extends WindowAdapter {
  ...
    Frame myFrame = new Frame("Experimental");
    myFrame.addWindowListener(this);
  ...
  public void windowOpened(WindowEvent evt) {
    ...
  } // windowOpened(WindowEvent)
  ...
} // class Experiment
```

Fortunately, `ActionListener`s are much easier. They need only support

```
public void actionPerformed(ActionEvent evt)
```

What can you do in this method? By calling `evt.actionCommand()` you can get a string that describes what action should be performed. For example, you might get the name of the button that has been pressed. You can then use that value to select what to do.

In some cases (e.g., in programs with only one button or in cases in which you have built a different listener for each object), your listener can simply do whatever is appropriate.

An important event

Are there any events that you must handle? In many cases, it is particularly important that you notice when a window is closing. For your simple applications, the close of a window will most likely signal the end of the application. Here is a `windowClosing` method that gets rid of the frame and exits the program when the current window closes. You will most likely include it (or something like it) in many of your early graphical applications.

```
/** React to the closing of the window. */
public void windowClosing(WindowEvent event) {
  // Get rid of the frame.
  myFrame.dispose();
  // And stop the program.
  System.exit(0);
} // windowClosing()
```

**Your first
graphical
application**

You should now be ready to create (or at least read) your first graphical application. We will start with a simple application that puts "Hello World" in a window.

```java
import java.awt.*;
import java.awt.event.*;
/**
 * Print "Hello World" using Java's AWT.
 * The class serves as the listener for its own frame
 * providing a windowClosing method.
 *
 * @author Samuel A. Rebelsky
 * @version 1.0 of February 1999
 */
public class HelloGUI
  extends WindowAdapter
{
  // +--------+------------------------------------------------
  // | Fields |
  // +--------+
  /** The frame used for interaction. */
  protected Frame gui;
  /** The area used for output. */
  protected Label out;

  // +--------------+------------------------------------------
  // | Constructors |
  // +--------------+
  /** Set up the frame for interaction. */
  protected HelloGUI() {
    // Create the frame (the window), set up its layout manager,
    // and listen to support "quit when closed".
    gui = new Frame("Greetings");
    gui.setLayout(new FlowLayout());
    gui.addWindowListener(this);
    // Create the output component.
    out = new Label("Hello World!");
    // Add the output area to the interface.
    gui.add(out);
    // Put it all together.
    gui.pack();
    // And we're ready to go.
    gui.show();
  } // HelloGUI()

  // +---------------+-----------------------------------------
  // | Event Handlers |
  // +---------------+
  /** React to the closing of the window. */
  public void windowClosing(WindowEvent event) {
    gui.dispose();
    System.exit(0);
  } // windowClosing()
```

```
// +------+---------------------------------------------------
// | Main |
// +------+
/* Start the ball rolling by creating an object. */
public static void main(String[] args) {
  new HelloGUI();
} // main(String[])
} // class HelloGUI
```

Let's consider the various parts of this class.

```
public class HelloGUI
  extends WindowAdapter
```

As we mentioned above, by extending `WindowAdapter` you automatically get handlers for all of the window events. `HelloGUI` will *override* window-Closing as above.

Next, we declare the two components of our GUI. We'll have a frame that we call `gui` and a label that we call `out`.

```
protected Frame gui;
protected Label out;
```

The primary work is done in the constructor. First, we create the frame, tell it what kind of layout manager to use, and give it a listener.

```
gui = new Frame("Greetings");
gui.setLayout(new FlowLayout());
gui.addWindowListener(this);
```

Next, we create the label for showing output.

```
out = new Label("Hello World!");
```

We must add that to the frame.

```
gui.add(out);
```

We then resize the window to hold all the components. There are other ways to set the size of windows, such as `setSize(int width, int height)`, but the `pack` method provides a good starting point.

```
gui.pack();
```

Finally, we show the window.

```
gui.show();
```

That covers everything significant in this class. You already know about the `windowClosing` handler. How do we use the class? We simply create a new `HelloGUI` object. We might build a separate class whose `main` method creates the object, or we can simply add the method to `HelloGUI`

```
public static void main(String[] args) {
  new HelloGUI();
} // main(String[])
```

Wait! Where's the rest of `main`? There seems to be nothing going on in the program. We create an object and then end. However, Java's event-driven model takes over once the main method completes. A frame is available, so Java observes events and calls appropriate handlers until the program terminates.

In Experiment G2.1, you will test this simple program. In Experiment G2.2, you will use this program to create multiple windows.

Adding a Quit button

As you may have observed, the mechanism for quitting our simple application may be less than obvious, particularly for novice users. Hence, it may be useful to add a Quit button. What do we need to do to add such a button to our interface?

- Add a field for the button since we have a field for each component.
- Create the button with `new` `Button(name)`.
- Give the button a listener to handle press events with `addAction-Listener(listener)`. We'll use the current object as the listener.
- Add the button to the frame.
- Add an `actionPerformed(ActionEvent  evt)` method to `HelloGUI` since `HelloGUI` objects must now serve as button listeners.
- Indicate that `HelloGUI` knows how to listen for actions by adding `implements` `ActionListener` to its declaration.

We consider each in turn.

To add a field for the button, you simply need to declare a field of type `Button` (more accurately, `java.awt.Button`).

```
/** A quit button. */
Button quit;
```

We'll build the button within the constructor with

```
quit = new Button("Quit");
```

We'll add the listener with

```
quit.addActionListener(this);
```

We'll add the button to the frame with

```
gui.add(quit);
```

All we have left to do is to write the `actionPerformed` handler and update the declaration. The handler is fairly straightforward.

```
/** Quit when the user clicks on the quit button. */
public void actionPerformed(ActionEvent evt) {
  gui.dispose();
  System.exit(0);
} // actionPerformed(ActionEvent)
```

Finally, we update the declaration.

```
public class HelloGUI
    extends WindowAdapter
    implements ActionListener
```

In Experiment G2.3, you will make and test these modifications, albeit in a different order.

Adding more buttons

Suppose we want to add more buttons to our program. For example, we might add a Help button to inform those who don't understand what to do. How might we add such a button?

We know how to create a new button.

```
help = new Button("Help");
help.addActionListener(this);
...
gui.add(help);
```

This means that whenever someone clicks on the button labeled Help, the program will call this object's `actionPerformed` method. We can update that method to replace the output with a help message.

```
/** React to a click on the button. */
public void actionPerformed(ActionEvent evt) {
  out.setText("Click quit!");
} // actionPerformed(ActionEvent)
```

Note that you can use the `setText` method to change the contents of a field.

But wait! We're using the same object (the current object) to listen for events on both the Quit button and the Help button. This means that we can't simply change the `actionPerformed` method to give help or the Quit button will give help and not quit.

What do we do? It's time to specialize the `actionPerformed` method. As noted earlier, by calling the `actionCommand` method of the action event, we can get a string that tells us which button was pressed. Hence, we might write

```
/** React to a click on the button. */
public void actionPerformed(ActionEvent evt) {
  // Get the command.
  String command = evt.getActionCommand();
  // Should we quit?
  if (command.equals("Quit")) {
    gui.dispose();
    System.exit(0);
  }
  // Should we give help?
  else if (command.equals("Help")) {
    out.setText("Click quit!");
  }
} // actionPerformed(ActionEvent)
```

In Experiment G2.4, you will add a Help button to the `HelloGUI` class. In Experiment G2.5, you will consider some improvements to this `action-Performed` handler.

Separate listeners

As you might expect, the test of the action command version of `action-Performed` begins to get cumbersome after you create more than about six components that need `ActionListeners`. What is the solution to this problem? One solution is to provide a separate `ActionListener` for each button you create, with the new action listener doing a call to the appropriate method of the frame.

Let's consider how we might rewrite `HelloGUI` to use such a strategy. We'll call the new version `ModularHelloGUI`. First, for convenience, we'll create separate `help` and `quit` methods.

```
public class ModularHelloWorld {
  ...
  public void help() {
    out.setText("Click quit!");
  } // help()
  public void quit() {
    gui.dispose();
    System.exit(0);
  } // quit()
  ...
} // ModularHelloWorld
```

Next, we'll need to create class objects that can listen for actions and call the appropriate methods. We'll call these two classes `HelpListener` (for the one that listens to the Help button) and `QuitListener` (for the one that listens to the Quit button). Each will call the corresponding method of `ModularHelloGUI`. Here is the `actionPerformed` method for `HelpListener`.

```
public void actionPerformed(ActionEvent evt) {
  base.help();
} // actionPerformed(ActionEvent)
```

What is `base`? It's the corresponding `ModularHelloWorld` object that provides the `help` method. How do we get `base`? Through the constructor for `HelpListener`.

```
/**
 * Create a new listener, especially designed to react by
 * calling the help method of a particular ModularHelloGUI.
 */
public HelpListener(ModularHelloGUI base) {
  this.base = base;
} // HelpListener(ModularHelloGUI)
```

We must then update `ModularHelloGUI` to use these listeners, rather than itself.

```
help.addActionListener(new HelpListener(this));
quit.addActionListener(new QuitListener(this));
```

What's left to do? That's about it. Now, when the user clicks on the Help button,

- Java finds the `HelpListener` and calls its `actionPerformed` method.
- That method calls the `help` method of `ModularHelloGUI`.
- The `help` method provides appropriate help.

Here's the code for `QuitListener` so that you can see how the various pieces fit together.

```java
import ModularHelloGUI;
import java.awt.event.ActionListener;
import java.awt.event.ActionEvent;
/**
 * React to quit messages for ModularHelloGUI.
 *
 * @author Samuel A. Rebelsky
 * @version 1.0 of February 1999
 */
public class QuitListener
  implements ActionListener
{
  // +--------+-------------------------------------------------
  // | Fields |
  // +--------+
  /** The base object that gets the message. */
  protected ModularHelloGUI base;

  // +--------------+-------------------------------------------
  // | Constructors |
  // +--------------+

  /**
   * Create a new listener, especially designed to react by
   * calling the quit method of a particular ModularHelloGUI.
   */
  public QuitListener(ModularHelloGUI base) {
    this.base = base;
  } // QuitListener(ModularHelloGUI)

  // +----------------+-----------------------------------------
  // | Event Handlers |
  // +----------------+

  /** Give help when the user clicks on the help button. */
  public void actionPerformed(ActionEvent evt) {
    base.quit();
  } // actionPerformed(ActionEvent)
} // class QuitListener
```

In Experiment G2.6, you will experiment with this more modular version of the program.

Experiments

Name: _____

ID: _____

**Experiment G2.1:
Your first AWT
program**

Required file:

- HelloGUI.java

Step 1. Make a copy of HelloGUI.java. Compile it, execute it, and describe what it does.

If you can't figure out how to quit, read the notes on this step.

Step 2. Read through the code for HelloGUI.java. What do you need to change in order to make the title bar of the window read "Fun with Java"?

Step 3. Make the change you described in Step 2. Recompile and execute HelloGUI. Were you correct?

Step 4. Read through the code for HelloGUI.java. What do you need to change in order to make the interior of the window display "GUIs are gooey"?

Step 5. Make the change you described in Step 4. Recompile and execute HelloGUI. Were you correct?

Step 6. Remove the line in `windowClosing` that reads

```
System.exit(0);
```

What do you expect to happen when you compile and execute `HelloGUI`?

Step 7. Compile and execute the modified `HelloGUI`. What happens when you close the window? What do you think this means?

Step 8. Reinsert the following line into `windowClosing`.

```
System.exit(0);
```

Experiment G2.2: Creating multiple windows

Required file:

- `HelloGUI.java`

Before you begin, if you have not done so already, make a copy of `HelloGUI.java`. Compile `HelloGUI`.

Step 1. As noted in the discussion, you can now create new `HelloGUI` objects in any `main` method. Create a new class, `HelloTwice`, which contains just the following `main` method.

```
/* Create two windows and let them take over. */
public static void main(String[] args) {
  new HelloGUI();
  new HelloGUI();
} // main(String[])
```

Note that you will need to import `HelloGUI`. What do you expect to happen when you compile and execute `HelloTwice`?

Step 2. Compile and execute `HelloTwice`. You may find that both windows appear in the same location, so try dragging one around to find the second. Do not close the windows yet.

Step 3. What do you expect to happen when you close one of these windows?

Step 4. Try closing one of the windows and report what happens. Explain why that happened.

When you are done, you may wish to consult the notes on this problem. In the post-laboratory problems, you will have the opportunity to consider how you might resolve this problem.

Experiment G2.3: Adding a Quit button

Required file:

- `HelloGUI.java`

Before you begin, if you have not done so already, make a copy of `HelloGUI.java`. Compile `HelloGUI`.

Step 1. Summarize the changes you will need to make in order to add a Quit button to `HelloGUI`.

Step 2. Change the declaration of `HelloGUI` to read

```
public class HelloGUI
  extends WindowAdapter
  implements ActionListener
```

What do you expect to happen when you try to compile and execute `Hel-loGUI`?

Step 3. Try to compile and execute `HelloGUI`. It should fail. Record and explain the failure.

If you are confused by this error, please refer to the notes on this step.

Step 4. Add the following method to `HelloGUI`.

```
/** Quit when the user clicks on the quit button. */
public void actionPerformed(ActionEvent evt) {
  gui.dispose();
  System.exit(0);
} // actionPerformed(ActionEvent)
```

What do you expect to happen when you try to compile and execute `Hel-loGUI`?

Step 5. Try to compile and execute `HelloGUI`. It should succeed. If you encounter any errors, attempt to resolve them. You need not record anything for this step.

Step 6. When will your new `actionPerformed` method be called? (Don't assume anything about future additions to the `HelloGUI` class or use of `HelloGUI` by other classes. Simply consider when it will be called in the current incarnation of the class as it stands by itself.)

After recording your answer, you may wish to examine the notes on this step.

Step 7. Add a field for the Quit button to the `HelloGUI` class.

```
/** A quit button. */
Button quit;
```

You need not record anything for this step.

Step 8. Add the following line to your `HelloGUI` constructor. This line creates the Quit button.

```
quit = new Button("Quit");
```

Where did you put the line?

Step 9. Add the following line to your `HelloGUI` constructor. This line adds the Quit button to the frame.

```
gui.add(quit);
```

Where did you put the line?

Step 10. What do you expect to happen when you compile and execute `HelloGUI`? What will happen when the user presses the Quit button?

Step 11. Compile and execute `HelloGUI`. You should not encounter any errors. What happens when the user presses the Quit button? Why?

After recording your answer, you may wish to refer to the notes on this problem.

Step 12. Add the following line to your `HelloGUI` constructor. This line sets up a listener for the Quit button.

```
quit.addActionListener(this);
```

Where did you put the line?

Step 13. What do you expect to happen when you compile and execute `HelloGUI`? What will happen when the user presses the Quit button?

Step 14. Compile and execute `HelloGUI`. You should not encounter any errors. What happens when the user presses the Quit button?

Step 15. Do you think it is still possible to quit `HelloGUI` by closing the window?

Step 16. Reflect on the design of this simple program. Now that we have installed a Quit button, should it still be possible to quit by closing the window?

Experiment G2.4: Adding a Help button

Required file:

- `HelloGUI.java` as modified in the previous experiment

Before you begin, confirm that you have a working version of `HelloGUI` as created in the previous experiment. If you did not do the previous experiment or had difficulty, use `NewHelloGUI.java`. We'll still refer to this program as `HelloGUI` in the following steps.

Step 1. Summarize the steps that you'll need in order to add a new, nonfunctional, Help button to `HelloGUI`.

Step 2. Update `HelloGUI` to add a nonfunctional Help button. Compile and test the modified `HelloGUI` and correct any errors. You need not record anything for this step.

Step 3. Add the following line to `HelloGUI`.

```
help.addActionListener(this);
```

Where did you put the line?

Step 4. What do you expect to happen when you compile and execute `Hel-loGUI` and then click on the Help button?

Step 5. What do you expect to happen when you compile and execute `Hel-loGUI` and then click on the Quit button?

Step 6. Confirm your answers to the two previous steps through testing. You need not record anything for this step.

Step 7. Replace the `actionPerformed` method with

```java
/** React to a click on the button. */
public void actionPerformed(ActionEvent evt) {
  out.setText("Click quit!");
} // actionPerformed(ActionEvent)
```

What difference do you expect this to make to the execution of the program?

Confirm your answer through testing.

Step 8. Replace the `actionPerformed` method with

```java
/** React to a click on the button. */
public void actionPerformed(ActionEvent evt) {
  // Get the command.
  String command = evt.getActionCommand();
  // Should we quit?
  if (command.equals("Quit")) {
    gui.dispose();
    System.exit(0);
  }
  // Should we give help?
  else if (command.equals("Help")) {
    out.setText("Click quit!");
  }
} // actionPerformed(ActionEvent)
```

What changes do you expect this to have on the execution of `HelloGUI.java`?

Confirm your answer through testing.

Experiment G2.5: Improving `actionPerformed`

Required file:

- `HelloGUI.java` as modified in the previous experiments

Before you begin, confirm that you have a working version of `HelloGUI` as created in the previous experiment. If you did not do the previous experiment or had difficulty, use `HelpfulHelloGUI.java`. We'll still refer to this program as `HelloGUI` in the following steps.

Step 1. Suppose we wanted to change the names of the Help and Quit buttons to "?" and "Bye" in `HelloGUI`. What changes would we have to make?

Step 2. Replace the line that reads

```
help = new Button("Help");
```

with one that reads

```
help = new Button("?");
```

What effect do you expect this to have on the appearance of the program?

Step 3. What do you expect to happen when the user clicks on the new "?" button?

Step 4. Confirm your answers to the previous steps by compiling and executing the modified `HelloGUI`. You need not record anything for this step.

If you are confused about the results, feel free to refer to the notes on this step.

Step 5. Add the following lines to the end of `actionPerformed`.

```
else {
  out.setText("Can't do " + command);
}
```

What do you expect to happen when the user clicks on the new "?" button?

Confirm your answer by compiling and executing the modified `HelloGUI`.

Step 6. Add a new Explode button to `HelloGUI`. This button, like the others, should use the current object as its listener. Summarize the changes you've made.

Step 7. What do you expect to happen when the user clicks on the new Explode button?

Confirm your answer by compiling and executing the modified `HelloGUI`.

Step 8. To better respond to the problem from Step 4 in which the "?" button no longer acts as a help button, we can check what string is currently assigned to the `help` button with the `getLabel` method. This method gets the label associated with a button.

Replace the line of `actionPerformed` that reads

```
else if (command.equals("Help")) {
```

with one that reads

```
else if (command.equals(help.getLabel())) {
```

What effect do you expect this change to have? Confirm your answer through testing.

After recording your answer, you may wish to look at the notes on this step.

Step 9. Replace the line that reads

```
quit = new Button("Quit");
```

with one that reads

```
quit = new Button("Bye!");
```

What effect do you expect this to have on the program? Confirm your answer through testing.

After recording your answer, you may wish to look at the notes on this step.

Step 10. As an alternative to the technique from Step 8, you can set the action command associated with a button. By setting the action command, you are easily able to make buttons with different names have the same effect. You can use `setActionCommand` to set the action command and `getActionCommand` to get it.

Add the line

```
quit.setActionCommand("Quit");
```

to the constructor for `HelloGUI`. What do you expect the result of this change to be? Confirm your answer through testing.

After recording your answer, you may wish to look at the notes on this step.

Experiment G2.6: Building separate listeners

Required files:

- `HelloListener.java`
- `ModularHelloGUI.java`
- `QuitListener.java`

Step 1. Make copies of `HelpListener.java`, `ModularHelloGUI.java`, and `QuitListener.java`. Compile the three files. Execute `ModularHello-GUI` and confirm that it works. You need not record anything for this step.

Step 2. Change the line of `ModularHelloGUI` that reads

```
help = new Button("Help");
```

to

```
help = new Button("?");
```

What effect do you expect this to have on the program?

Recompile and execute `ModularHelloGUI` to confirm your answer.

Step 3. Change the line of `ModularHelloGUI` that reads

```
help.addActionListener(new HelpListener(this));
```

to one that reads

```
help.addActionListener(new QuitListener(this));
```

What effect do you expect this to have on the program?

Recompile and execute `ModularHelloGUI` to confirm your answer. Once you have done so, return the line to

```
help.addActionListener(new HelpListener(this));
```

Step 4. Change the name of `ModularHelloGUI`'s `help` method to `give-Help`. What effect do you expect this to have on the program?

Recompile and execute `ModularHelloGUI` to confirm your answer.

Post-Laboratory Problems

**Problem G2-A:
A customizable
alert**

Create a new class, `Alert`, that displays a simple alert message on the screen. Your class should provide one constructor, `Alert(String title, String message)` that supplies a title for the window and a message for the interior of the window.

Note that this class will be quite similar to `HelloGUI`, except that you will not hard code the title and message. It is also likely that your class will not need a `main` method.

**Problem G2-B:
Multiple frames**

As you may have observed in the experiments, one problem with our standard `windowClosing` handler is that it quits the program when any window closes. Suggest a strategy one might use so that the program only quits when the last window closes. (You need not write any code for this problem; your goal is to think about the problem in general terms.)

**Problem G2-C:
Multiple frames,
revisited**

Using your strategy from Problem G2-B, create a program that builds three frames, each with a different word. Your program should continue to keep each frame on the screen until the user closes it. Closing one frame should not affect the other frames.

**Problem G2-D:
Separate frames**

Rewrite `HelloGUI` so that it uses two frames: one for output and one for the Help and Quit control buttons.

**Problem G2-E:
Layout managers**

Consult the Java documentation to learn about the other layout managers provided by the AWT. Select one of them and write a short introduction that your fellow students might use in creating new programs.

**Problem G2-F:
Widgets**

A widget is something that you put in a graphical user interface, such as a window, menu, or button. Pick a program with a graphical user interface and make a list of the kinds of widgets it contains.

**Problem G2-G:
AWT widgets**

Consult the Java documentation to determine how many of the widgets you listed in the previous problem are included as classes within the AWT. For each widget you listed, give the corresponding AWT class or note that you could not find an appropriate class.

Notes

Experiment G2.1, Step 1. As mentioned in the discussion, you quit this application by closing the window.

Experiment G2.2, Step 4. When you close one window, the other window also closes because the `windowClosing` handler terminates the program with `System.exit(0)`.

Experiment G2.3, Step 3. When you indicate the `HelloGUI`, it implements the `ActionListener` interface, you are making a commitment to implement the `actionPerformed` method. Since you have not yet added such a method, the Java compiler complains.

Experiment G2.3, Step 6. Since we've never made `HelloGUI` a listener for any object that can encounter `ActionEvent`s, the new `actionPerformed` method will never be executed.

Experiment G2.3, Step 11. We have not yet added a listener for the Quit button, so nothing happens when we click on it.

Experiment G2.5, Step 4. Since `actionPerformed` looks for the string Help and the Help button now reports the string "?", nothing happens when you press the new button.

Experiment G2.5, Step 8. The "?" button should now work.

Experiment G2.5, Step 9. For the same reason that the "?" button previously failed to give help, the "Bye!" button should fail to quit the program. It will, however, cause the program to report that it Can't do Bye!

Experiment G2.5, Step 10. The "Bye!" button should now work.

Session G3: Java's Abstract Windowing Toolkit, Continued

In this laboratory session, you will continue your investigations into Java's Abstract Windowing Toolkit. In a previous laboratory, you considered how to build windows, provide output for the user, and react to buttons. In this laboratory, you will focus on getting input from the user. The goals of this laboratory are to

- refine your understanding of Java's AWT;
- introduce some of the AWT's input mechanisms;
- refine your understanding of the `String` class; and
- consider some error-handling mechanisms.

Your instructor will tell you which of the proposed experiments you are to perform.

Prerequisite skills:

- Objects and classes in Java
- Applets and graphics (optional)
- Inheritance and interfaces
- Java's numeric classes, such as `java.lang.Integer`
- Exceptions and exception handling
- AWT basics

Note that many of these skills are optional if you're willing to accept "I'm not sure what this means, but I can just copy it" rather than a deeper understanding. (At some point, you'll need to develop the deeper understanding in any case; however, you may find it best to delay such understanding until later.)

Required files:

- `FieldModifier.java`
- `FirstWord.java`

- GreetGUI.java
- HelpfulHelloGUI.java
- MakeUpperCase.java
- Quote.java
- SimpleCalc.java
- StringFun.java
- StringModifier.java

Discussion

Obviously a user interface is more than buttons, windows, and labels. From a practical perspective, there are a number of other interface components. In addition, the design of a good interface involves careful consideration of the interaction paradigm, appropriate placement and design of the various interface components, and testing with actual users. But in order to build a good interface, you certainly need more components.

In particular, you need a way to get input from the user. Clearly, buttons provide one mechanism for getting input, but there are also a number of others. For example, menus also transmit information from the user to the program. Perhaps the most important input mechanism is the *input field,* in which users can type information.

The AWT, reviewed

As you may recall from the previous laboratory, the AWT takes a component-based approach to the construction of graphical user interfaces. You build components and place them inside of other components. Your programs will typically be based on `Frame` objects, which provide windows on the screen. A *layout manager* specifies how the objects are placed within the frame.

For example, here is how one might create a new `Frame` with two buttons labeled Help and Quit.

```
Frame myFrame = new Frame("Example");
Button help = new Button("Help");
Button quit = new Button("Quit");
myFrame.setLayout(new FlowLayout());
myFrame.add(help);
myFrame.add(quit);
myFrame.pack();
myFrame.show();
```

Importantly, the AWT provides an event-based control paradigm. When things happen to the various components of an interface, Java calls the appropriate method in the listener for the component. For example, we might create an object, `Helper`, that listens to the Help button and have it listen with

```
Helper helper = new Helper(...);
help.addActionListener(helper);
```

The `Helper` class will have the following structure.

```
import java.awt.*;
import java.awt.event.*;
public class Helper
  implements ActionListener {
  ...
  public actionPerformed(ActionEvent evt) {
    ...
  } // actionPerformed(ActionEvent)
} // class Helper
```

One program design strategy we have used is to have the primary class listen for events on the various components it creates.

Putting it all together, here is a class that puts up a small piece of information along with Help and Quit buttons.

```
import java.awt.*;
import java.awt.event.*;

/**
 * Print "Hello World" using Java's AWT.
 * Includes quit and help buttons.
 * <p>
 * The class serves as the listener for its own frame,
 * providing a windowClosing method.  It also serves as
 * a listener for the quit button.
 *
 * @author Samuel A. Rebelsky
 * @version 1.0 of February 1999
 */
public class HelpfulHelloGUI
  extends WindowAdapter
  implements ActionListener
{
  // +--------+------------------------------------------------
  // | Fields |
  // +--------+
  /** The frame used for interaction. */
  protected Frame gui;
  /** The area used for output. */
  protected Label out;
  /** The help button. */
  protected Button help;
  /** The quit button. */
  protected Button quit;

  // +--------------+------------------------------------------
  // | Constructors |
  // +--------------+

  /** Set up the frame for interaction. */
  protected HelpfulHelloGUI() {
    // Create the frame (the window).
    gui = new Frame("Greetings");
```

```
    gui.setLayout(new FlowLayout());
    gui.addWindowListener(this);

    // Create the output component.
    out = new Label("Hello World!");

    // Create the help button.
    help = new Button("Help");
    help.addActionListener(this);

    // Create the quit button.
    quit = new Button("Quit");
    quit.addActionListener(this);

    // Add the output area to the interface.
    gui.add(out);
    gui.add(help);
    gui.add(quit);
    gui.pack();

    // And we're ready to go.
    gui.show();
  } // HelpfulHelloGUI()

  // +----------------+-----------------------------------------
  // | Event Handlers |
  // +----------------+

  /** Decide what to do when the user clicks on a button. */
  public void actionPerformed(ActionEvent evt) {
    // Get the command.
    String command = evt.getActionCommand();
    // Should we quit?
    if (command.equals("Quit")) {
      gui.dispose();
      System.exit(0);
    }
    // Should we give help?
    else if (command.equals("Help")) {
      out.setText("Click quit!");
    }
  } // actionPerformed(ActionEvent)

  /** React to the closing of the window. */
  public void windowClosing(WindowEvent event) {
    gui.dispose();
    System.exit(0);
  } // windowClosing()

  // +------+-------------------------------------------------
  // | Main |
  // +------+

  /* Start the ball rolling by creating an object. */
  public static void main(String[] args) {
    new HelpfulHelloGUI();
  } // main(String[])
} // class HelpfulHelloGUI
```

In Experiment G3.1, you will refresh your memory of the Java AWT using this class.

Getting user input

You can generate output and observe when the user clicks on buttons. It is now time to consider other ways of getting input from the user. One particularly appropriate mechanism for getting user input is the *text input field,* an area on the screen in which users can type information. As you may recall from your own interactions with graphical user interfaces, one typically types information in the field and then clicks a button to key some action. (It is also possible to react as the user types in the field; we leave that as a topic for further study.) In Java's AWT, text input fields are provided by the `TextField` class.

You create these objects just as you would create any other component.

```
TextField myField = new TextField("Initial text");
```

Importantly, you can both get the contents of a text field with `getText()` and set the contents with `setText(new-text)`. For example, here is some code that converts what the user typed into all upper-case letters.

```
// Get the contents of the field.
String contents = myField.getText();
// Replace the contents of the field with the contents in
// upper-case.
myField.setText(contents.toUpperCase());
```

As an alternate example, here is a class that greets the user, based on a name typed in a field.

```
import java.awt.*;
import java.awt.event.*;
/**
 * Greet the user.
 *
 * The class serves as the listener for its own frame,
 * providing a windowClosing method.  It also serves as
 * the listener for its buttons, providing an appropriate
 * actionPerformed method.
 *
 * @author Samuel A. Rebelsky
 * @version 1.0 of February 1999
 */
public class GreetGUI
    extends WindowAdapter
    implements ActionListener
{
    // +--------+------------------------------------------------
    // | Fields |
    // +--------+

    /** The frame used for interaction. */
    protected Frame gui;
```

```
/** The field in which the user enters a name. */
protected TextField userName;
/** The button the user presses. */
protected Button greet;
/** The area used for output. */
protected Label out;

// +-------------+---------------------------------------
// | Constructors |
// +-------------+

/** Set up the frame for interaction. */
protected GreetGUI() {
  // Create the frame (the window).
  gui = new Frame("Greetings");
  gui.setLayout(new FlowLayout());
  gui.addWindowListener(this);
  // Create the entry field.  Initialized to have a number of
  // spaces so that there is room for the user to enter a name.
  userName = new TextField("              ");
  // Create the button.
  greet = new Button("Hi!");
  greet.addActionListener(this);
  // Create the output field.  Right now, we'll use it for
  // instructions.
  out = new Label("Enter your name and press the button.");
  // Add the components to the interface.
  gui.add(userName);
  gui.add(greet);
  gui.add(out);
  gui.pack();
  // And we're ready to go.
  gui.show();
} // GreetGUI()

// +--------------+---------------------------------------
// | Event Handlers |
// +--------------+

/** React to a click on the button. */
public void actionPerformed(ActionEvent evt) {
  // Update the output
  out.setText("Hi there " + userName.getText() +
              ", welcome to this program.");
} // actionPerformed(ActionEvent)
/** React to the closing of the window. */
public void windowClosing(WindowEvent event) {
  gui.dispose();
  System.exit(0);
} // windowClosing()

// +------+---------------------------------------------
// | Main |
// +------+
```

```
/* Start the ball rolling by creating an object. */
public static void main(String[] args) {
  new GreetGUI();
} // main(String[])
} // class GreetGUI
```

In Experiment G3.2, you will consider some of the details of this class. In Experiment G3.3, you will develop a class that can manipulate the contents of a text field.

Getting numeric input

What if we want to read a number rather than a string? We'll need to convert the string to a number. Fortunately, Java provides a number of library classes with methods that can be used for such conversions. These include `Integer.valueOf(String str)` and `Double.valueOf(String str)`. Unfortunately, each of these methods can fail (say, for example, you used the string `One` or `Hello`). Hence, you must catch the exception that results from erroneous use of the method.

For example, here is how you might extract a double value from a field.

```
String numStr = numberField.getText();
double num = 0.0;
try {
  num = Double.valueOf(num);
}
catch (Exception e) {
  // Do whatever is appropriate to handle the error.
}
```

Putting it all together, here is a simple calculator that lets the user enter two integers and computes their sum.

```
import java.awt.*;
import java.awt.event.*;

/**
 * A very simple calculator.  This will read two integers from the
 * user and display their sum.
 *
 * Uses a simple graphical user interface, rather than textual
 * input and output.
 *
 * The interface will present two text areas in which the user can
 * enter numbers, an "equals" button that the user presses to
 * request a result, and an area in which the program can write
 * output.
 *
 * The class serves as the listener for its own frame and button,
 * providing actionPerformed and windowClosing methods.
 *
 * @author Samuel A. Rebelsky
 * @version 1.1 of February 1999
 */
```

```java
public class SimpleCalc
  extends WindowAdapter
  implements ActionListener
{

  // +--------+--------------------------------------------------
  // | Fields |
  // +--------+

  /** The frame used for interaction. */
  protected Frame gui;
  /** The field used for input of the first value. */
  protected TextField val1;
  /** The field used for input of the second value. */
  protected TextField val2;
  /** The area used to show the plus sign. */
  protected Label plus;
  /** The area used for output. */
  protected Label out;
  /** The area used for messages (errors and others). */
  protected Label messages;
  /** The button used to tell it to compute. */
  protected Button equals;

  // +--------------+-------------------------------------------
  // | Constructors |
  // +--------------+

  /** Set up the frame for interaction. */
  protected SimpleCalc() {
    // Create the frame.
    gui = new Frame("Add");
    gui.setLayout(new FlowLayout());
    gui.addWindowListener(this);
    // Create the output field.  Leave sufficient space for output.
    out = new Label("        ");
    // Create the messages field.  Begin with instructions.
    messages = new Label("Enter two integers and click the =
                          button.");
    // Create the input fields.  Note that we initialize them to have
    // some spaces to ensure that the layout manager gives us enough
    // space.  A little later, we'll clear them out.
    val1 = new TextField("    ");
    val2 = new TextField("    ");
    // Create the addition symbol.
    plus = new Label("+");
    // Create the button.
    equals = new Button("=");
    equals.addActionListener(this);
    // Add the various components
    gui.add(messages);
    gui.add(val1);
    gui.add(plus);
    gui.add(val2);
    gui.add(equals);
```

```java
        gui.add(out);
        gui.pack();
        // Clear the text fields (see above).
        val1.setText("");
        val2.setText("");
        // And we're ready to go.
        gui.show();
    } // SimpleCalc()

    // +---------------+-------------------------------------------
    // | Helper Methods |
    // +---------------+

    /** Do the simple computation. */
    public void doComputation() {
        // The two values we'll use to compute.
        int num1 = 0;
        int num2 = 0;
        // Read the strings the user entered.
        String str1 = val1.getText();
        String str2 = val2.getText();
        // Convert the first value to a number.
        try {
            num1 = Integer.valueOf(str1).intValue();
        }
        catch (Exception e) {
            // Whoops!  Bad input.  Tell the user.
            messages.setText("The left operand is not an integer!");
            // Reset the input.
            val1.setText("");
            // Give up.
            return;
        }
        // Convert the second value to a number.
        try {
            num2 = Integer.valueOf(str2).intValue();
        }
        catch (Exception e) {
            // Whoops!  Bad input.  Tell the user.
            messages.setText("The right operand is not an integer!");
            // Reset the input.
            val2.setText("");
            // Give up.
            return;
        }
        // Display the result.
        out.setText(Integer.toString(num1+num2));
    } // doComputation()

    // +---------------+-------------------------------------------
    // | Event Handlers |
    // +---------------+

    /** React to a click on the button. */
    public void actionPerformed(ActionEvent evt) {
```

```
    doComputation();
  } // actionPerformed(ActionEvent)
  /** React to the closing of the window. */
  public void windowClosing(WindowEvent event) {
    gui.dispose();
    System.exit(0);
  } // windowClosing()

  // +------+--------------------------------------------------------
  // | Main |
  // +------+

  /* Start the ball rolling by creating an object. */
  public static void main(String[] args) {
    new SimpleCalc();
  } // main(String[])
} // class SimpleCalc
```

In Experiment G3.4, you will investigate this class. In Experiment G3.5, you will update this class to compute with real numbers instead of just integers. In Experiment G3.6, you will consider the ramifications of adding a Quit button to this class.

Experiments

Name: _____

ID: _____

Experiment G3.1: The AWT, reviewed

Required file:

- `HelpfulHelloGUI.java`

Step 1. Make a copy of `HelpfulHelloGUI.java`. Compile and execute it. Describe what the application does.

Step 2. Change the line that reads

```
help =user new Button("Help");
```

to one that reads

```
help = new Button("?");
```

What effect do you expect this change to have?

After recording your answer, recompile and execute the modified program to confirm that answer. You may also want to read the notes on this problem.

Step 3. Keeping the change from the previous step, update the line that reads

```
else if (command.equals("Help"))
```

to one that reads

```
else if (command.equals(help.getLabel())
```

What effect do you expect this second change to have?

After recording your answer, recompile and execute the modified program to confirm that answer. You may also want to read the notes on this problem.

Step 4. Change the text of the help button back to Help. What changes would you need to make to `HelpfulHelloGUI.java` so that the help message would be "Please click on the quit button to exit"?

Step 5. Update the line that reads

```
out.setText("Click quit!");
```

to one that reads

```
out.setText("Please click on the quit button to exit");
```

What effect do you expect this change to have when the user clicks on the Help button?

After recording your answer, recompile and execute the modified program to confirm that answer. You may also want to read the notes on this problem.

Step 6. As you may have noted, the label for the help message isn't big enough. We might guess that repacking the frame might do it. Update the appropriate portion of `actionPerformed` to read

```
out.setText("Please click on the quit button to exit");
gui.pack();
```

Does this make any difference?

Step 7. As you may have noted, the addition of the line that reads

```
gui.pack();
```

does not seem to have made a difference. This is because the layout manager only looks at the size of things once, when they're added to the frame. What we need to do is re-add the output label so that the layout manager notices the new size. You do this with a variant of the `add` command, which takes a second parameter giving the position of the added component. Since we want the label to stay at the beginning, we use

```
out.setText("Please click on the quit button to exit");
gui.add(out,0);
gui.pack();
```

Make this change. Does it make any difference to how `HelpfulHelloGUI` acts? If so, describe the difference.

After recording your answer, you may wish to look at the notes on this problem.

Step 8. As you saw in the previous step, you can choose where to add components. Suppose we had used

```
gui.add(out,2);
```

instead of

```
gui.add(out,0);
```

What do you expect the differences will be in what happens when the user clicks on the Help button?

Step 9. Recompile and execute `HelpfulHelloGUI` and explain the differences.

After recording you answer, you may wish to look at the notes on this problem.

Step 10. Suppose we had instead used

```
gui.add(out,10);
```

What do you expect the differences will be in what happens when the user clicks on the Help button?

After recording you answer, you may wish to look at the notes on this problem.

Step 11. The AWT also permits you to remove components with the remove method. What do you expect the effect of the following lines to be?

```
out.setText("Please click on the quit button to exit");
gui.add(out,0);
gui.remove(help);
gui.pack();
```

Experiment G3.2: Getting input from the user

Required file:

* GreetGUI.java

Step 1. Make a copy of GreetGUI.java. Compile and execute it. Describe what the application does.

If you can't figure out how to quit the program, look at the notes on this problem.

Step 2. As you may have observed in Step 1, there are some extra spaces in the input field that interfere with data entry. This is because in GreetGUI, the instruction to create the input field reads

```
userName = new TextField("          ");
```

What do you expect to happen if you replace this by the following line?

```
userName = new TextField("");
```

Confirm your answer by making the change, recompiling `GreetGUI`, and executing `GreetGUI`. After you have done so, restore the line that reads

```
userName = new TextField("          ");
```

Step 3. As you may have observed in Step 2, deleting all the spaces results in insufficient space for data entry. How can we balance the need for an empty field and the need for an initial size? One strategy is to clear the field at an appropriate time.

How might you clear the contents of text field `userName`?

Step 4. The appropriate time to clear the field is after you've done the layout because once the layout has been done, the space for the field is fixed. Try adding the following lines to `GreetGUI.java` directly after `gui.pack()`.

```
// Clear the field.
userName.setText("");
```

What effect do you expect this change to have?

Confirm your answer by making the change, recompiling `GreetGUI`, and executing `GreetGUI`.

Step 5. What do you expect to happen when you run `GreetGUI` and enter a particularly long name, such as John Doe, the Everyman?

Confirm your answer by executing GreetGUI and entering a long name. Does expanding the window make any difference?

Step 6. How do we recover from the previous problem? We'd like to expand the size of the out label. One possibility is to add it to the frame again. (Each object can only appear once in the frame.)

Update the actionPerformed method to read

```
/** React to a click on the button. */
public void actionPerformed(ActionEvent evt) {
   // Update the output
   out.setText("Hi there " + userName.getText() +
             ", welcome to this program.");
   // The size may have changed, so add it again.
   gui.add(out);
} // actionPerformed(ActionEvent)
```

Does this have any effect? Does expanding the window make any difference?

Step 7. As you may have observed in the previous step, by re-adding out, we were able to expand the size it is given. Unfortunately, we did not expand the window, too. (This may be a good thing; some users will find it disconcerting if windows keep changing sizes.) Can we also expand the window? Yes! With the pack method.

Update the actionPerformed method to read

```
/** React to a click on the button. */
public void actionPerformed(ActionEvent evt) {
   // Update the output
   out.setText("Hi there " + userName.getText() +
             ", welcome to this program.");
   // The size may have changed, so add it again.
   gui.add(out);
   // And then redraw the frame (perhaps enlarging it).
   gui.pack();
} // actionPerformed(ActionEvent)
```

Does this have the intended effect? What is your aesthetic judgment of the results?

Experiment G3.3: String manipulation

Required files:

- `FieldModifier.java`
- `FirstWord.java`
- `MakeUpperCase.java`
- `Quote.java`
- `StringFun.java`
- `StringModifier.java`

In this experiment, you'll consider a technique for having different classes (or, more precisely, different objects) listen to different buttons. The technique we use in this experiment is to attach a `FieldModifier` to each button.

Step 1. Read and explain the code for `FieldModifier.java`.

```java
import java.awt.*;
import java.awt.event.*;
import StringModifier;

/**
 * Objects that listen to buttons and, in response, modify a
 * TextField in an AWT application.  You need one FieldModifier
 * per type of modification per field.
 *
 * @author Samuel A. Rebelsky
 * @version 1.0 of February 1999
 */
public class FieldModifier
  implements ActionListener
{
  // +--------------------------------------------------------
  // | Fields |
  // +--------+

  // No, this doesn't modify these kinds of fields; it modifies
  // the text in a TextField in an AWT.
  /** The field to modify. */
  protected TextField field;
  /** The string modifier used to modify its contents. */
  protected StringModifier stringmod;

  // +--------------+------------------------------------------
  // | Constructors |
  // +--------------+

  /**
   * Build a new FieldModifier that can modify a particular field
   * using a particular modifier.
   */
  public FieldModifier(TextField field, StringModifier stringmod)
  {
      this.field = field;
      this.stringmod = stringmod;
```

```
} // FieldModifier(TextField,StringModifier)

// +--------+----------------------------------------------------
// | Methods |
// +--------+

/**
 * When asked to perform an action, modify the field.  Used a
 * "long form" for the code, which could be expressed more
 * succinctly.
 */
public void actionPerformed(ActionEvent evt) {
  // Get the contents of the field.
  String str = field.getText();
  // Update the string
  str = stringmod.modify(str);
  // And replace the contents of the field.
  field.setText(str);
} // actionPerformed(ActionEvent)
} // class FieldModifier
```

Step 2. Make a copy of all the required files. Compile all the files and then execute `StringFun`. Summarize what the program does.

Step 3. As you may have noted, when we create a `FieldModifier`, we supply two parameters to the constructor, as in

```
upperCase.addActionListener(
  new FieldModifier(info, new MakeUpperCase()));
```

The first parameter is the field to modify when the button is clicked (when the `FieldModifier` is activated); the second is a `StringModifier` that will be used to modify the field. What do you expect to happen if we change `new MakeUpperCase()` to `new Quote()`? (You should also add an appropriate `import` statement.)

Confirm your answer by making the change, recompiling, and executing. Once you've confirmed your answer, restore the code.

Step 4. What changes do you expect to have to make in order to add a second button that puts quotes around the string?

Step 5. Make the changes to add this new Quote button. The changes are as follows.

a. Add an <u>import</u> statement of the form

```
import Quote;
```

b. Add a new field called quote, using

```
/** The "put quotes around" button. */
protected Button quote;
```

c. In the constructor for StringFun, build that button with

```
quote = new Button("Put in quotes");
```

d. In the constructor for StringFun, add a listener for that button with

```
quote.addActionListener(
   new FieldModifier(info,
                      new Quote()));
```

e. Add that button to the interface with

```
gui.add(quote);
```

After making the changes, confirm that the revised StringFun supports both conversion to uppercase and quoting.

Step 6. Create a MakeLowerCase class. You may want to refer to the code for MakeUpperCase.java when doing so. Summarize the class here.

Step 7. Update `StringFun` to include a button that converts the field to lowercase. Summarize the changes here.

Step 8. Update `StringFun` to include a button that uses the `FirstWord` class. What does that class (and therefore that button) do? Note that you should try various strings, such as "Hello" (just one word), "Hello World" (two words), and "Hello Cool World" (three words).

Step 9. You may have noted that `FirstWord` uses the `substring` method provided by the `String` class. What are the parameters to that method? (You may need to refer to the Java documentation.)

Step 10. You may have noted that `FirstWord` uses one form of the `indexOf` method from the `String` class. What other forms are there?

Experiment G3.4: A simple calculator

Required file:

- `SimpleCalc.java`

Step 1. Make a copy of `SimpleCalc.java`. Compile and execute it. Enter the values 2 and 3 and click on the = button. Enter the values 5 and 10 and click on the = button. Summarize the appearance and features of this application.

If you can't figure out how to quit the program, look at the notes on this problem.

Step 2. What do you expect to happen if you enter the values "two" and "three" and click on the = button?

Step 3. What does happen if you enter the values "two" and "three" and click on the = button?

Step 4. Read through the code for SimpleCalc.java and identify the part of the code that does this error checking. Summarize the design of that code.

Experiment G3.5: Supporting real numbers

Required file:

- SimpleCalc.java

Step 1. Before you begin, if you have not already done so, make a fresh copy of SimpleCalc.java and compile it. What do you expect will happen if you try to add 1.5 and 2 with SimpleCalc?

Step 2. What happens if you try to add 1.5 and 2 with SimpleCalc?

Step 3. As you may have observed in the previous step, SimpleCalc is only designed to input and add integers. In order to add 1.5 and 2, we would have to expand SimpleCalc to input and add real numbers (either floats or <u>double</u>s). Read through the code for `SimpleCalc.java` and note the places in which `SimpleCalc` makes assumptions that it's working with integers.

After doing so, you may wish to refer to the notes on this problem.

Step 4. Update `SimpleCalc` so that it can accept real numbers (i.e., <u>dou-ble</u>s) as input. Summarize the changes you've made.

**Experiment G3.6:
Adding a quit
button**

Note: You may have completed a similar experiment in the previous labora-tory. This experiment is intended to help reinforce some of the AWT con-cepts.

Required file:

- `SimpleCalc.java`

Step 1. Make a fresh copy of `SimpleCalc.java`. Compile and execute it to ensure that it still works.

Step 2. Read through the code for `SimpleCalc.java` and make notes on what lines you'd have to add (and where) in order to add a Quit button.

Step 3. Add a Quit button to `SimpleCalc`. You will need to add a new field, `quit`.

```
/** The button used to tell it to quit. */
protected Button quit;
```

You will also need to add code to create the button.

```
// Create the quit button.
quit = new Button("Quit");
quit.addActionListener(this);
```

Finally, you will have to add it to the frame.

```
gui.add(quit);
```

Compile the modified `SimpleCalc` and correct any compiler errors you encounter.

Step 4. What do you expect will happen when someone clicks on the Quit button?

Step 5. Run the modified `SimpleCalc` and determine what happens when someone clicks on the Quit button. Explain why.

Step 6. Update the `actionPerformed` method to quit the program.

```
/** Quit when the user clicks on the quit button. */
public void actionPerformed(ActionEvent evt) {
  gui.dispose();
  System.exit(0);
} // actionPerformed(ActionEvent)
```

Recompile `SimpleCalc`.

Step 7. What do you expect will now happen when someone clicks on the Quit button?

After entering your answer, run the modified `SimpleCalc` to verify that answer.

Step 8. What do you expect will now happen when someone clicks on the = button?

Step 9. Run the modified `SimpleCalc` and determine what happens when someone clicks on the = button. Explain why.

Post-Laboratory Problems

Problem G3-A: Observing the user

Read the documentation for the `TextField` class and determine what events are sent when the user types, what kind of listener can react to those events, and how the listener can react. Write a short summary that your classmates should be able to understand and use.

Problem G3-B: Capitalization

Using your answer from Problem G3-A, write a simple GUI that observes what the user types and capitalizes every letter typed.

Problem G3-C: Passwords

Using your answer from Problem G3-A, write a simple GUI that reads in a password typed in a text field, putting some special symbol in the field in place of each character typed.

Problem G3-D: Setting the size of text fields

Java provides a `setSize` method for text fields as well as for other components. Read and report on the use and abuse of this method. Can you use it to create a blank field, as we needed in Experiment G3.2?

Problem G3-E: Beginning a real calculator

Build a new graphical user interface class, `Calculator`, which displays eleven buttons corresponding to the ten decimal digits (0, 1, ..., 9) and clear. Your class should also display a field. When the user clicks on a digit, you should add it to the end of the field.

Problem G3-F: Adding calculation

Extend your `Calculator` class to support an `add` and `equals` button. The `add` button should remember the current value in the display field and clear that field. The `equals` button should add the contents of the display field and added it to the remembered value. If this seems odd to you, consider the interface for a typical desktop calculator.

Notes

Experiment G3.1, Step 2. Since the string associated with the Help button has changed, clicking on it no longer has any apparent effect.

Experiment G3.1, Step 3. Now we check which string is associated with the Help button and can therefore accommodate any changes to that button we'd like.

Experiment G3.1, Step 5. Because the space for the label was predetermined, the new help message overflows the label. We'll need to figure out a way to expand the label and possibly the window.

Experiment G3.1, Step 7. The label should expand, and the window should also expand to make room for the expanded label, with everything else shifting slightly.

Experiment G3.1, Step 9. The label moved. This suggests that each component can only be added once. If you try to add it a second time, the original copy is removed.

Experiment G3.1, Step 10. You should get an exception. The problem is that you can only add components at an appropriate position. If there are n components, they should be at positions 0 through $n - 1$.

Experiment G3.2, Step 1. As mentioned in the previous laboratory session, you quit this application by closing the window.

Experiment G3.4, Step 1. As mentioned in the previous laboratory session, you quit this application by closing the window.

Experiment G3.5, Step 4. There are a number of places in which it is assumed that we're adding integers.

- The initial message says to enter two integers.
- The declarations for `num1` and `num2` indicate that they are integers.
- The conversion from `String` to number is done with `Integer.valueOf(...).intValue()`.
  - Using the `Integer` class.
  - Extracting an integer with `intValue`.
- The sum is converted back to a number with `Integer.toString(...)`.

Session O1: Object-Oriented Design

In this laboratory session you will investigate the process of object-oriented design by considering the design of a computerized Othello game. The goals of this laboratory are to

- reinforce your skills in building and designing objects;
- introduce techniques for doing object-oriented design; and
- have some fun.

Your instructor will tell you which of the proposed experiments you are to perform.

Prerequisite skills:

- Objects and classes in Java
- Graphics in Java (optional)
- Inheritance (optional)

Required files:

- `Player.java`

Discussion

You have learned that Java is an object-oriented language. You have also seen a number of reasons to use object-oriented languages. For example, objects provide a natural mechanism for modeling many problems and solutions. In addition, well-designed objects provide a natural mechanism for supporting reuse. But how does one do good object design? There is no real substitute for practice and experience: you learn object design by designing the objects for programs and then reflecting (and re-reflecting) on your designs. However, there are a number of processes by which beginning designers can develop the basic skills. We will investigate a few of those in this laboratory session.

The processes we will investigate include narratives, question and answer sessions, drawing diagrams, and generalization through related examples. You will find that it is often best to do design in dialog with others, as one person may find both flaws and additional possibilities in the design of another person.

Since design skills come from experience, it is important that you record your design decisions when you make them. Then, as you work on your project, you should reflect on those decisions and continue to record observations. If you have made a bad decision, it helps to have the implications documented so that you can avoid making similarly inappropriate decisions in the future. If you have made a good decision, it helps to have it documented so that you can reuse the ideas that led to that decision.

These strategies are certainly not the only ones you can use to improve your design skills. For example, you may find it helpful to study the design of larger systems. You might read about the design of such a system or even attempt to replicate that design.

Narratives

As an example, we will consider the game of Othello. In particular, we will think about how we might design a program that allows people to play Othello. If you do not know Othello, do not worry; here is a description:

> Othello is a two-person game played on an eight-by-eight board. It is often convenient to number the rows of the board 1–8 and the columns A–H. The game begins with two black pieces and two white pieces on the center four squares of the board (D4, D5, E4, and E5). There is a black piece in the top-left and bottom-right of those four squares (D4 and E5). There is a white piece in the top-right and bottom-left of those four squares (D5 and E4). Players alternate turns, with each player making a legal move when it is his or her turn. A legal move consists of placing a piece so that two of pieces surround a row, column, or diagonal of the opponent's pieces. All of the opponent's pieces are then flipped (from black to white or from white to black). If a player cannot make a legal move, that player loses his or her turn. Play continues until there are no longer blank squares on the board or neither player can make a legal move. The player with the most pieces is the winner.

Note that this is, in effect, a short *narrative* describing the game. Such narrative descriptions are good first steps in object design. As with all pieces of prose, this narrative included both nouns and verbs. It is often the case that nouns correspond closely to the objects and classes in a program and that verbs correspond closely to the methods these objects and classes provide. If you circle the nouns, you are on your way to determining which objects and classes belong in your program. If you box the verbs, you are also on your way to determining the methods.

For example, you might note that the description uses the nouns *player, piece,* and *move.* This makes it likely that a program that simulates an Othello game will include the classes `Player`, `Piece`, and `Move`. What methods will these classes provide? Now we can turn our attention to the verbs. We see that players make *moves* and that pieces *flip.* This suggests that the `Player` class will most likely include a `makeMove` or `chooseMove` method and that the `Piece` class will include a `flip` method.

Other nouns might suggest particular objects. For example, "black" is presumably an instance of `Color`, or at least the state of a `Piece` (or both). Still other nouns may be extraneous. For example, while the description of Othello uses the term "opponent", it is unlikely that we will need an `Opponent` class or even an `opponent` object in class `Player`. However, it is possible that some methods might benefit from an `opponent` variable.

In Experiment O1.1, you will begin to consider the design of an Othello class.

Question and answer sessions

The objects, classes, and methods one develops through narratives are often somewhat sketchy and are usually insufficient to form a whole program. We have not yet determined what attributes or fields each class needs, nor have we determined what parameters the methods will need. In addition, there are often a number of implicit objects in every description. How do we garner this additional information? We can garner information through a more careful reading of the narrative, asking questions as we go. What types of questions should we ask?

- For various actions, you might ask "What object does this action?"
- You might also ask "What information do we need in order to do this?"
- For objects and classes, you might ask "How would I normally describe such objects and what would they normally do?"

For example, closer reading of the description of Othello suggests that someone needs to determine whose turn it is. It may be helpful to use a `Referee` class that selects the current player. It may also be that the class that runs the game makes this determination.

Similarly, you note that there are many references to legal moves. What determines whether a move is legal? A set of `Rules`. The `Rules` also determine when the game is over and, in effect, who moves next.

Now let us consider the `makeMove` method. What information does a player need to make a move? The player certainly needs to know his or her color, the state of the board, and the applicable rules. Since a player always has the same color, we might make that a field in the `Player` class. On the other hand, the state of the board changes, so we might make that a parameter of the `makeMove` method. The rules are consistent, so we might also make those a field in the `Player` class.

Are these the only decisions we could have made? Certainly not. We might have instead chosen to make all color, board, and rules all parameters to the `makeMove` method or all fields in the `Player` class, or some other combination. How do you decide what is best to do? Again, experience will tell you. For now, a good strategy is to make things that can be changed by other objects (e.g., the board) parameters, while things that will remain consistent throughout the game (e.g., the rules) can be fields.

You might note that we have not begun to specify *how* `makeMove` operates, we have only specified what it does. At this point, it is appropriate to stay at this level of abstraction. In part, the how will be determined by our further steps. In part, the how may differ depending on other issues. For example, in a text-based Othello game, `makeMove` might draw the board and prompt for the player to type in a move; in a graphical Othello game, `makeMove` might wait for the player to click on a legal square; in a game against the computer, the computer player will make a move by running an algorithm that chooses an appropriate space.

Finally, we might ask ourselves what constitutes a move. Basically, it is the placement of a piece on the board at a particular position. This suggests that the `Move` class will have at least two attributes: a `Piece` and a `Position`. We also note that moves update the board. This suggests that the `Board` class will need an `update` method that takes a `Move` as a parameter.

In Experiment O1.2, you will refine your descriptions.

Beginning coding

At this stage in your design, you should have a rough outline of the classes you will need in the program, some of the methods those classes will need to provide, and some of the fields each class will use. You can use this information to start writing the code for your programs. For example, I've determined that each `Player` will need a `Color` for its pieces and a `makeMove` method. I might also note that I'll need the `Color` in order to create a particular player, giving me an idea of what the constructor will look like. This analysis leads to the following class description.

```
import Color;
/**
 * A person playing an Othello game (or, perhaps, any game).
 *
 * @author Samuel A. Rebelsky
 * @version 1.1 of September 1998
 */
public class Player {
```

```
// +--------+-----------------------------------------------
// | Fields |
// +--------+

/** The color of the pieces the player places on the board. */
protected Color mycolor;

// +-------------+-----------------------------------------------
// | Constructors |
// +-------------+

/**
 * Create a new player that uses a particular color of
 * piece.
 */
public Player(Color piececolor) {
  this.mycolor = piececolor;
} // Player(Color)

// +---------+-----------------------------------------------
// | Methods |
// +---------+

/**
 * Choose a move to make (but don't make the move).
 */
public Move makeMove(Board b) {
  // Code not yet available.
} // makeMove(Board)

} // class Player
```

In Experiment O1.3, you will begin to develop classes for the project.

Narrating interactions

Our descriptions up to this point have ignored an important component: interaction with the user or users. While not all programs, classes, objects, or methods will interact with the user, many will. How do we determine what role such interactions play in the design of our program? We write more detailed narratives that describe how we envision users interacting with the program.

For example, we might describe two players using our Othello game as follows.

> Two players, William and Jonathan, start the game. The game prompts for the player name. William enters his name for white; Jonathan enters his name for black. The game displays the game board (with white pieces at D5 and E4 and black pieces at D4 and E5). It then prompts William for his move. William places a white piece at C4, surrounding the black piece at D4. The game automatically flips the piece at D4 and then prompts Jonathan for his move. Jonathan chooses to place a black piece at A1. The game determines that this is not a legal move, informs Jonathan, and then asks for another move.

You'll note that we used "the game" a great deal in this narrative. You will often find that you use a similar noun (perhaps "the program") in describing interaction. Often, this will be your controlling object, or even the `main` routine in that object.

Why do we use such narratives? Sometimes it is to identify additional objects and classes (as in the `Game` class suggested in the previous paragraph). More frequently, it is to identify additional classes and methods that are necessary. For example, we might note that we need to draw boards, perhaps with a `draw` method provided by the `Board` class.

Again, it helps to ask questions. For example "*How* does it display the game board?" or "*How* does it prompt for moves?" You might also ask "*What* object does the prompting?" In this case, it is likely that the `Player` object prompts for moves as part of its work for the `makeMove` method. In order to do this, it may need additional parameters or fields, such as a `SimpleOutput` object to write to and a `SimpleInput` object to read from.

As we progress toward a full implementation, we can turn our narrative and questions into pseudocode, as in

```
To play Othello:
  create the board, rules, and players
  while the rules do not indicate that the game is over
    if the current player has an available move then
      repeatedly
        ask the current player to select a move
      until the player selects a legal move
      make that move, updating the board
      switch players
    else // the current player has no legal moves
      switch players
    end if
  end while
  count the pieces and report the winner
```

Thinking of alternative situations is also helpful. For example, one might describe an interaction between one player and the computer as follows.

> Michelle starts the Othello game. It asks her whether she wants to play against the computer or another player. She selects the computer as an opponent. The game then asks for her name. She enters her name, Michelle. The game tells her that it will play white and she will play black. It then displays the board. The computer moves first and places a white piece at C4.

Again, we may want to ask some questions. For example, "*How* does the computer make a move?" One method would be to check every square on the board, identify all the legal moves, and pick one using some heuristic (a simple one is "the first legal move I find"; a more interesting one might be "the one that flips the most pieces"; better ones may pay attention to the placement of pieces and the number of pieces on the board).

Comparing alternate narratives can also help identify some objects. For example, if we read the second narrative again, we may ask ourselves "*Which* object computes the computer's move?" Since objects in class Player develop moves in the first scenario, it may make sense to use related objects in the second scenario. In particular, we might consider building a subclass of the Player object, such as ComputerPlayer.

In Experiment O1.4, you will develop narratives for some of the interactions in the game. In Experiment O1.5, you will continue coding the Othello game.

Diagrams of relationships

As you may have guessed, most object-oriented programs are not just collections of random objects, interacting chaotically. Rather, the interactions between objects are carefully scripted. How does one script these interactions? We can develop scripts by thinking carefully about the relationships between objects, again based on our earlier narratives.

The interaction narratives give a good beginning. For example, we can tell that:

- Some method of the Game object calls the display method of the Board object.
- Some method of the Game object calls the makeMove method of a Player object, which returns a Move object.
- The makeMove method of some Player objects request a Move from some type of interaction object or objects.

Many programmers find it helpful to diagram these relationships, representing them visually in addition to, or instead, of textually. Often, it is best for each programmer to decide on the visualization that is most appropriate for him or her. Typically, a diagram will include a box for each object in the program, with sub-boxes for each of the methods. A call to a method is represented by a line from calling object or method to callee. The response may be represented by a dotted line.

In Experiment O1.6, you will practice drawing diagrams.

Generalization and encapsulation

As we saw earlier, one of the primary reasons to do object-oriented programming is that it can easily support reuse. That is, well designed objects that work in one program should also be usable in another program. Similarly, by changing just one or two objects in a program, one might make it do something somewhat different.

In our Othello game, we might decide to support other sized boards (e.g., 10x10 or 6x6), more than two players, or alternate starting positions. Each change may affect multiple classes. It is our goal to minimize the number of classes affected.

For example, if we had finished coding the Othello game and later decided to support different sized boards (and we were not careful about the original design of the game), it is likely that we will need to change

- the `makeMove` method of the `Player` class, since there are a wider variety of spaces to select;
- the `Rules` class to support the different sized boards; and
- the `Board` class to include a constructor that takes the board size as a parameter.

If we design the various classes in such a way that they make fewer assumptions, these updates might be easier. For example, if we had written the `makeMove` method so that it queried the board for its size or for a list of legal spaces, then it might not be necessary to update `makeMove` at all when we changed the size of the board. The secret is to think about these alternatives before coding, rather than afterwards.

As another example, consider the pseudocode for a game of Othello that we developed earlier. Could we reuse this code for other games simply by changing the board, players, and rules? No. The pseudocode includes a number of assumptions about the rules of Othello. For example, it assumes that players alternate turns (except when one player cannot make a move). If we were going to support other games, such as chess, we would need to write a new description. Hence, it might be better to rewrite the algorithm as follows:

```
To play a game
  create the game board, rules, and players
  while the rules do not indicate that the game is over
    determine the current player
    let that player make a move
  end while
  determine the winner
```

In fact, we could even make this a parameterized method

```
To play a game given a board, rules, and players
  while the rules do not indicate that the game is over
    determine the current player
    let that player make a move
  end while
  determine the winner
```

In Experiment O1.7, you will consider other generalizations for the design of the Othello game.

Experiments

Name: _____

ID: _____

**Experiment O1.1:
Determine
potential objects
and classes for
an Othello
simulation**

Here is the description of Othello that appeared previously.

Othello is a two-person game played on an eight-by-eight board. It is often convenient to number the rows of the board 1–8 and the columns A–H. The game begins with two black pieces and two white pieces on the center four squares of the board (D4, D5, E4, and E5). There is a black piece in the top-left and bottom-right of those four squares (D4 and E5). There is a white piece in the top-right and bottom-left of those four squares (D5 and E4). Players alternate turns, with each player making a legal move when it is his or her turn. A legal move consists of placing a piece so that two of pieces surround a row, column, or diagonal of the opponent's pieces. All of the opponent's pieces are then flipped (from black to white or from white to black). If a player cannot make a legal move, that player loses his or her turn. Play continues until there are no longer blank squares on the board or neither player can make a legal move. The player with the most pieces is the winner.

Step 1. Circle all of the nouns.

Step 2. For each noun, decide whether that noun represents something you need to represent in the program or something not necessary to the program. If the noun represents something necessary to the program, decide whether it is an object or a class. If the noun represents something unnecessary, suggest why.

Step 3. Box all of the verbs.

Step 4. For each verb, decide whether the verb represents a method a class might implement. Then attach each verb to the appropriate class or classes.

**Experiment O1.2:
Refining your
descriptions**

Step 1. Reread the description of Othello and make a list of at least two new questions of the form "who does this?" What additional objects or classes, if any, do the answers to these questions suggest?

Step 2. Look at your list of methods and, for each method, ask "What information do I need in order for this method to succeed?" Make a list of methods and their required pieces of information.

Step 3. Look at the required pieces of information you developed in Step 2 and for each piece decide whether it is more appropriately a parameter to the method or a field in the object.

Step 4. Consider each of the classes you developed in this experiment and in Experiment O1.1. For each class, consider what fields you will need. This may require you to reflect on how you would normally describe the object or on how the object operates.

Experiment O1.3: Beginning coding

Step 1. Based on your analysis of Othello, create a `Move` class. Your class need only include fields, constructors, and empty methods. You need not enter the bodies of any methods you include. Summarize the design of your class.

Step 2. Based on your analysis of Othello, create a `Board` class. Again, include only fields, constructors, and empty methods. Summarize the design of your class.

Step 3. Based on your analysis of Othello, create a `Rules` class. Once again, include only fields, constructors, and empty methods. Summarize the design of your class.

Experiment O1.4: Narrating interactions

Step 1. Write a narrative describing the interaction with the `Game` object at the end of a game. You may need to play a game of Othello by hand to reach an end state, or you may find it appropriate to make one up. Try to consider other aspects of the rules as you write this narrative. Your narrative should be between one hundred and two hundred words.

Step 2. The original interaction narrative (the one describing the beginning of the game) is woefully lacking in details, as is illustrated by the questions we asked earlier. For example, it does not describe how the board is displayed or how input is read from the players. Rewrite the narrative so as to clarify these issues. Your new narrative should be approximately two hundred words.

Step 3. Expand your narrative from Step 1 to include more details, as suggested in Step 2.

Step 4. Pick at least two new classes, methods, method parameters, or fields suggested by these narratives, and update your code from the previous experiment to include the updates. Enter your changes here.

Experiment O1.5: Selective coding

Step 1. Earlier, we developed pseudocode for a game of Othello. Translate this into Java code. In particular, create an `Othello` class with a `main` routine that corresponds to this pseudocode. Your `main` routine should contain real Java code, although it need not work yet (since the other classes are unlikely to be complete).

Step 2. Consider whether any of the pieces of the `main` routine would be better represented as separate objects or methods. Enter your suggestions here.

Step 3. Write a `makeMove` method for the `Player` class. Your method will need to prompt for the move to make and return a corresponding `Move`. Describe your algorithm here.

Experiment O1.6: Diagramming

Step 1. Make a list of eight method calls that might appear in an implementation of an Othello game. For each call, note which method of which object would make the call and which object would provide the called method. For example, it is likely that the `main` method of `OthelloGame` will call the `display` method of `Board`.

Step 2. Draw a picture showing the interactions between the objects described in Step 1. Feel free to use whatever form you deem most appropriate.

Experiment O1.7: Generalization

Step 1. Describe an interesting alternate board on which we might play Othello.

Step 2. Suggest an alternate game (other than chess) in which we might use the Othello board.

Step 3. What other classes will need to be changed if we play Othello on different boards? Why?

Step 4. What does this suggest about the design of the `Board` class in your Othello game? In particular, what fields are truly needed, and what belong in subclasses? More importantly, what methods should `Board`s include?

Post-Laboratory Problems

Problem O1-A: Describe a game

Pick a game and write a short two paragraph description of the game comparable to the description of Othello from this laboratory. Using this description, identify the objects and classes that might be used in a simulation of that game.

Problem O1-B: A simple Othello interface

We are on our way to a working Othello game. The first step is to get a working interface. You will need

- Frameworks for all the appropriate classes: Othello, Rules, Player, Board, and Piece. A framework contains only class definition, constructors (possibly empty), and methods (again, possibly empty). You may have written some of these frameworks for Experiment O1.3. When a method needs to return a value, it returns a "reasonable" default value. For example, the isLegal method of the Rules class might always return <u>true</u>.
- An Othello class with a main routine. You may have written this for Experiment O1.5.
- A makeMove method for the Player class that prompts for a move and returns a corresponding Move object. You may have written this for Experiment O1.5.
- A display method for the Board class. You will need to write that now.
- An initialize method for the Rules class that places pieces on the board. You will need to write that now.

By filling in the details, you should be able to get a simple working interface for the Othello game in which players can enter moves and see a board. At this point, the pieces should not flip and may not even display.

Note that as you fill in the details, you may realize that you need additional methods. For example, although we have not discussed it, the Board class will clearly need a placePiece method.

Problem O1-C: Update Board

Update the Board class so that it will remember where pieces are placed on the board and display them appropriately.

Problem O1-D: Update Rules

Finish the Rules class. You will need to ensure that it is able to

- check whether or not a move is legal;
- determine if a player has a legal move;
- determine whether the game is over;
- identify the winner when the game is over;
- place pieces in the initial configuration; and
- update the board after a move is made.

This problem is perhaps the most difficult in this assignment.

Problem O1-E: Changing Othello's board

Using your code from the previous problems, update Othello so that it is played on a rectangular 6x8 board. What classes did you need to change?

Problem O1-F: Changing Othello's rules

Using your code from the previous problems, update Othello so that the initial state of the board contains two black pieces and two white pieces on the center four squares, with the black pieces forming a row and the white pieces forming a row. What classes did you need to change?

Problem O1-G: Changing Othello's pieces

Using your code from the previous problems, update Othello so that pieces have three colors: white, black, and red. Assume that they flip in sequence: white to black, black to red, red to white. What classes did you need to change? What other questions did you need to ask in order for these updates to be successful and useful?

Session O2: Inheritance

In this laboratory session, you will learn about inheritance, one of the key characteristics of object-oriented languages. The goals of this laboratory session are to

- examine selected issues in good software design, particularly code reuse;
- motivate and introduce inheritance; and
- investigate Java's primary inheritance mechanism.

Your instructor will tell you which of the experiments you are to perform.

Prerequisite skills:

Note: It is possible to do this lab directly after J3, although some post-laboratory problems also require J4 (Boolean Expressions and Conditionals).

- Java objects and classes

Required files:

- NewPoint.java
- Point.java
- PointFun.java
- SimpleInput.java
- SimpleOutput.java
- TaxicabPoint.java

Discussion

We use object-oriented languages for a number of reasons. Often, objects provide a natural mechanism for modeling the domain of the problem. For example, when we are writing a program to simulate a game, like chess, we might create an object for each component of the program (e.g., pieces, game board, user interface).

Reuse

In addition, object-oriented languages support reuse. After you design an object to use in one program, you will often find that you can reuse it in another program. For example, after building a `Board` class for chess, you could reuse that object in a checkers game. This is the simplest form of reuse.

But what if we want to not only reuse a class, but also extend that class to add new capabilities? For example, suppose we wanted to have a class like `Point`, but one that had a `toString()` method that converted points to strings. What could we do?

We could obtain the source code for `Point` (i.e., the file `Point.java`) and modify that source code. An advantage of this solution is that we need not change any of the programs that already use the `Point` class. A disadvantage is that there will soon be many different versions of the `Point` class. For example, while you may decide to add a `toString` method, someone else might decide to add a `distanceFrom(Point other)` method and someone else might decide to add both. In addition, the source code for a class is not always available.

We could build a new class, `NewPoint`, which contains the same methods as `Point`, as well as the new methods we want to add. Rather than reimplementing all of `Point`'s methods, we could include a field that contains a base point and simply call the appropriate method based on that field. For example, we might have the following attribute declaration

```
/**
 * The point that this point is based on.
 */
protected Point base;
```

When creating a new `NewPoint`, we just need to create a new `Point`, as in

```
/**
 * Build the point (x,y).
 */
public NewPoint(double x, double y) {
  base = new Point(x,y);
} // NewPoint(double, double)
```

To get the x coordinate of a `NewPoint` we might use

```
/**
 * Get the X coordinate of a point.
 */
```

```
public double getX() {
  return base.getX();
} // getX()
```

Similarly, to move a `NewPoint` right, we might use

```
/**
 * Shift the point right by a particular amount.
 */
public void shiftRight(double amt) {
  base.shiftRight(amt);
} // shiftRight(double)
```

Look at `NewPoint.java` for additional details.

There are a number of disadvantages to this strategy, too. In particular, there is a lot of busy work writing a number of methods with just one call to the base object. In addition, you cannot use a `NewPoint` where you had previously used a `Point`.

You will discover some of these disadvantages in Experiment O2.1.

Inheritance

Because experience shows that many times programmers need to build extended versions of existing classes, and because of the problems described in the previous section, most object-oriented languages provide a more sophisticated reuse mechanism called *inheritance*. What is inheritance? Put most simply, it is a way to add functionality to a class without changing the underlying class. A class that inherits from another class automatically includes essentially all of the methods and fields of the class that it inherits from. For example, if we based an `ExtendedPoint` class on our `Point` class, then `ExtendedPoint` would automatically include `getX`, `getY`, `shiftLeft`, and all of the other methods provided by the `Point` class *without requiring any additional code.*

A class that inherits from another class is also said to extend that class. The original class is called the `superclass` and the class that inherits from that class is called the `subclass`.

Inheritance is so important to object-oriented programming that some computer scientists do not consider a language object-oriented unless it supports inheritance. However, as we will see, there are a number of alternative notions of inheritance.

How do you build a subclass in Java? Using the `extends` in the class declaration. For example

```
public class ExtendedPoint
  extends Point {
  ...
} // ExtendedPoint
```

What needs to go in a subclass? Officially, nothing, in which case the subclass behaves identically to the superclass. However, there is little purpose to extending a class if you are not going to add some functionality through additional or modified methods. In addition, you will almost always need to add new constructors to a subclass because a subclass does not inherit the constructors of the superclass.

For example, we might write

```
/**
 * Build the point (x,y).
 */
public ExtendedPoint(double x, double y) {
  setValue(x,y);
} // ExtendedPoint(double, double)
```

This does lead to a question. What should we do if we want to use one of the constructors defined in the superclass? Fortunately, Java provides a solution. If you want to use one of the superclass's constructors, you use

```
super(parameters);
```

For example, if the superclass is `Point` and the two parameters are of type `double`, then the `Point(double,double)` constructor will be used.

Taking advantage of this feature, we might instead define the constructor for `ExtendedPoint` as

```
/**
 * Build the point (x,y).
 */
public ExtendedPoint(double x, double y) {
  super(x,y);
} // ExtendedPoint(double, double)
```

You will experiment with a simple extension of the `Point` class in Experiment O2.2. In Experiment O2.3 you will add additional functionality to that new class.

Overriding methods

Most frequently, we extend classes to add additional functionality. For example, we might build an `ExtendedPoint` to extend `Point` with a method like `toString`, which provides a printable version of the point, or `distanceFrom`, which computes the distance between a point and another point.

However, sometimes we want to modify the functionality of an existing method. For example, `Point` includes a `distanceFromOrigin` method that gives the straight-line distance of a point from the origin. What should we do if we'd like to have points that use taxicab distance in which distance is measured along horizontals and verticals, but not diagonals? In object-oriented terminology, we *override* the original method. We do that by creating a new method with the same name as the overridden method. For example,

```
/**
 * A point on the plane that uses taxicab distance rather than
 * standard distance.  Intended as a simple example of inheritance
 * and overriding in Java.
```

```
 *
 * @version 1.1 of October 1999
 * @author Samuel A. Rebelsky
 */
public class TaxicabPoint extends Point {

   // +--------------+----------------------------------------------
   // | Constructors |
   // +--------------+

   /**
    * Build the point (x,y).
    */
   public TaxicabPoint(double x, double y) {
      super(x,y);
   } // TaxicabPoint(double, double)

   /**
    * Build the point (0,0).
    */
   public TaxicabPoint() {
      super(0,0);
   } // TaxicabPoint()

   // +---------+----------------------------------------------
   // | Methods |
   // +---------+

   /**
    * Compute the distance of a point from the origin.  Overrides
    * corresponding method from the Point class.
    */
   public double distanceFromOrigin() {
      return this.getX() + this.getY();
   } // distanceFromOrigin

} // class TaxicabPoint
```

In Experiment O2.4 you will conduct a short experiment with Taxicab-
Points. In Experiment O2.5 you will override the toString method we've
added to ExtendedPoint.

From rectangles to squares

Let us turn to a more complicated form of inheritance. Suppose we were
extending the Rectangle class to develop a Square class. Is this a reasonable thing to do? Some would argue yes, since squares are particular kinds
of rectangles. Others would argue no, since squares provide somewhat different semantics than do rectangles (e.g., if you change the width of a rectangle, you do not affect its height; however, if you change the width of a
square, you must also change its height). We will assume that this is a reasonable extension and consider how to build the Square class.

What are the potential difficulties of such an extension? In general, they
relate to ensuring that the square remains a square. For example, when we

set the width to a particular value, we also need to set the height to the same value (and vice versa).

In Experiment O2.6 you will build a `Square` class from a `Rectangle` class.

Multiple inheritance

At times, you may find that you want to create a class that inherits methods from multiple classes. For example, if you've extended `Point` to `PrintablePoint` (adding a `toString` method) and also extended `Point` to `ComparablePoint` (adding `equals` and `lessThan` methods), you might consider writing a `PrintableAndComparablePoint` by extending both `PrintablePoint` and `ComparablePoint`. This is called *multiple inheritance*.

Unfortunately (or fortunately, depending on your perspective), Java does not support multiple inheritance. Why not? Primarily, because it can be complicated to understand. For example, if class `AB` extends both `A` and `B` and both `A` and `B` provide a `toString` method, then which does `AB` use? In addition, it turns out that multiple inheritance is difficult to implement efficiently.

As an alternative to multiple inheritance, Java provides *interfaces,* which are discussed in a subsequent laboratory session. It turns out that most of the multiple inheritance that is done in practice can be handled more elegantly, more appropriately, and more efficiently by interfaces.

Experiments

Name: _____

ID: _____

**Experiment O2.1:
Building a new
point class**

Required files:

- NewPoint.java
- Point.java
- PointFun.java

Step 1. Make copies of Point.java, PointFun.java, and NewPoint.java. Compile all three and execute PointFun. Record your results.

Step 2. Replace the line in PointFun that reads

```
Point pt = new Point(2,3);
```

with

```
Point pt = new Point();
```

Recompile PointFun and execute it. Record your results.

Step 3. Make a copy of PointFun.java called NewPointFun.java (you'll also have to change PointFun to NewPointFun within the code). Update NewPointFun to use a NewPoint wherever it used a Point. Summarize your changes here.

Step 4. Compile and execute `NewPointFun`. Record your results. Are they the same as in Step 2?

Step 5. Update the zero-parameter constructor for `Point` to read

```
/**
 * Build the point (1,1).
 */
public Point() {
  this.xcoord = 1;
  this.ycoord = 1;
} // Point()
```

Do not change `NewPoint` or `NewPointFun`. Recompile `Point` and run `New-PointFun`. Record and explain the output.

Step 6. As you may have observed, the zero-parameter constructor for `New-Point` no longer creates the point (0,0). Update that constructor so that it always creates that point. Summarize your changes here.

Step 7. Record any general observations you have about the process of creating a variant of the `Point` class in this experiment.

**Experiment 02.2:
A simple
extension of the
Point class**

Required files:

- `Point.java`
- `PointFun.java`

Step 1. Make fresh copies of `Point.java` and `PointFun.java`. Compile the two programs. Execute `PointFun`. Record the results.

Step 2. Build a new `ExtendedPoint` class containing only the following lines along with an appropriate introductory comment.

```
public class ExtendedPoint
   extends Point {
} // class ExtendedPoint
```

Compile the new class and record any error messages you receive. After doing so, read the notes on this step.

Step 3. Modify `PointFun` to use an `ExtendedPoint` in place of each `Point`. Summarize your changes.

Step 4. Attempt to compile the new class and record any error messages you receive. What do these error messages suggest? After writing your answer, read the notes on this step.

Step 5. Change the line in `PointFun`'s `main` method that creates the point from

```
ExtendedPoint pt = new ExtendedPoint(2,3);
```

to

```
ExtendedPoint pt = new ExtendedPoint();
```

Recompile and execute `PointFun`. Record the output. What does this suggest?

Step 6. Add the following constructor to `ExtendedPoint`.

```
/**
 * Build the point (x,y).
 */
public ExtendedPoint(double x, double y) {
  setValue(x,y);
} // ExtendedPoint(double, double)
```

Recompile both `PointFun` and `ExtendedPoint`. If you are successful, record and explain the results. If you are not successful, record and explain the error messages.

Step 7. Add the following constructor to `ExtendedPoint`.

```
/**
 * Build the point (1,1).
 */
public ExtendedPoint() {
  setValue(1,1);
} // ExtendedPoint()
```

Recompile both `PointFun` and `ExtendedPoint`. If you are successful, record and explain the results. If you are not successful, record and explain the error messages.

Step 8. Change the line in `PointFun`'s `main` method that creates the point from

```
ExtendedPoint pt = new ExtendedPoint();
```

to

```
ExtendedPoint pt = new ExtendedPoint(4,1);
```

Recompile and execute `PointFun`. Record the output. What does this suggest?

Step 9. Replace the appropriate constructor in `ExtendedPoint` with

```
/**
 * Build the point (x,y).
 */
public ExtendedPoint(double x, double y) {
  super(x,y);
} // ExtendedPoint(double, double)
```

Recompile both `PointFun` and `ExtendedPoint`. Run `PointFun`. If you are successful, record and explain the results. If you are not successful, record and explain the error messages.

Experiment O2.3: Adding functionality to `ExtendedPointS`

Required files:

- `Point.java`
- `PointFun.java`
- `ExtendedPoint.java` (created in the previous experiment)

Obviously, we want subclasses to do more than their superclasses do, otherwise there is no purpose to having subclasses. In particular, we often want to add new methods to subclasses. In this experiment, we will add a `toString` method that will convert points to printable strings.

Step 1. Make copies of `Point.java`, `PointFun.java`, and `Extended-Point.java`. If you have not already done so, update `PointFun.java` to use `ExtendedPoints` rather than `Points`. Compile and execute `PointFun` and record the results.

Step 2. Add the following `toString` method to `ExtendedPoint`.

```
/**
 * Convert the point to a string for ease of printing.
 */
public String toString() {
    return "x=" + getX() + ", y=" + getY();
} // toString()
```

Recompile `ExtendedPoint` and `PointFun`. Execute `PointFun`. Record your results. Are they what you expected? Why or why not?

Step 3. Update the `main` method of `PointFun` so that every line that read

```
out.println("(" + pt.getX() + "," + pt.getY() + ")");
```

now reads

```
out.println(pt.toString());
```

Recompile and execute `PointFun`. Record your results. Are they what you expected? Why or why not?

Step 4. In addition to inheriting the methods of its superclass, a subclass also inherits the fields of its superclass (subject to some restrictions that you do not yet need to understand). We can see this by updating the `toString` method to use `xcoord` and `ycoord` rather than `getX` and `getY`.

Replace the line in `toString` that reads

```
return "x=" + getX() + ", y=" + getY();
```

with one that reads

```
return "X:" + this.xcoord + ",Y:" + this.ycoord;
```

Recompile `ExtendedPoint` and execute `PointFun`. Record your results. Are they what you expected? Why or why not?

Step 5. The previous steps suggest that we often have the choice of using the methods of the superclass (e.g., `getX`) to obtain the fields of the superclass (e.g., `xcoord`) or directly using the fields of the superclass. Which strategy do you think is better and why? You may want to consider which of the `toString` methods you prefer in answering this question, but you should also try to think about other issues.

Experiment O2.4: Overriding methods

Required files:

- `Point.java`
- `PointFun.java`
- `TaxicabPoint.java`

In addition to adding new methods to subclasses (as in Experiment O2.3), we may also want to change what methods do. For example, we might want to create a variant of `Point`s that use different distance metrics or a variant of `ExtendedPoint`s that print points in a different way. We will make the distance extension in this experiment and the printing extension in the next experiment.

Step 1. Make copies of `Point.java`, `PointFun.java`, and `Taxicab-Point.java`. Compile all three files. Execute `PointFun` and record the results.

Step 2. Read the source code for `Point` and `TaxicabPoint` and, in your own words, describe how `TaxicabPoint`s differ from `Point`s.

Step 3. Update `PointFun` to use `TaxicabPoint`s instead of regular `Point`s. Compile and execute `PointFun` and record your results. Are they the same as in Step 1? If so, why? If not, why not?

Experiment O2.5: Overriding the `toString` method

Required files:

- `Point.java`
- `PointFun.java`
- `ExtendedPoint.java` (created in the previous experiment)

Step 1. Make copies of `Point.java`, `PointFun.java`, and `Extended-Point.java`. If you have not already done so, add the following `toString` method to `ExtendedPoint`.

```
/**
 * Convert the point to a string for ease of printing.
 */
public String toString() {
  return "x=" + getX() + ", y=" + getY();
} // toString()
```

Update the `main` method of `PointFun` to use `ExtendedPoint`s and the `toString` method, as in

```
/**
 * Build a point and move it around.
 */
public static void main(String[] args) {
    // We'll be generating some output.
    SimpleOutput out = new SimpleOutput();
    // The point we'll be playing with.
    ExtendedPoint pt = new ExtendedPoint(2,3);
    // Print some basic information
    out.println(pt.toString());
    out.println("  distance from origin: " +
            pt.distanceFromOrigin());
    // Move it right a little bit.
    out.println("Shifting right by 0.7");
    pt.shiftRight(0.7);
    // Print current information
    out.println(pt.toString());
    out.println("  distance from origin: " +
            pt.distanceFromOrigin());
    // Move it right a little bit.
    out.println("Shifting up by 2.5");
    pt.shiftUp(2.5);
    // Print current information
    out.println(pt.toString());
    out.println("  distance from origin: " +
            pt.distanceFromOrigin());
    // Move it left a little bit.
    out.println("Shifting left by 10.2");
    pt.shiftLeft(10.2);
    // Print current information
    out.println(pt.toString());
    out.println("  distance from origin: " +
            pt.distanceFromOrigin());
} // main(String[])
```

Compile the files. Execute `PointFun` and record the results.

Step 2. Build a new `ReextendedPoint` class containing only the following lines (along with an appropriate introductory comment and constructors).

```
public class ReextendedPoint
    extends ExtendedPoint {
} // class ReextendedPoint
```

Compile the new class and correct any errors. What methods do you expect `ReextendedPoint` to provide?

After you've answered this question, read the notes on this step.

Step 3. Update `PointFun` to use `ReextendedPoint`s instead of `Extended-Point`s. Recompile and execute `PointFun`. Record and explain the results.

Step 4. Add the following `toString` method to `ReextendedPoint`.

```
/**
 * Convert the point to a string for ease of printing.
 */
public String toString() {
  return "(" + getX() + "," + getY() + ")";
} // toString()
```

Recompile `ReextendedPoint` and execute `PointFun`. Record and explain the results.

Experiment O2.6: From `Rectangle` to `Square`

Required files:

- `Rectangle.java`

Step 1. Make a copy of `Rectangle.java`. Build a subclass of `Rectangle` called `Square`. You need not put anything in `Square` (yet). Build a class,

SquareTester, that you will use for testing your Square class. The main method of SquareTester should include

```
SimpleOutput out = new SimpleOutput();
Square box = new Square();
out.println("The area of the square is: " + box.area());
```

Are you able to compile all three files? If not, why not? If so, record and explain the output.

Step 2. Add a constructor to Square that takes one parameter: the length of a side. Update SquareTester to use that constructor. Compile the various components of your program and correct any errors. Enter the code for your constructor here.

Step 3. Add the following line to the main method of SquareTester. Recompile SquareTester and record the results. Explain those results.

```
box.setWidth(2);
out.println("The height of the box is now: " + box.getHeight());
```

Step 4. Look through the code for Rectangle. Make a list of the methods it provides. Highlight the methods that you expect to need to change, but don't change any methods.

Step 5. In order to correctly set the width of a square, we'll need to override the `setWidth` method. But we also need to access the width and height in the `Rectangle` class, preferably with the `setWidth` and `setHeight` of that class. How do we distinguish the two versions of `setWidth`? We can use `super`.`setWidth` to indicate the appropriate method of the superclass.

Write a new `setWidth` method that updates both width and height, which is what should happen in a square. Enter the code for that method here.

Post-Laboratory Problems

Note: Most of these problems require conditionals.

Problem O2-A: Extending Points

Build `ComparablePoint`, a subclass of the `Point` class that includes `equals(Point other)` and `lessThan(Point other)` methods. The `equals` method should return <u>true</u> if the other point is equal to the current point. The `lessThan` method should return true if the current point is closer to the origin than the other point.

Write a small test program that uses your `ComparablePoint`s.

Problem O2-B: Putting Points on a grid

Build `GridPoint`, a subclass of the `Point` class that puts points on a grid, rather than anywhere on the plane. For example, if the grid has a spacing of 1, then the point (0.7,2.3) is placed at (1,2). If the grid has a spacing of 0.5, then the point (1.2, 2.3) is placed at (0.5, 2.5). The constructor for your class should take the spacing as a parameter.

Write an appropriate program to test your new class.

Problem O2-C: Validating Squares

One of the drawbacks to the `Square` and `Rectangle` classes we developed in the experiments is that they do not verify that their width and height are reasonable. In particular, they will admit negative or zero-valued widths and heights, something we traditionally do not accept for squares and rectangles.

a.   Develop a new `SafeSquare` class that extends the `Square` class.

b.   Develop a new `SafeRectangle` class that extends the `Rectangle` class. Extend `SafeRectangle` to build a `NewSafeSquare` class.

c.   Which of a and b is a better way of building a safe square class?

Problem O2-D: A hierarchy of shapes

Often, we use subclassing to build hierarchies of objects. For example, we might begin with `Book`s, subclass them to `Textbook`s, `Novel`s, and `Collections` (obviously not a comprehensive list of types of books). We could then subclass `Textbook`s to `Introductory` and `Advanced` or perhaps by discipline. Similarly, we might subclass `Collections` into `ShortStories` and `Essays` or perhaps into single author and multiple author collections. And so on and so forth.

Design a hierarchy of shapes. That is, begin with a generic `Shape` class including notes as to which methods it might provide, such as `area`. Then list the subclasses and sub-subclasses of the `Shape` class. At each stage, note which methods you may need to override.

Notes

Experiment O2.2, Step 2. The compilation of `ExtendedPoint` should be successful. If it isn't, you have most likely made a typographical error in entering the code for the new class.

Experiment O2.2, Step 4. It is likely that the Java compiler will complain that you are attempting to use a parameterized constructor for `Extended-Point` when no such constructor exists.

Experiment O2.5, Step 2. `ReextendedPoint` extends `ExtendedPoint`. This means that it automatically provides any methods that `ExtendedPoint` provides. `ExtendedPoint` extends `Point`, so it automatically provides all the methods that `Point` provides. `ExtendedPoint` also provides a `toString` method. Hence, `ReextendedPoint` provides all the methods of `Point` (`getX`, `getY`, etc.) plus `toString`.

Session O3: Interfaces and Polymorphism

In a previous laboratory, you examined Java's mechanisms for inheritance in which a subclass automatically inherits all the methods provided by its superclass. In this laboratory, you will investigate a related mechanism, Java's *interfaces*. You will also learn about polymorphism, one of the key attributes of object-oriented programming. The goals of this laboratory are to

- consider a second form of reuse: reuse through polymorphism;
- learn how Java's inheritance mechanism supports this form of reuse;
- investigate Java's interface mechanism, which also supports this form of reuse; and
- compare interfaces and inheritance.

Your instructor will tell you which of the experiments to perform.

Prerequisite skills:

- Objects and classes
- Conditionals
- Inheritance

Required files:

- DateHelper.java
- NewPoint.java
- Point.java
- PointFun.java
- PointPrinter.java
- Printable.java
- SimpleDate.java
- SimpleInput.java
- SimpleOutput.java
- SimpleTime.java

Discussion

You may recall from the discussion of inheritance that inheritance provides an elegant mechanism for reuse. In particular, by extending a class, you automatically reuse all the methods in that class with no additional effort. But are there other ways in which we may want to reuse code? Yes! Often, we would like to write general methods that will work on a variety of related objects. For example, we might design a `printIndented` method that should print any object or at least any printable object, indented by an appropriate number of spaces. Similarly, we might design a `sort` method that can sort any collection of elements or at least any collection of elements in which we can compare the individual elements.

In some languages, it is impossible or exceedingly difficult to design such methods. Fortunately, Java's inheritance mechanism and an accompanying feature called interfaces simplify the design of general methods. Together with polymorphism, interface and inheritance support generalized methods.

Polymorphism

What is polymorphism? It seems that there are hundreds of related definitions. You can think of polymorphism as the ability to use an object in a subclass in place of an object in a superclass, with the choice of methods to execute based on the actual class of the object.

For example, consider the `SimpleDate` class that we have used in the past. Here is a sample implementation of such a class.

```java
/**
 * A very simple implementation of dates using Gregorian-style
 * calendars (with year, month, and day).
 *
 * @author Samuel A. Rebelsky
 * @version 1.2 of September 1998
 */
public class SimpleDate {

    // +--------+------------------------------------------------
    // | Fields |
    // +--------+

    /** The year. */
    protected int year;
    /** The month.  Use 1 for January, 2 for February, ...  */
    protected int month;
    /** The day in the month.  */
    protected int day;

    // +--------------+------------------------------------------
    // | Constructors |
    // +--------------+

    /**
     * Build a new date with year, month, and day.  The month should be
     * between 1 and 12 and the day between 1 and the number of days in
     * the month.
```

```
      */
    public SimpleDate(int y, int m, int d) {
      this.year = y;
      this.month = m;
      this.day = d;
    } // SimpleDate(int,int,int)

    // +-----------+-------------------------------------------------
    // | Extractors |
    // +-----------+

    /**
     * Get the year.
     */
    public int getYear() {
      return this.year;
    } // getYear()

    /**
     * Get the month.
     */
    public int getMonth() {
      return this.month;
    } // getMonth()

    /**
     * Get the day.
     */
    public int getDay() {
      return this.day;
    } // getDay()

    /**
     * Convert to a string (American format: MM/DD/YYYY)
     */
    public String toString() {
      return this.month + "/" + this.day + "/" + this.year;
    } // toString()

} // class SimpleDate
```

Suppose we want to subclass `SimpleDate` to provide more precise time information including not just the day, month, and year, but also minute and second on that day. Here is a class that does just that.

```
/**
 * Extended time/date information, including not just the day, but
 * also the time of day.  (Alternately, including not just the time,
 * but the day on which that time falls.)
 *
 * @author Samuel A. Rebelsky
 * @version 1.0 of January 1999
 */
public class SimpleTime extends SimpleDate {
```

```
// +--------+-----------------------------------------------------
// | Fields |
// +--------+

/** The hour of the day.  */
public int hour;
/** The minute of the day.  */
public int minute;

// +--------------+---------------------------------------------
// | Constructors |
// +--------------+

/**
 * Create a new time, specifying all the components.
 */
public SimpleTime(int year, int month, int day, int hour, int
                  minute) {
  // Set up the day without the time
  super(year,month,day);
  // Fill in the remaining information
  this.hour = hour;
  this.minute = minute;
} // SimpleTime(int,int,int,int,int)

/**
 * Create a new time, specifying only the day.  Use 0:00 as the
 * hour and minute.
 */
public SimpleTime(int year, int month, int day) {
  // Set up the day without the time
  super(year,month,day);
  // Fill in the remaining information
  this.hour = 0;
  this.minute = 0;
} // SimpleTime(int,int,int)

// +------------+-----------------------------------------------
// | Extractors |
// +------------+

/**
 * Get the hour.
 */
public int getHour() {
  return this.hour;
} // getHour()

/**
 * Get the minute.
 */
public int getMinute() {
  return this.minute;
} // getMinute()
```

```
/**
 * Convert to a string.
 */
public String toString() {
  if (this.minute < 10) {
    return this.hour + ":0" + this.minute + "," + super.toString();
  } // if the minute is a single digit
  else {
    return this.hour + ":" + this.minute + "," + super.toString();
  } // if the minute is multiple digits
} // toString()
} // class SimpleTime
```

The calls to super(year,month,day) in the constructors are calls to the constructors of the superclass. As you may recall, the constructors in a subclass must begin with an explicit or implicit call to a constructor for the superclass.

The call to super.toString in the new toString says to use the toString method of the superclass, giving a string for the year, month, and day.

Now suppose a programmer wants to write a method to print a range of dates. The method might print the first date, a dash, and then the second date. The method might print the word "from", the first date, the word "to", and the second date. Here is some code that might do the latter. (You can find this code in DateHelper.java.)

```
public void printRange(SimpleOutput out,
                       SimpleDate first,
                       SimpleDate second) {
  out.println("From " + first.toString() +
              " to " + second.toString());
} // printRange(SimpleOutput,SimpleDate,SimpleDate)
```

What happens if we call this with two SimpleDates, as in

```
helper.printRange(out, new SimpleDate(1964,6,17),
                  new SimpleDate(1964,12,3));
```

As you might expect, it prints the range using just the dates, giving

```
From 6/17/1964 to 12/3/1964
```

What happens if we call this with two SimpleTimes, as in

```
helper.printRange(out, new SimpleTime(1964,6,17),
                  new SimpleTime(1964,12,3));
```

Even though printRange expects two SimpleDates, it ends up using the toString method of SimpleTime. The output will then be

```
From 0:00, 6/17/1964 to 0:00, 12/3/1964
```

In some object-oriented languages (such as C++), the default action would have been for printRange to use SimpleDate's toString method in both cases.

Polymorphism is very important. In fact, many computer scientists consider polymorphism to be one of the three key building blocks of object-oriented programming, the three being objects, inheritance, and polymorphism.

In Experiment O3.1, you will experiment with polymorphism.

Interfaces

As the asides in the introduction suggest, it would be nice if we could just say *this method* works on any object that provides *these methods*. For example, `printIndented` works on any object that provides `getX` and `getY` methods. It would seem that polymorphism, or something similar, should support such descriptions.

Let us consider the `print` method provided by the `PointPrinter` class. You may recall that that method is defined as

```
out.println("(" + pt.getX() + "," + pt.getY() + ")");
out.println("   distance from origin: " +
            pt.distanceFromOrigin());
```

(While this method might be improved by using the `toString` method developed in a previous lab, note that by default `Point`s do not include such a method.)

It seems that this method should be able to work on any class that provides `getX`, `getY`, and `distanceFromOrigin` methods. However, as you will see in Experiment O3.2, this is not the case.

Generalized methods

In particular, Java's type-checking mechanism, which verifies that when you call a method, the arguments match the types of the parameters to the method, will prevent you from using a `NewPoint` where a `Point` is called for. That is, even though `NewPoint` provides the same methods as `Point`, the type-checking system is unable or unwilling to check this.

At the same time, Java needs some way to provide generalized methods, since the solution of rewriting the method with the same code but a different method header is not only inelegant, but also not always possible. As a simple example, consider the `Plane` or `TextPlane` classes used in the introductory laboratories. If we only had access to the files `Plane.class` or `TextPlane.class` and not to `Plane.java` or `TextPlane.java`, then there would be no way to plot `NewPoint`s without first converting them to `Point`s.

As you begin to use more code written by others, you will soon learn that a large number of professional programmers only distribute their compiled code and not their source code. For example, Microsoft will be happy to sell you a copy of the executable (i.e., compiled) versions of Word or Excel, but you will be unable to convince them to let you see the inner workings of the programs (i.e., their source code). At the same time, it is becoming increasingly likely that people will want to extend large programs with custom components, such as a new drawing tool to be used in a drawing program.

Fortunately, Java provides two mechanisms for writing generalized functions: inheritance and interfaces.

Generality through inheritance

The designers of Java decided that successful programming involved more formal mechanisms for indicating that a class has certain capabilities. Since every method provided by a class is automatically inherited or overridden by the subclass, inheritance provides a simple and elegant way for indicating just this. In particular, Java permits you to use an object from a subclass wherever an object for the superclass is called for. Hence, because `Plane` and `Text-Plane` provide a `plot(Point)` methods, you can also plot `ExtendedPoint`s. Similarly, because `PointPrinter` provides a `print(Point)` method, you can print `ExtendedPoint`s.

You will investigate this type of reuse in Experiment O3.3.

Building generalized methods with Java's interfaces

As you've seen, there are two reasons to use inheritance. First, by extending another class, we can automatically provide all the methods of the class. Second, we can use a member of a subclass anywhere we can use a member of the superclass. We can take advantage of this second property to build generalized methods that act on a variety of objects. For example, `Plane` can plot anything that acts like a point.

What other generalized methods might we build? Typically, sorting and searching methods are written so that they can sort or search sequences of a wide variety of types. As long as you can compare two values, you can search or sort.

On a more practical level, we might want to improve `SimpleOutput` (or `MyOutput`, if you've done Lab O3.4) to print a wider variety of values, not just strings and numbers, but also other objects. For example, we might define a class, `Printable`, that includes a `makePrintabale` method used to convert the current object to a string. We can then say that it is possible to print any subclass of `Printable` using the following method

```
/**
 * Print a printable object.
 */
public void print(Printable printme) {
  this.print(printme.makePrintable());
} // print(Printable)
```

Unfortunately, it is awkward to use `Printable`. In particular, what should the default `makePrintable` method (the one provided by `Printable`) do? More importantly, what happens if we want to subclass a nonprintable class, such as `Point` and also make a printable class? As mentioned in the previous laboratory session, Java does not permit you to subclass two classes.

Java provides an alternate mechanism for writing and using generalized functions. Rather than writing a superclass, you can instead write an interface. An interface definition looks surprisingly like a class definition except that

- the keyword interface is used instead of the keyword class, and
- the methods in an interface have no bodies.

With inheritance, you indicate that a class extends another class. With interfaces, you indicate that a class implements another class. For example, we might indicate that a PrintablePoint implements the Printable interface with

```
public class PrintablePoint
  implements Printable
```

An interface is a contract between you and the compiler in which you assert that I have implemented all of the methods defined in the interface, and the compiler can trust your class to implement all of the methods declared in the interface.

You use interfaces similarly to the way you use superclasses except that,

- one class can implement multiple interfaces;
- one class can both implement an interface (or interfaces) and extend another class; and
- a class must define all of the methods declared in any interface it implements.

For example, we can define a Printable interface as follows

```
/**
 * A simple interface used to describe classes that include a
 * toString method (and are therefore printable).
 *
 * @author Samuel A. Rebelsky
 * @version 1.0 of September 1998
 */
public interface Printable {
  /**
   * Convert the current object to a string.
   */
  public String makePrintable();
} // interface Printable
```

We can now declare a printable point (i.e., something that extends Point but is also printable) with

```
/**
 * A point that can be printed.
 */
public class PrintablePoint
  extends Point
  implements Printable
{
} // class PrintablePoint
```

In Experiment O3.4, you will improve SimpleOutput by permitting it to print any class that implements Printable. In Experiment O3.5, you will perform other comparisons of interfaces and superclasses.

Experiments

Name: _____

ID: _____

Experiment O3.1: Polymorphism

Required files:

- DateHelper.java
- SimpleDate.java
- SimpleTime.java

Before you begin, make copies of DateHelper.java, SimpleDate.java, SimpleTime.java. Compile all three files.

Step 1. Create a new program, NewDateTester.java, with a main method that contains the following lines.

```
SimpleOutput out = new SimpleOutput();
DateHelper helper = new DateHelper();
helper.printRange(out, new SimpleDate(1964,6,17),
                       new SimpleDate(1964,12,3));
```

Compile and execute NewDateTester. Record the results.

Step 2. Add the following lines to the main method of NewDateTester.

```
helper.printRange(out, new SimpleTime(1964,6,17),
                       new SimpleTime(1964,12,3));
```

Recompile and execute NewDateTester. Record the new results.

Step 3. Were the results in Steps 1 and 2 the same? If so, why? If not, why not?

Step 4. Add the following lines to the `main` method of `NewDateTester`.

```
helper.printRange(out, new SimpleTime(1964,6,17,5,0),
                       new SimpleTime(1964,12,3,11,30));
```

What do you expect the new output to be?

Step 5. Recompile and execute `NewDateTester`. Record the new results. Were they what you expected? Why or why not?

Step 6. Add the following lines to the `main` method of `NewDateTester`.

```
helper.printRange(out, new SimpleDate(1964,6,17),
                       new SimpleTime(1964,12,3,11,30));
```

What do you expect the new output to be?

Step 7. Recompile and execute `NewDateTester`. Record the new results. Were they what you expected? Why or why not?

Experiment O3.2:
`NewPoint`s and
`PointPrinter`s

Required files:

- `NewPoint.java`
- `Point.java`
- `PointFun.java`
- `PointPrinter.java`

Step 1. Make copies of `Point.java`, `PointFun.java`, and `New-Point.java`. Change the body of the `main` method of `PointFun.java` to read

```
// We'll be generating some output.
SimpleOutput out = new SimpleOutput();
// The point we'll be playing with.
Point pt = new Point(2,3);
// Something to help us print
PointPrinter printer = new PointPrinter();
// Print some basic information
printer.print(out,pt);
// Move it right a little bit.
out.println("Shifting right by 0.7");
pt.shiftRight(0.7);
// Print current information
printer.print(out,pt);
// Move it right a little bit.
out.println("Shifting up by 2.5");
pt.shiftUp(2.5);
// Print current information
printer.print(out,pt);
// Move it left a little bit.
out.println("Shifting left by 10.2");
pt.shiftLeft(10.2);
// Print current information
printer.print(out,pt);
```

Compile all three classes and execute `PointFun`. Record your results.

Step 2. Update `PointFun` to use a `NewPoint` wherever it used a `Point`. Summarize your changes here.

Step 3. Try to compile `PointFun`. What happens?

After writing your answer, you may want to look at the notes.

Step 4. Update `PointPrinter` so that it can print both `Points` and `New-Points`. Recompile `PointPrinter`. Summarize your changes here.

You may also want to look at a suggested update.

Step 5. Recompile `PointFun`. Are you successful? If so, why would you have been successful here and not in Step 3? If not, why not?

After recording your answer, look at the notes on the subject.

Step 6. Execute the newly compiled `PointFun` and record your results. Are they what you expected? Why or why not?

Step 7. Record any general observations you have about the process of creating and using variants of the `Point` class in this experiment.

Experiment O3.3: Using ExtendedPointS

Required files:

- `Point.java`
- `PointFun.java`
- `PointPrinter.java`
- `ExtendedPoint.java` (created and modified in previous laboratory sessions)

Step 1. Make copies of `Point.java`, `PointFun.java`, `PointPrinter.java`, and `ExtendedPoint.java`. The body of the `main` method of `PointFun` should be identical to that of Step 1 of Experiment O3.2. Compile all four classes. Execute `PointFun`. Record your results.

Step 2. Update the `main` method of `PointFun` so that it uses `ExtendedPoints` instead of `Points`. *Do not modify PointPrinter!* Summarize your changes.

Step 3. Compile and execute `PointFun`. Were you successful? If not, summarize and explain the error messages. If you were successful, compare your answer to Step 3 of Experiment O3.2. When you are done, read the notes on this step.

Step 4. Record any general observations you have about the process of creating and using a subclass of the `Point` class in this experiment.

Experiment O3.4:
Printing points

- `Point.java`
- `SimpleOutput.java`

Step 1. Make copies of the two files and compile them.

Step 2. Create the following `Printable` class

```
public class Printable {
  /**
   * Convert the current object to a string.
   */
  public String makePrintable() {
    ...
  } // toString()
} // class Printable
```

You will need to fill in something appropriate for the ellipses. Compile this class and correct any errors you encounter. What did you use in place of the ellipses?

Step 3. Update `SimpleOutput.java` to include a `println(Printable)` method. Summarize the changes you've made to add such a method.

After doing so, you may want to read the notes on this step.

Step 4. Create a new class, `PrintablePoint` that extends `Point`. Add a `makePrintable` method to `PrintablePoint`. Compile `PrintablePoint` and correct any errors. Summarize the structure of `PrintablePoint`.

Step 5. Create a new class, `PointPrinter`, that creates and prints a `PrintablePoint`. The `main` method of `PointPrinter` should be similar to

```
SimpleOutput out = new SimpleOutput();
PrintablePoint pt = new PrintablePoint(1,4);
out.print("The point is ");
out.println(pt);
```

What do you expect to happen if you try to compile or execute `PointPrinter`? Why?

Step 6. Compile and execute `PointPrinter`. What happened? Is this what you expected? Explain the results.

Step 7. Update `PrintablePoint` so that it extends both `Point` and `Printable`. The class header will read

```
public class PrintablePoint
  extends Point
  extends Printable {
  ...
} // class PrintablePoint
```

What happens when you try to compile this new class? Why?

Step 8. Change `Printable` from a class to an interface. Summarize the changes you've made.

Step 9. Try to compile `PrintablePoint`. What happens? How does this result differ from the result in Step 7, and why?

Step 10. Update `PrintablePoint` so that it implements `Printable` rather than extending it. Try to compile the revised class. How do your results differ from those in Steps 7 and 9? Why do they differ?

Step 11. Execute `PointPrinter` and record the results. Are they what you expected? Why or why not?

Experiment O3.5: Printing revisited

Required files:

- `Printable.java` (the interface, not the class)
- `SimpleOutput.java` (as modified in the previous experiment)

Step 1. If you have not already done so, make a copy of the required files and add a `println(Printable)` method to `SimpleOutput`.

Step 2. Create a new class, `Person`, which implements `Printable`. `Person` should have one field, a string representing the name of the person. Make sure you include an appropriate constructor for setting that name. *Do not include a* `makePrintable` *method!* Summarize your design for the class.

Step 3. Create a new class, `PersonPrinter`, with a `main` method that reads

```
SimpleOutput out = new SimpleOutput();
Person author = new Person("Mary P. Boelk");
out.print("The author is ");
out.println(author);
```

Compile and execute `PersonPrinter`. Record the results. Are they what you expected? Why or why not?

Step 4. Add a `makePrintable` method to `Person` that returns the name of the person. Recompile `Person` and execute `PersonPrinter`. Record the results. Were they the same as in the previous step? Why or why not?

Step 5. Change the keyword <u>implements</u> in `Person` to <u>extends</u>. Attempt to recompile `Person`. What happens? Why do you think this is? After writing your answer, restore the <u>implements</u>.

Step 6. Build a `Student` class that extends `Person`. Students should include majors in addition to names. Do not explicitly indicate that `Student` implements `Printable` and do not include a `makePrintable`. Compile `Student` and correct any errors you encounter. Summarize the design of your class.

Step 7. Update the `main` method of `PersonPrinter` to print a `Student` rather than a `Person`. For example, you might write

```
Student generic = new Student("Gen R. Ic", "None");
out.print("This is what we know about the student: ");
out.println(generic);
```

Compile and execute the revised `PersonPrinter`. Were you successful? What might success indicate?

Step 8. Add a `makePrintable` method to `Student`. Recompile `Student` and execute `PersonPrinter`. Record your results. What do they suggest? Note that you never explicitly indicated that `Student`s are printable.

Post-Laboratory Problems

Problem O3-A:
`makePrintable`
vs. `toString`

Java recommends that you use `toString` rather than `makePrintable` when converting objects to strings. In fact, Java will often automatically use `toString`, if available, to convert an object to a string. Write an appropriate class or classes to test this assertion. (Note that the instructions for this problem are purposefully left vague so that you will make some effort to understand both the assertion and how you might check it.)

Given this experience, it behooves you to update the classes from the experiments to define and use `toString` rather than `makePrintable`.

**Problem O3-B:
Cloning points**

One of the difficulties with using members of subclasses in place of members of superclasses is that the methods that use these objects sometimes make copies. For example, the `Plane` class includes the line

```
Point copy = new Point(pt.getX(), pt.getY());
```

This means that even if we call `plot` on a `GridPoint` or a `Comparable-Point`, it ends up turning the point into a normal `Point`. How do we avoid this? By adding a `clone` method to all of our classes. This method makes a copy of the current object. That is, if `Point`, `GridPoint`, and `Comparable-Point` all provide `clone` methods, then the methods that use `Point`s can easily make copies using the `clone` method, rather than explicitly making a new copy.

Update `Point`, `GridPoint`, `ComparablePoint`, and any other descendants of the `Point` class to include `clone` methods.

Update `TextPlane` and `Plane` to use those methods.

**Problem O3-C:
Abstract classes**

Java provides a third inheritance-like mechanism through abstract classes. Investigate the uses of abstract classes and summarize their similarities to and differences from both normal inheritance and interfaces.

**Problem O3-D:
Interfaces vs.
inheritance**

Describe an instance (other than the ones in the laboratories) in which it is more appropriate to use inheritance rather than interfaces.

Describe an instance (other than the ones in the laboratories) in which it is more appropriate to use interfaces rather than inheritance.

In a few sentences, summarize guidelines a programmer might use in deciding whether to use interfaces or inheritance.

**Problem O3-E:
Defining
polymorphism**

There are a number of ways in which computer scientists define polymorphism. See how many you can find. Are they all essentially equivalent, or are there substantial differences among the different definitions?

Notes

Experiment O3.2, Step 3. Because `PointPrinter`'s `print` method was designed to work with `Point`s and not `NewPoint`s, Java won't let you call the `print` method on a `NewPoint`.

Experiment O3.2, Step 4. Since `PointPrinter` needs to support both `Point`s and `NewPoint`s, it makes sense to maintain the existing method and add an additional method that differs only in that we use `NewPoint` instead of `Point`. The method might look like

```
/**
 * Print a point using a particular output object.
 */
public void print(SimpleOutput out, NewPoint pt) {
  out.println("(" + pt.getX() + "," + pt.getY() + ")");
  out.println("  distance from origin: " +
              pt.distanceFromOrigin());
} // print(SimpleOutput, NewPoint)
```

Experiment O3.2, Step 5. If you have done everything appropriately, compilation should be successful in this step. Why? Before there was no `print` method that could accept a `NewPoint` as a parameter. Now there is.

Experiment O3.3, Step 3. In Experiment O3.2, you found that it is not possible to pass a `NewPoint` as a parameter to the `print` method of `PointPrinter`. In this experiment, you found that it is possible to pass an `ExtendedPoint` as a parameter to the same function *without modifying* `print`! This illustrates the principle that you can use an element of a subclass wherever an element of a superclass is called for.

Experiment O3.4, Step 3. You will need to create the appropriate method using code similar to that which appears in the discussion. In addition, you will need to import the new `Printable` class.

Session X1: Primitive Types

In this laboratory session, you will develop and execute a number of small programs intended to reveal issues about the ways in which Java stores and manipulates its primitive types, like integers and real numbers. The goals of this laboratory session are to

- investigate Java's primitive types;
- learn about type coercion; and
- consider operator precedence in Java.

Your instructor will tell you which of the experiments you are to perform.

Prerequisite skills:

Note: If appropriate, this can be held after Lab J1.

- Basic Java programming
- Loops (optional)

Required files:

- `BasicComputations.java`
- `CastingAbout.java`
- `FactsAboutCharacters.java`
- `FactsAboutIntegers.java`
- `FactsAboutReals.java`
- `IntegerLimits.java`
- `SimpleInput.java`
- `SimpleOutput.java`

Discussion

As you may have noticed, two kinds of values are used in Java: the *primitive values,* like integers and real numbers, and the *compound values* we build from them, like arrays and classes. While much of the focus in object-oriented programming is on classes and objects, it is also useful for you to have a firm grasp on the primitive types.

In Java, as in most computer languages, primitive values are represented by a fixed number of *binary digits* or *bits.* A binary digit is a zero or a one. Given a limit on the length of sequences of binary digits, there are only a restricted number of values that one can represent. For example, if one is only allowed to use two binary digits, there are only four different values one can represent (00, 01, 10, and 11). Similarly, if one is only allowed to use four binary digits, there are only sixteen different values that one can represent (0000, 0001, 0010, 0011, 0100, 0101, 0110, 0111, 1000, 1001, 1010, 1011, 1100, 1101, 1110, 1111). An *encoding* or *notation* is used to convert each sequence of binary digits to a corresponding value. For example, one might say that the sequence 0101 represents the integer 5. Clearly, there are limits to what one can represent.

Representing integers

Today's computer systems use more than four bits for storage. The designers of Java realized that there are times in which programmers need only a small range of integers and other times in which programmers need larger ranges. Although computer memories are growing, it is important for programmers to be able to use only as much space as they need for the particular range they need. Hence, Java provides four representations of integers, each of which uses a different number of bits and therefore provides a different range of allowable values. These are `byte`, `short`, `int`, and `long`.

In some languages, the encoding and size of the primitive types may vary from implementation to implementation. In Java, they are fixed. Java requires that an implementation use two's complement notation (don't worry, if you don't know what it is, then you don't need to) and that each integral type have a particular size (which we'll leave it to you to figure out). To aid programmers, Java provides system-defined constants that give the smallest and largest integer values permitted. For `int`, they are `Integer.MAX_VALUE` and `Integer.MIN_VALUE`, respectively.

In Experiment X1.1 you will investigate details of the primitive `int` type used to represent integers. In Experiment X1.2, you will consider the three other representations. In Experiment X1.3, you will investigate what happens when you try to exceed the bounds of allowable integer values.

Representing reals

As with the storage of integers, only a finite number of bits are used for the storage of real numbers. Hence, only a finite number of different real numbers can be represented in a computers memory. Java uses a so-called *floating-point* representation of real numbers. In a floating point representation, some bits are used to represent the digits in the number and some are used to represent the position of the decimal point. (If you've ever used scientific notation, this should be familiar.) This means (more or less) that the precision of the number is based on the size of the number. You can represent very large numbers, but the last few digits will be approximate. Similarly, you can also represent very small numbers, but again the last few digits may be approximate. For example, you can represent 100,000,000 with Java's `float` type, but it may treat 100,000,000 and 99,999,999 as the same number. Similarly, you can represent 0.000000001 using `float`, but Java may not be able to distinguish 0.000000001 and 0.00000001000000001.

In effect, these values are rounded to a value that can be easily represented. Thus, a value stored as type `float` is often merely an approximation of the actual value. The type `double` gives better approximations, but at a cost of more memory. As with integers, the predefined constants `Float.MIN_VALUE` and `Float.MAX_VALUE` set the boundaries for floating-point storage.

In Experiment X1.4 you will investigate the bounds of real numbers in Java, and in Experiment X1.5 you will investigate what happens at and near those bounds.

Coercion and casting

The term *coercion* refers to the interpretation of data as a type other than that originally intended. A common instance of coercion occurs when adding a numeric value of type `int` to another value of type `float`. In this case, the integer value must be converted to a floating-point representation before the addition can be performed.

In the example mentioned above, Java performs coercion without an explicit request to do so. In other cases, the programmer must designate that coercion is to take place. In Java terminology, this is known as casting. Casting is indicated by enclosing the variable containing the value to be coerced in parentheses and preceding it with the name of the new type. Thus, if `r` were a value of type `float`, `(int) r` would produce an integer value corresponding to `r`, presumably by rounding.

In general, relying on coercion is not considered good programming style. The argument is that if data types are chosen correctly, then there should be no need for coercion. On the other hand, sometimes coercion is a logical way of handling a problem. In these cases, it is best to document the fact that coercion is taking place. In this light, many software designers insist that casting be used, even in those cases in which the language would perform the coercion anyway.

In Experiment X1.6, you will investigate the effects of casting in Java.

Representing characters

In Java, data items of type character are often stored as bit patterns according to the ASCII code. Thus, the letter a is stored as the integer 97. However, it is also possible to use Unicode characters in Java, particularly through the `Character` class.

For your initial experiments with characters in Java, you will work with the ASCII representations. How do you convert a character to an integer? Some languages provide a function to do just that. In Java, you can simply cast the character to an integer. How do you convert an integer back to a character? Again, you cast the integer to a character.

In Experiment X1.7 you will explore issues in the representation of characters.

Precedence

As you might expect, Java permits you to write fairly complex arithmetic expressions, such as

```
a * b - c + d / e * f
```

Arguably, this expression is somewhat ambiguous, as it is not immediately clear in which order the operations are performed. It is, of course, a dangerous thing for a computer language to be ambiguous. Hence, Java, like most languages, specifies an order of evaluation. Java uses a precedence-based evaluation order: higher-precedence operations (such as multiplication and division) are executed first, then lower-precedence operations are executed next. For most operations, equal precedence operations are executed left-to-right. For example, in `1-2-3`, the `1-2` is evaluated first, giving `-1`, and then three is subtracted, giving `-4`. (If Java were to evaluate negation right-to-left, we'd get `1-(-1)`, which is `2`.)

Since Java converts types when computing (e.g., when multiplying a float and an integer, it treats the result as an integer), the order-of-evaluation can have a significant effect on the outcome, as you will explore in Experiment X1.8. Since the plus (+) operator can also be used with strings, precedence leads to some odd outcomes when strings and numbers are combined, as you will see in Experiment X1.9.

Experiments

Name: _____

ID: _____

Experiment X1.1: Facts about integers

In this experiment you will investigate the storage of integer values on your own particular machine. (In Java, the machine you are on should not matter, but it is still useful to explore the limitations directly.)

Required file:

- `FactsAboutIntegers.java`

Step 1. Make a copy of `FactsAboutIntegers.java`, which is given by

```java
import SimpleOutput;
/**
 * A program that prints simple "facts" about integer values.
 *
 * @author Samuel A. Rebelsky
 * @author Your Name Here
 * @version 1.1 of January 1999
 */
public class FactsAboutIntegers {
  /**
   * Print some interesting facts about integers in Java.
   */
  public static void main(String[] args) {
    SimpleOutput out = new SimpleOutput();
    out.println("The smallest allowable integer (int) value is " +
              Integer.MIN_VALUE);
  } // main(String[])
} // class FactsAboutIntegers
```

Compile and execute the program and record the value of the minimum integer.

Step 2. Modify the program in Step 1 to find the value for the largest integer. Record what you learn.

Step 3. Since integers are represented in two's complement notation, the maximum and minimum integer values should be one less than some power of two ($2^n - 1$, for some integer n). For what value of n is the value of the maximum integer on your machine equal to $2^n - 1$?

Step 4. Use the information collected in Steps 1 through 3 to determine the number of bits used in Java to represent data of type integer. Explain your answer.

Experiment X1.2: Other integer types

Required file:

- `FactsAboutIntegers.java`

Step 1. Make appropriate modifications to `FactsAboutIntegers` to help you fill in the appropriate values. Note that the base types are <u>byte</u>, <u>short</u>, <u>int</u>, and <u>long</u>. The corresponding maximum values are `Byte.MAX_VALUE`, `Short.MAX_VALUE`, `Integer.MAX_VALUE`, and `Long.MAX_VALUE`.

Note that the number of distinct values is traditionally the number of values that fall between the minimum and maximum value (inclusive).

Minimum and maximum values of various forms of integers

Type	Minimum Value	Maximum Value	# of Distinct Values
byte			
short			
int			
long			

Step 2. What, if anything, can you say about the relationship of the numbers of distinct values (the final column in the table from Step 1)?

Step 3. Given the evidence from Steps 1 and 2, and any other evidence you can develop, determine the number of bits used to represent each of the primitive integer types.

**Experiment X1.3:
Exceeding limits**

Required file:

- `IntegerLimits.java`

In this experiment you will determine how your computer system responds to programs that try to produce integer values that exceed the limits of the particular representation.

Step 1. Make a copy of `IntegerLimits.java`. Here is the code for that program.

```java
import SimpleOutput;
/**
 * Compute some information on what happens when we work near
 * the limits for the values of integers.
 *
 * @author Samuel A. Rebelsky
 * @author Your Name Here
 * @version 1.0 of January 1999
 */
public class IntegerLimits {
  /**
   * The various tests.
   */
  public static void main(String[] args) {
    // The following lines are to be used in a future experiment.
    int i = Integer.MIN_VALUE;
    SimpleOutput out = new SimpleOutput();
    i--;  // Shorthand for i = i - 1
    out.println("When we subtract one from " + Integer.MIN_VALUE +
                " we get " + i);
  } // main(String[])
} // class IntegerLimits
```

Compile and execute `IntegerLimits`. Record the result. What does this suggest?

Step 2. Test the limits of each of the four integer types. For example, to test what happens when we subtract 1 from the smallest byte, we would use

```java
byte i = Byte.MIN_VALUE;
i--;
out.println("When we subtract one from byte " + Byte.MIN_VALUE +
            " we get + " i);
```

Use the results from your program to fill in the following table.

```
Results of subtracting one from smallest value

type      smallest value      one less
byte
short
int
long
```

Step 3. What do those results suggest?

Step 4. What happens if you use

```
i = i - 1;
```

rather than

```
--i;
```

Check the modification on each of the four integer types and record any error messages you receive. What do these messages suggest?

When you have completed your answer, you may wish to check the notes on this problem.

Step 5. Repeat Step 2 using two less than the smallest value. Use the results from your program to fill in the following table.

```
Results of subtracting two from smallest value
```

type	smallest value	two less
byte		
short		
int		
long		

Step 6. Repeat Step 2 using one more than the largest value, two times the largest value, and two times the smallest value. You can use ++ to increment values. You may not be able to fill in all of the spaces in the table for the reasons given in Step 4.

```
Exceeding the smallest and largest values
```

type	smallest	smallest-1	smallest*2	largest	largest+1	largest*2
byte						
short						
int						
long						

Step 7. What do the results of Step 6 suggest?

Step 8. Update `IntegerLimits` to count up from `Integer.MAX_VALUE-10` for twenty steps. You might use

```
int num = Integer.MAX_VALUE - 10;
int i;
out.println("Printing the twenty one values starting with " + num);
for (i = 0; i <= 20; ++i) {
  out.println(num);
  ++num;
} // for
```

Recompile and execute `IntegerLimits`. Summarize and explain the results.

Step 9. Repeat the previous step, counting down from the smallest integer plus ten. Again, summarize and explain your results.

Experiment X1.4: Facts about reals

In this experiment you will investigate the storage of real values on your own particular machine. (In Java, the machine you are on should not matter, but it is still useful to explore the limitations directly.)

Required file:

- `FactsAboutReals.java`

Step 1. Make a copy of `FactsAboutReals.java`, which is given by

```java
import SimpleOutput;
/**
 * A program that prints simple "facts" about real values.
 *
 * @author Samuel A. Rebelsky
 * @author Your Name Here
 * @version 1.0 of September 1998
 */
public class FactsAboutReals {
  /**
   * Print some interesting facts about real numbers in Java.
   */
  public static void main(String[] args) {
    SimpleOutput out = new SimpleOutput();
    out.println("The smallest allowable real (float) value is " +
            Float.MIN_VALUE);
    out.println("The smallest allowable real (double) value is " +
            Double.MIN_VALUE);
  } // main(String[])
} // class FactsAboutReals
```

Compile and execute the program and record the value of the minimum `float` and `double`.

Step 2. Modify the program in Step 1 to find the value for the largest `float` and `double`. Record what you learn.

Step 3. How do the values from Steps 1 and 2 relate?

Step 4. Update your program to compute 1 + the largest value of the particular type. Recompile and execute your program. What do you find? Why might this be?

Experiment X1.5: The limits of reals

Step 1. Add the following lines to `FactsAboutReals`, but do not recompile or execute the program.

```
int i;
float f;
f = 1;
for (i = 0; i < 200; ++i) {
  f = f*100;
  out.println(f);
}
```

What do you expect those lines to do?

Step 2. Recompile and execute `FactsAboutReals`. Record your output. What does this output suggest? Would doing more repetitions help you? If so, try that.

Step 3. Update `FactsAboutReals` so that it squares `f` at each step, rather than multiplying by 100. What do your results suggest?

Step 4. Add the following lines to the loop.

```
g = f + 1;
out.println(g);
```

Recompile and execute `FactsAboutReals`. Record and explain your results.

Step 5. Update `FactsAboutReals` to repeatedly divide by 100, rather than multiplying by 100. What do you expect the results to be? What are the results? Explain any differences.

Step 6. Repeat the previous step, dividing by two rather than 100. What do these results suggest?

Experiment X1.6: Casting

Required file:

- `CastingAbout.java`

Step 1. Here are the beginnings of the `CastingAbout` program, which is used to cast values.

```java
import SimpleOutput;

/**
 * A number of tests of casting in Java.
 *
 * @author Samuel A. Rebelsky
 * @author Your Name Here
 * @version 1.0 of September 1998
 */
public class CastingAbout {
  public static void main(String[] args) {
    SimpleOutput out = new SimpleOutput();
    byte b = 1;
    short s = 2;
    int i = 3;
    long l = 4;
    float f = 1.1;
    double g = 2.3;
  } // main(String[])
} // class CastingAbout
```

Try to compile the program and record any error messages. What do these error messages suggest?

Step 2. Update `CastingAbout` so that none of the variables is initialized. Does this correct the problems from Step 1? Why or why not?

Step 3. Add the following lines to `CastingAbout`.

```
i = 3;
l = i;
out.println("l is " + l);
```

Recompile and execute the program. Record your results. Are they what you would expect? Why or why not?

Step 4. Add the following lines to `CastingAbout`.

```
l = 3;
i = l;
out.println("i is " + i);
```

Recompile and execute the program. Were you successful? Why or why not?

Step 5. Replace the line that reads

```
i = l;
```

with one that reads

```
i = (int) l;
```

Recompile and execute the program. Were you successful? If so, record and explain the output. If not, explain why not.

Step 6. Instead of assigning 3 to 1, assign `Long.MAX_VALUE`. What happens? Why?

Step 7. Add the following lines to `CastingAbout`.

```
l = 3;
f = l;
out.println("f is " + f);
```

Recompile and execute the program. Were you successful? Why or why not? If you were successful, what do the results suggest?

Step 8. Try assigning a float to an integer, instead of vice versa. Note that you may need an explicit coercion. What happens with fractional float values? Float values larger than `Long.MAX_VALUE`? Other special cases?

**Experiment X1.7:
Facts about
characters**

Required files:

- `FactsAboutCharacters.java`

Step 1. Here is the `FactsAboutCharacters.java` program.

```java
import SimpleOutput;
/**
 * A program that prints out some very simple "facts" about
 * characters in Java.
 *
 * @author Samuel A. Rebelsky
 * @author Your name here
 * @version 1.0 of September 1998
 */
public class FactsAboutCharacters {
  /**
   * Print some interesting facts about characters in Java.
   */
  public static void main(String[] args) {
    SimpleOutput out = new SimpleOutput();
    // Build a few characters to consider
    char s1 = 'a';
    char s2 = 'A';
    char s3 = '3';
    char s4 = '.';
    // Print some information on those characters
    out.println("The integer that corresponds to " + s1 + " is " +
                (int) s1);
    out.println("The integer that corresponds to " + s2 + " is " +
                (int) s2);
    out.println("The integer that corresponds to " + s3 + " is " +
                (int) s3);
    out.println("The integer that corresponds to " + s4 + " is " +
                (int) s4);
    // Some alternate information for further experiments.
    out.println("The 100th character is " + (char) 100);
  } // main(String[])
} // class FactsAboutCharacters
```

Compile and execute the program and record the results.

Step 2. Modify the program so that it finds codes for the characters >, b, B, and the space. Summarize your work and findings below.

Step 3. It is also possible to convert codes back to characters by casting them as characters. Modify the program from Step 1 to find the characters immediately before and after the characters a, 2, and Z in the ASCII order. Summarize your modifications and record your findings below.

Step 4. Given the results of the previous steps, does Java use ASCII encoding? Why or why not?

Experiment X1.8: Precedence

Step 1. Create a new program, PrecedenceFun.java, with a main routine that contains the following lines

```
SimpleOutput out = new SimpleOutput();
out.println(1-2-3);
out.println(1-(2-3));
out.println((1-2)-3);
```

What do you expect the output of this program to be?

Step 2. Compile and execute your program, correcting any compilation errors if you discover any. Record the result. Were they what you expected? What did the results suggest?

Step 3. Add the following lines to your `main` routine.

```
out.println(2*2-2);
out.println(2-2*2);
out.println(2*(2-2));
out.println((2-2)*2);
```

What do you expect the new output to be?

Step 4. Compile and execute your program, correcting any compilation errors if you discover any. Record the result. Were they what you expected? What did the results suggest?

Step 5. Add the following lines to your program.

```
out.println(5/2);
out.println(5.0/2.0);
out.println(5.0/2);
out.println(5/2.0);
```

Recompile and execute the program. Record the results. Explain the results.

After you are finished answering this question, read the notes on this problem.

Step 6. Add the following lines to your program.

```
out.println(3/2*1.0);
out.println(1.0*3/2);
```

Recompile and execute the program. Record the results. Explain the results.

After you are finished answering this question, read the notes on this problem.

Experiment X1.9: Concatenating strings and numbers

Required files:

• `BasicComputations.java`

Before you begin, obtain fresh copies of `SimpleInput.java`, `SimpleOutput.java`, and `BasicComputations.java`.

Step 1. After the line that prints the square in `BasicComputations.java`, add a line that reads

```
out.println(val + " + 1 is " + (val+1));
```

What do you think this will do? Will the output be different from that in the previous step? Compile and execute the program to test your hypothesis. Record any discrepancies and suggest why such discrepancies might occur.

After doing so, you may want to look at the notes on this problem.

Step 2. Remove the parentheses from around `(val+1)`. What, if anything, do you think this will do? Compile and execute the program to test your hypothesis. Record any discrepancies and suggest why such discrepancies might occur.

After doing so, you may want to look at the notes on this problem. Reinsert the parentheses when you are done with this step.

Step 3. Remove the parentheses around `val*val` in

```
out.println(val + " squared is " + (val*val));
```

What, if anything, do you think this will do? Compile and execute the program to test your hypothesis. Record any discrepancies and suggest why they might have occurred.

After doing so, you may want to look at the notes on this problem.

Post-Laboratory Problems

Problem X1-A:
Converting cases

Write a program that asks the user for a lowercase letter of the alphabet and then prints its equivalent uppercase letter.

Problem X1-B:
Rounding or truncation?

You may not know whether Java rounds or truncates numbers when it approximates them as <u>float</u>s or <u>double</u>s. If it rounds, it chooses the nearest representable value. If it truncates, it chooses the next smallest (or closest to zero) representable value. Write a program that might help you determine whether Java rounds or truncates.

Problem X1-C:
Rounding or truncation, revisited

Consult the official Java documentation to find an answer to Problem X1-B.

Problem X1-D:
Encryption

Write an encrypting program that converts each character received into the next character in the alphabet. As a special case, convert z into a.

Problem X1-E:
Coercion

Make a table that indicates which types of coercion are done automatically. The row labels should indicate the type coerced to and the column labels should indicate the type coerced from. An entry in the table should be a plus sign if coercion is done automatically and empty otherwise.

Problem X1-F:
Unicode representation

Unlike languages such as C++ which use ASCII representation exclusively, Java also uses Unicode representation of characters. Investigate Unicode and suggest why the designers of Java might have chosen this alternate representation.

Problem X1-G:
Operators and precedence

Find or develop a table of all the valid arithmetic operators in Java and their relative precedence.

Problem X1-H:
Big integers and big reals

As we saw in the experiments, there are limitations to all of the primitive Java data types. What if we want more precision or larger ranges? We could build our own types from Java's primitive types. Or we could use two utility classes, `BigInteger` and `BigFloat`. Find documentation on those two classes and summarize their capabilities.

Notes

Experiment X1.3, Step 3. Since 1 is an <u>int</u>, Java treats the result of i+1 as an <u>int</u>. It is illegal to assign an <u>int</u> to a <u>byte</u> or a <u>short</u> without casting it first.

Experiment X1.8, Step 5. The first result will be 2. The remaining results will be 2.5. In the first case, Java does integer division, since both parts are integers. In the other cases, at least one of the parts is a real number, so Java does real division.

Experiment X1.8, Step 6. The first result will be 1.0. The second result will be 1.5. Since Java does equal-precedence operators left-to-right, in the first case, the 3/2 is treated as integer division, giving 1. In the second case, the 1.0*3 is done first, giving the real number 3.0. Hence, real division is done.

Experiment X1.9, Step 1. Since we're simply concatenating outputs with plus, this should have the same results as in the previous step. Note that the plus sign in quotes is ignored. This is because parts of a string are treated only as parts of a string and not as operators.

Experiment X1.9, Step 2. Strangely enough, if you remove the parentheses, you should not get an error message, but you won't get the output you expect. Why? Because Java adds left to right. This means it reads the expression as *(string+val)+1*. When you add a string and an integer, you get the string that results from concatenating the integer to the end of the string. This gives a new string, to which you concatenate 1. So, the unparenthesized code results in concatenating val and 1 to the end, rather than adding them and then concatenating.

Yes, this is an odd and somewhat subtle problem. However, experience shows that it is likely to be one you'll encounter if you're not careful, and it is best to know about such problems early.

Experiment X1.9, Step 3. In this case, removing the parentheses should not affect the output. Since the normal order of operations says that multiplication is done first, Java implicitly parenthesizes this as string + (val*val).

Session X2: Vectors

In this session, you will explore another of Java's standard classes. The vector class, `java.util.Vector` provides an alternative to arrays for creating collections. The goals of this laboratory are to:

- consider some limitations of arrays;
- motivate dynamic data structures;
- introduce the `java.util.Vector` class;
- compare arrays and vectors;
- show how to determine the types of objects with <u>instanceof</u>
- explore explicit typing of objects, and
- visit some object equivalents of Java's primitive types.

Prerequisite skills

- Objects and classes
- Arrays
- Primitive types and coercion
- Loops

Required files

- `ClassList.java`
- `CourseManager.java`
- `HetArray.java`
- `ModTester.java`
- `SimpleDate.java`
- `SimpleInput.java`
- `SimpleOutput.java`
- `Student.java`
- `VectorMod.java`

Discussion

As you've seen, arrays provide a useful mechanism for collecting different pieces of information and working with the collection. In particular, arrays let you create collections of a specified size, add and remove elements, and refer to elements by number (the index in the array). Arrays provide *homogeneous* collections: all the elements in an array are of the same type. For example, although you can have an array of `int`s and an array of `float`s, you cannot have an array that contains both `int`s and `float`s.

In Experiment X2.1, you will investigate what happens when you try to treat arrays as heterogeneous structures.

Vectors

What are the disadvantages of arrays? We've already seen one. Arrays are homogeneous. What if we want a *heterogeneous* collection, one in which different elements can have different types? It will be difficult to use arrays for such cases.

But even if we want to collection only one type of information, there are drawbacks to using arrays. In particular, arrays require you to prespecify the *capacity,* the number of elements you expect to use. A programmer who is not sure how much space to specify runs the risk of wasting memory by overspecifying the capacity or of running out of space by underestimating the needed capacity. How does one get around this? Traditionally, programmers use *dynamic data structures,* which are data structures whose size can change dynamically while the program is running.

Java includes a number of common programming structures as utility classes for the language. One of these, `java.util.Vector`, is a dynamic data structure quite similar to arrays, but which can grow dynamically. (For a comment on the term "vector", see the notes.) Like arrays, vectors permit you to add and look up elements and to refer to elements by number.

What methods do vectors provide?

- The `size()` method gives the number of elements in the vector.
- The `capacity()` method gives the current capacity of the vector, the number of elements that can be stored in the vector before the vector needs to grow further; vectors often grow in chunks.
- The `addElement(element)` method adds an element at the end of the vector, expanding the vector if necessary.
- The `elementAt(position)` method gets the element at a particular position in the vector. The position should be less than the size of the vector.
- The `setElementAt(element,position)` method replaces an element in the vector. The position must be nonnegative and less than the size of the vector. For example, if the size is 5, the position can be 0, 1, 2, 3, or 4.
- The `removeElementAt(position)` method removes an element from the vector, shifting the remaining elements down one position. This also shrinks the size of the vector by 1.

How do vectors differ from arrays?

- Arrays are a fixed size; vectors grow dynamically as elements are added to them.
- Arrays are homogeneous; vectors are heterogeneous: one vector can store a variety of types of objects.
- Vectors can store only objects; arrays can also store primitive values.
- Arrays provide a default initial value for each element, based on the type (normally 0 for numeric types and <u>null</u> for objects); vectors do not.
- Arrays permit gaps: you can assign to the third element of an array without first assigning to the second element; vectors do not permit gaps: in order to assign a value to the nth element, you must first assign values to the 0th, 1st, 2nd, 3rd, ..., $n - 1$st element.
- The elements in an array do not move; the elements in a vector may shift as other elements are deleted. This shifting is necessary to prevent gaps.

The first two attributes are perhaps the most important. When you create an array, you must know in advance how much space you'll need and what you'll be storing in it. When you create a vector, you can let it grow as the needs of the program dictate, and store whatever is appropriate.

In Experiment X2.2, you will study the basic operations on vectors. In Experiment X2.3, you will consider some of the limits and limitations of vectors.

Other vector capabilities

Vectors also provide a number of methods that are not immediately available for arrays (but that you could probably implement if called upon to do so). These special methods include:

- The `contains(element)` method, which determines whether a vector contains a particular element.
- The `indexOf(element)` method, which returns the first index of an element equal to the specified element. If the element is not in the vector, this method returns -1.
- The `removeElement(element)` method, which removes an element from the vector.

As you can tell, such methods are useful when you want to get information about the collection. For example, if we built a collection of students (e.g., for a class list), we might want to check whether a particular student is in that collection. In effect, these are similar to the methods provided by `java.util.Hashtable`, except that there is not a separate key for each value. In some situations, it makes more sense to build a table of objects without creating separate keys.

For example, here is a class used to implement a list of students enrolled in a particular course.

```
import java.util.Vector;
import Student;
```

```
/**
 * A list of students enrolled in a particular course.  Developed as
 * an illustration of a use of vectors.
 *
 * @author Samuel A. Rebelsky
 * @version 1.0 of January 1999
 */
public class ClassList {

  // +--------+---------------------------------------------------
  // | Fields |
  // +--------+

  /** The members of the class.  */
  protected Vector members;
  /** The name of the class.  */
  protected String name;

  // +--------------+---------------------------------------------
  // | Constructors |
  // +--------------+

  /**
   * Build a new class list, specifying the name of the class.
   */
  public ClassList(String name) {
    this.name = name;
    this.members = new Vector();
  } // ClassList(String)

  // +-----------+--------------------------------------------------
  // | Modifiers |
  // +-----------+

  /**
   * Add a student to the class list.  Does not add a student
   * who is already in the class.
   */
  public void addStudent(Student student) {
    if (this.members.contains(student)) {
      // Already in the class, do nothing.
    }
    else {
      this.members.addElement(student);
    }
  } // addStudent(Student)

  /**
   * Remove a student from the class.
   */
  public void removeStudent(Student student) {
    this.members.removeElement(student);
  } // removeStudent(Student)

  /**
   * Set the grade of a student in the class.
   */
```

```
public void setGrade(Student student, int grade) {
  // Look up the index of the student.
  int index = this.members.indexOf(student);
  // Declare a member of the class.
  Student member;

  // Did we find the student?
  if (index != -1) {
    member = (Student) this.members.elementAt(index);
    member.setGrade(grade);
  } // if the student is in the class
} // setGrade(Student, int)

// +-----------+-------------------------------------------
// | Extractors |
// +-----------+

/**
 * Get the grade assigned to a particular student.  Returns
 * -1 if there is no such student in the class.
 */
public int getGrade(Student student) {
  // Look up the index of the student.
  int index = this.members.indexOf(student);
  // Declare a member of the class.
  Student member;
  // Did we find the student?
  if (index != -1) {
    member = (Student) this.members.elementAt(index);
    return member.getGrade();
  } // if the student is in the class
  else { // the student is not in the class
    return -1;
  } // the student is not in the class
} // getGrade(Student)

/**
 * Generate a string listing the members of the class.
 */
public String toString() {
  return this.name + ": " + this.members.toString();
} // toString()

} // class ClassList
```

Note that most of these methods were relatively trivial to write, as they could rely on the corresponding methods in java.util.Vector. The most complex methods are setGrade and getGrade. It may seem odd that each is passed a Student, and then modifies or uses a different Student. However, the Student passed as an argument, is used only to match the student record stored in the class list. Success in finding the actual student depends on the operation of the equals method of the Student class.

The following is the corresponding class used to implement the students in the course.

```
/**
 * A record for a student in a particular class.
 *
 * @author Samuel A. Rebelsky
 * @version 1.0 of January 1999
 */
public class Student {
  // +--------+----------------------------------------------------
  // | Fields |
  // +--------+

  /** The student's first name. */
  protected String firstName;
  /** The student's last name.  */
  protected String lastName;
  /**
   * The student's current grade.  Set to -1 if the student does
   * not have a grade.
   */
  protected int grade;

  // +-------------+---------------------------------------------
  // | Constructors |
  // +-------------+

  /**
   * Create a new student record.
   */
  public Student(String firstName, String lastName) {
    this.firstName = firstName;
    this.lastName = lastName;
    this.grade = -1;
  } // Student(String)

  // +----------+---------------------------------------------
  // | Modifiers |
  // +----------+

  /**
   * Set the grade of a student.
   */
  public void setGrade(int newgrade) {
    this.grade = newgrade;
  } // setGrade()

  // +-----------+---------------------------------------------
  // | Extractors |
  // +-----------+

  /**
   * Determine if this student is the same as another student.
   * Relies on names to make this determination.  (It may also
   * be appropriate to rely on identification number or something
   * else.)
   */
  public boolean equals(Student other) {
```

```
      return (this.firstName.equals(other.firstName) &&
             this.lastName.equals(other.lastName));
   } // equals(Student)

   /**
    * Determine if this student is the same as another object.
    * That object must be a student.
    */
   public boolean equals(Object other) {
     if (other instanceof Student) {
       return this.equals((Student) other);
     }
     else {
       return false;
     }
   } // equals(Object)

   /**
    * Get the grade assigned to the particular student.  Returns
    * -1 if the student does not yet have an assigned grade.
    */
   public int getGrade() {
     return this.grade;
   } // getGrade()

   /**
    * Generate a string giving the name of the student.
    */
   public String toString() {
     return this.firstName + " " + this.lastName;
   } // toString()

} // class Student
```

In Experiment X2.4, you will test these new methods. In Experiment X2.5, you will use and modify the ClassList and Student classes.

Determining the class of vector elements

Vectors are heterogeneous. This means that each element of the vector may have a different class. This isn't really a problem if all one needs to do is print elements, or find elements, in which case we know the type. What if you don't know the type of an element, and want to do different things depending on the type? For example, let's consider how one might scan through the elements of a vector, capitalizing the strings, and resetting each date to the first of the month. In pseudocode, this is not difficult.

```
for i = 0 to the number of element in the vector
  e = vec.elementAt(i)
  if e is a string, then
    vec.setElementAt(e.toUpperCase(), i)
  else if e is a date, then
    vec.setElementAt(makeNewDate(e), i)
```

How does one write this in Java? Fortunately, Java includes an <u>instanceof</u> operator that does the same thing as "is a" in the pseudocode above.

The following is the Java equivalent.

```
int i; // A counter
String s; // A string in the vector
SimpleDate d; // A date in the vector
for(i = 0; i < vec.size(); ++i) {
  // Replace each string by its uppercase equivalent
  if (vec.elementAt(i) instanceof String) {
    s = (String) vec.elementAt(i);
    vec.setElementAt(e.toUpperCase(), i);
  } // it's a string
  // Replace each date by the first of the month
  else if (vec.elementAt(i) instanceof SimpleDate) {
    d = (SimpleDate) vec.elementAt(i);
    vec.setElementAt(new SimpleDate(d.getYear(), d.getMonth(), 0),
                     i);
  } // it's a date
} // for
```

Note that we were able to cast the elements of the vector, just as we can cast primitive types. What happens if we cast elements incorrectly? You will explore that further in Experiment X2.6.

Storing primitive values in vectors

We've seen that it's possible to use vectors to store a wide variety of objects, including strings, dates, and student records. What if we want to store primitive types, such as `int`, <u>float</u>, or <u>boolean</u>. It turns out that vectors can only store objects, and not primitive types.

What if we'd like to create a collection of numbers, characters, or boolean values? One option would be to implement our own `IntVector`, `CharVector`, and such. However, this will be time consuming, and the resultant classes will not be heterogeneous.

Fortunately, Java provides a solution to our problem. For every primitive type, there is a corresponding class. These primitive classes include `java.lang.Integer` (for `int`), `java.lang.Byte`, `java.lang.Short`, `java.lang.Long`, `java.lang.Float`, `java.lang.Double`, `java.lang.Character` (for <u>char</u>), and `java.lang.Boolean`. Because they are part of the `java.lang` package, you do not need to explicitly <u>import</u> these classes.

How do you create one of these objects? You pass in the corresponding value. For example, to create the `Integer` with value 1, you could use `new Integer(1)`. Similarly, to create the `Character` with value 'z', you would use <u>new</u> `Character('z')`.

How do you extract the primitive values from these types? For the `Character` class, you can use the `charValue` method. For example

```
Character charobj;
char ch;
...
ch = charobj.charValue();
```

For the `Boolean`, you can use the `booleanValue` method. For all of the numeric types, you can use one of `byteValue`, `shortValue`, `intValue`, `longValue`, `floatValue`, or `doubleValue`. You can also use these methods to convert between types (e.g., to get a `long` from a `Double`).

You will work with these primitive objects in Experiment X2.7.

Experiments

**Experiment X2.1:
Heterogeneity
and arrays**

Required files:

- `HetArray.java`
- `SimpleDate.java`

Step 1. Make a copy of `HetArray.java`. Here is the code for that class:

```java
import SimpleOutput;

/**
 * An experiment with trying to use arrays heterogeneously.
 *
 * @author Samuel A. Rebelsky
 * @author Your Name Here
 * @version 1.0 of January 1999
 */
public class HetArray {
  /**
   * Here are our experiments.
   */
  public static void main(String[] args) {
    // Set up primary variables
    SimpleOutput out = new SimpleOutput();
    float[] stuff = new float[5];
    int i = Integer.MAX_VALUE - 3;
    // Fill in a few elements of the array
    stuff[0] = (float) 3.4;
    stuff[1] = i;
    stuff[2] = Integer.MAX_VALUE;
    // Print out some information
    out.println("i is " + i);
    out.println("stuff[0] is " + stuff[0]);
    out.println("stuff[1] is " + stuff[1]);
    out.println("stuff[2] is " + stuff[2]);
    // Treat the elements as integers
    out.println("The integer version of stuff[0] is " + (int)
            stuff[0]);
    out.println("The integer version of stuff[1] is " + (int)
            stuff[1]);
    out.println("The integer version of stuff[2] is " + (int)
            stuff[2]);
  } // main(String[])
} // class HetArray
```

What do you expect the output of this program to be? Note that the maximum integer value is 2147483647.

Step 2. Compile and execute `HetArray`. Record the output. Is it the same as what you expected? Explain the output.

If you are somewhat confused by the output, you may want to read the notes on this problem.

Step 3. Note that once we've stored values in the array, there is no obvious way to tell what type of value we stored, since Java treats them all as _float_s. How might you keep track of the type?

Once you've thought about the problem, you may want to read the notes on this problem.

Step 4. Replace the line that reads

```
float[] stuff = new float[5];
```

with one that reads

```
float[] stuff = new int[5];
```

What do you expect will happen when you try to compile and run the program?

Step 5. Compile the changed program. What errors, if any, are reported during compilation or execution? What does this suggest? After answering this question, restore the line you changed in the previous step.

Step 6. Extend `HetArray` so that it imports `SimpleDate`. (If you don't already have a copy of `SimpleDate.java`, make a copy and compile it.) Then add the following lines to the `main` method of `HetArray`.

```
stuff[3] = new SimpleDate(1987,8,29);
...
out.println("stuff[3] is " + stuff[3]);
...
out.println("The integer version of stuff[3] is " + (int) stuff[3]);
```

What effect do you think these lines will have?

Step 7. Try to recompile and execute `HetArray`. What errors, if any, are reported during compilation or execution? What does this suggest?

After writing your answer, you may want to check the notes on this problem.

Experiment X2.2: Vector basics

Required files:

- `SimpleDate.java`

Step 1. Create a new class, `VectorTester`, with a `main` method that includes the following code. (You will also need to make sure that `Vector-Tester` imports `java.util.Vector`.)

```
// Step 1.  Build a new vector and print some information.
SimpleOutput out = new SimpleOutput();
Vector vec = new Vector();
out.println("The size of a new vector is: " + vec.size());
out.println("The capacity of a new vector is: " + vec.capacity());
```

Compile and execute `VectorTester`. Record the results.

Step 2. Add the following lines to the `main` method of `VectorTester`.

```
// Step 2. Add an element to the vector.
vec.addElement("Alpha");
out.println("After adding one element, the size of the vector is: "
            + vec.size());
out.println("After adding one element, the capacity of the vector
            is: " + vec.capacity());
out.println("The initial element of the vector is: "
            + vec.elementAt(0));
```

Compile and execute `VectorTester`. Record the results.

Step 3. If you have not done so already, make a copy of `SimpleDate.java`. Compile `SimpleDate`. Add the following lines to the `main` method of `VectorTester`.

```
// Step 3.  Add another element.
vec.addElement(new SimpleDate(1964,6,17));
out.println("Added element " + vec.elementAt(1));
out.println("The size of the vector is now: "
            + vec.size());
out.println("The capacity of the vector is now: "
            + vec.capacity());
```

Recompile and execute `VectorTester`. Record the results. What do these results suggest?

Step 4. Add the following line to the `main` method of `VectorTester`.

```
// Step 4.  Print the elements.
out.println("The elements of the vector are: " + vec.toString());
```

Recompile and execute `VectorTester`. Record the results. What does this suggest?

After entering your answer, you may wish to examine the notes on this problem.

Step 5. Add the following lines to the end of the `main` method of `Vector-Tester`.

```
// Step 5.  Change element 1.
vec.setElementAt("Zebra", 1);
out.println("The elements of the vector are now: " + vec.toString());
```

Recompile and execute `VectorTester`. Record the results. What does this suggest?

Step 6. Add the following lines to the end of the `main` method of `Vector-Tester`. What do you expect the output to be?

```
// Step 6. Add a few more elements.
vec.addElement("Aardvark");
vec.addElement("Piano");
out.println("The elements of the vector are now " + vec.toString());
```

Step 7. Add the following lines to the end of the `main` method of `Vector-Tester`.

```
// Step 7. Delete element 1.
vec.removeElementAt(1);
out.println("Deleted element 1");
out.println("The elements of the vector are now " + vec.toString());
out.println("Element 1 of the vector is now " +
            vec.elementAt(1));
out.println("The size of the vector is now " + vec.size());
```

What do you expect the output to be? (Do not compile and run the program. Rather, try to predict the output.)

Step 8. Compile and execute the modified `VectorTester`. Record the output. What does this output suggest?

After answering this question, you may wish to look at the notes on this problem.

Experiment X2.3: Testing limits

Note: In this experiment, you will see what happens when you start reaching the limits of the size of the vector or use the vector in ways other than specified.

Step 1. Create a new file, `NewVectorTester.java` with a `main` method that contains the following lines.

```
// Step 1.  Build a new vector and add some elements.
SimpleOutput out = new SimpleOutput();
Vector vec = new Vector();
vec.addElement("World");
vec.addElement("Wide");
vec.addElement("Web");
out.println("Original vector: " + vec.toString());
out.println("  Capacity: " + vec.capacity());
vec.setElementAt("Web", 2);
out.println("Fixed second element: " + vec.toString());
```

Compile and execute `NewVectorTester`. Record the results.

Step 2. Add the following lines to the end of the `main` method of `New-VectorTester`.

```
// Step 2. Add element 3.  Is this legal?
vec.setElementAt("WWW", 3);
out.println("Modified vector: " + vec.toString());
out.println("  New size: " + vec.size());
```

What do you expect to happen when the modified program is executed?

Step 3. Compile and execute the modified `NewVectorTester`. Record any results or errors. What do the results or errors suggest?

After entering an answer, you may wish to look at the notes on this problem. You should also comment out any erroneous code.

Step 4. Add the following lines to the end of the `main` method of `New-VectorTester`.

```
// Step 4. Delete and then set element 2.  Is this legal?
vec.removeElementAt(0);
vec.setElementAt("WWW", 2);
```

What do you expect to happen when the modified program is executed?

Step 5. Compile and execute the modified `NewVectorTester`. Record any results or errors. What do the results or errors suggest?

After entering an answer, you may wish to look at the notes on this problem. You should also comment out any erroneous code.

Step 6. Add some lines to `main` that fill the vector to its capacity. (Don't overfill the vector! If the vector can hold only ten elements, put ten elements total in the vector, not ten more elements.) Test your code. Summarize the code you wrote here:

After writing and testing the code, you may want to look at the notes on this problem.

Step 7. Add a line to `main` to print the filled vector. Compile and execute the modified `NewVectorTester` and record the results.

Step 8. Add the following lines to the end of the `main` method of `NewVectorTester`.

```
vec.addElement("Overflow");
out.println("Overfilled vector: " + vec.toString());
out.println("  Capacity: " + vec.capacity());
```

What do you expect to happen?

Step 9. Recompile and execute the modified `NewVectorTester`. Record the results. Were they what you expected? What do these results suggest?

Step 10. Add the following lines to the end of the `main` method of `NewVectorTester`.

```
// Step 10.  Delete a few elements.
vec.removeElementAt(0);
vec.removeElementAt(0);
vec.removeElementAt(0);
vec.removeElementAt(0);
out.println("Shrunk vector: " + vec.toString());
out.println("  Capacity: " + vec.capacity());
```

What do you expect to happen?

Step 11. Recompile and execute the modified `NewVectorTester`. Record the results. Were they what you expected? What do these results suggest?

After recording your answer, you may wish to look at the notes on this problem.

Step 12. Add the following lines to the end of the `main` method of `NewVectorTester`.

```
// Step 12.  Delete the last element.
vec.removeElementAt(vec.size());
out.println("Modified vector: " + vec.toString());
```

Recompile and execute the modified `NewVectorTester`. Record the results. Were they what you expected? What do these results suggest?

After recording your answer, you may wish to look at the notes on this problem.

Experiment X2.4: Additional vector methods

Step 1. Create a new file, `NameGame.java`, with a `NameGame` class containing a `main` method with the following lines.

```
// Prepare for writing output.
SimpleOutput out = new SimpleOutput();
// Build a vector to play with.
Vector names = new Vector();
// Add some names to the vector.
vec.addElement("John");
vec.addElement("Jane");
vec.addElement("Jack");
vec.addElement("Janet");
vec.addElement("John");
vec.addElement("Jane");
vec.addElement("John");
out.println("Original vector: " + vec.toString());
```

Compile and execute `NameGame`. Record the output.

Step 2. Add the following lines to the `main` method of `NameGame`.

```
// Step 2.  See if Jan is in the list.
if (names.contains("Jan")) {
  out.println("Jan is in the name list.");
}
else {
  out.println("Jan is not in the name list.");
}
```

What do you expect the new output to be?

Step 3. Compile and execute the modified `NameGame`. Record and explain the output.

Step 4. Add the following lines to the `main` method of `NameGame`.

```
// Step 4.  See if Jane is in the list.
if (names.contains("Jane")) {
  out.println("Jane is in the name list.");
}
else {
  out.println("Jane is not in the name list.");
}
```

What do you expect the new output to be?

Step 5. Compile and execute the modified `NameGame`. Record and explain the output.

Step 6. Add the following lines to the `main` method of `NameGame`.

```
// Step 6.  Change an instance of "John" to "Jonathan".
int johnsIndex = names.indexOf("John");
if (johnsIndex != -1) {
  names.setElementAt("Jonathan", johnsIndex);
}
out.println("After changing 'John' to 'Jonathan': " +
            names.toString());
```

What do you expect the new output to be?

Step 7. Compile and execute the modified `NameGame`. Record and explain the output.

Step 8. Add the following lines to the `main` method of `NameGame`.

```
// Step 8.  Delete Janet.
 names.removeElement("Janet");
 out.println("After deleting Janet: " + names.toString());
```

What do you expect the new output to be?

Step 9. Compile and execute the modified `NameGame`. Record and explain the output.

Step 10. Add the following lines to the `main` method of `NameGame`.

```
// Step 10.  Delete John.
 names.removeElement("John");
 out.println("After deleting John: " + names.toString());
```

What do you expect the new output to be?

Step 11. Compile and execute the modified `NameGame`. Record and explain the output.

Experiment X2.5: Course management

Required files:

- `ClassList.java`
- `CourseManager.java`
- `Student.java`

Step 1. Make copies of `ClassList.java`, `CourseManager.java`, and `Student.java`. Here is the definition of `CourseManager.java`.

```java
import SimpleOutput;    // So we can print output
import Student;         // So we can create students
import ClassList;       // So we can list students

/**
 * A simple test of course management.
 *
 * @author Samuel A. Rebelsky
 * @author Your Name Here
 * @version 1.0 of January 1999
 */
public class CourseManager {
  /**
   * Manage the class.
   */
  public static void main(String[] args) {
    // Prepare to print output.
    SimpleOutput out = new SimpleOutput();
    // Set up the course.
    ClassList cs1 = new ClassList("CS1");
```

```
   // Add some students to the class.
   cs1.addStudent(new Student("Sam", "Rebelsky"));
   cs1.addStudent(new Student("Julie", "Dunn"));
   cs1.addStudent(new Student("Susan", "Hartman"));
   cs1.addStudent(new Student("Henry", "Walker"));
   // Print out the class list
   out.println(cs1.toString());
 } // main(String[])
} // class CourseManager
```

What do you expect the output to be?

Step 2. Compile the three files and execute `CourseManager`. Record the output. Was it what you expected? Why or why not?

Step 3. Add the following lines to the end of the `main` method of `Course-Manager`.

```
// Step 3.  Add a duplicate entry.
cs1.addStudent(new Student("Sam", "Rebelsky"));
out.println("After adding Sam Rebelsky: " + cs1.toString());
```

What do you expect the new output to be?

Step 4. Compile and execute the modified `CourseManager`. Are the results what you expected? Why or why not?

After entering your answer, you may wish to check the notes on this problem.

Step 5. Add the following lines to the end of the `main` method of `Course-Manager`.

```
// Step 5.  Delete an entry.
cs1.deleteStudent(new Student("Julie", "Dunn"));
out.println("After deleting Julie Dunn: " + cs1.toString());
```

What do you expect the new output to be?

Step 6. Compile and execute the modified `CourseManager`. Are the results what you expected? Why or why not?

After entering your answer, you may wish to check the notes on this problem.

Step 7. In the code added in Step 5, why did we create a new student when we were actually deleting the student?

After entering your answer, you may wish to check the notes on this problem.

Step 8. Add the following lines to the end of the `main` method of `Course-Manager`.

```
// Step 8.  Change a grade.
cs1.setGrade(new Student("Henry", "Walker"), 95);
out.println("Henry Walker's grade is now: " +
          cs1.getGrade("new Student("Henry", "Walker")));
```

Compile and execute the modified `CourseManager`. Record the results.

Step 9. Add the following lines to the end of the `main` method of `Course-Manager`.

```
// Step 9.  Try to change a grade.
Student samr = new Student("Sam", "Rebelsky");
samr.setGrade(80);
out.println("Sam Rebelsky's grade is now: " + cs1.getGrade(samr));
```

Compile and execute the modified `CourseManager`. Record and explain the results.

After recording your answer, you may wish to look at the notes on this problem

Experiment X2.6: Modifying vector elements

Required files:

- `ModTester.java`
- `SimpleDate.java`
- `VectorMod.java`

Before you begin, make copies of `ModTester.java`, `SimpleDate.java`, and `VectorMod.java`. Compile the three classes.

Step 1. `VectorMod.java` is a collection of methods to modify the elements of vectors. Here is the code for that class.

```java
import SimpleDate;
import java.util.Vector;

/**
 * Methods for affecting the elements of a vector.  Ideally, these
 * would be provided by extending Vector class, but we may not yet
 * have the appropriate skills for doing so
 *
 * Warning!  Some methods in the class are initially erroneous.
 *
 * @author Samuel A. Rebelsky
 * @author Your Name Here
 * @version 1.0 of January 1999
 */
public class VectorMod {
  /**
   * Put all of the strings in the vector into all caps.
   */
  public void allCaps(Vector vec) {
    int i;      // Counter variable for loop
    String s; // A string found in the vector
    // Step through the elements of the vector
    for(i = 0; i < vec.size(); ++i) {
      // if the ith element is a string
      if (vec.elementAt(i) instanceof String) {
        // then put the string into upper case
        s = (String) vec.elementAt(i);
        vec.setElementAt(s.toUpperCase(), i);
      } // if it's a string
```

```
      } // for each element of the vector
    } // allCaps(Vector)

    /**
     * Reset all of the dates in the vector to the beginning of
     * the month.
     */
    public void firstOfMonth(Vector vec) {
      int i;          // Counter variable for the loop
      SimpleDate d;   // A date found in the vector
      // Step through the elements of the vector
      for (i=0; i < vec.size(); ++i) {
        d = (SimpleDate) vec.elementAt(i);
        vec.setElementAt(new SimpleDate(d.getYear(),d.getMonth(),1),
                         i);
      } // for each element of the vector
    } // firstOfMonth(Vector)
} // class VectorMod
```

Summarize the methods that this class provides.

Step 2. `ModTester.java` is a program intended to test `VectorMod.java`.
Here is the code for `ModTester.java`.

```
import VectorMod;
import SimpleDate;
import java.util.Vector;

/**
 * Test VectorMod's methods for modifying the elements of vectors.
 *
 * @author Samuel A. Rebelsky
 * @author Your Name Here
 * @version 1.0 of January 1999
 */
public class ModTester {
  /**
   * The tests.
   */
  public static void main(String[] args) {
    // Prepare for generating output
    SimpleOutput out = new SimpleOutput();
    // Prepare for modifying vectors
    VectorMod mod = new VectorMod();
    // Build a vector to modify
    Vector vec = new Vector();
```

```
      // Fill in some elements
      vec.addElement("Hello");
      vec.addElement("Hi");
      vec.addElement(new SimpleDate(1995,7,31));
      vec.addElement(new SimpleDate(1998,8,6));
      vec.addElement("hello");
      // Print out the vector.
      out.println("*** Original vector ***");
      out.println(vec.toString());
      // Convert the strings in the vector to upper case
      mod.allCaps(vec);
      // Print out the modified vector.
      out.println("*** After converting strings to upper case ***");
      out.println(vec.toString());
   } // main(String[])
} // class ModTester
```

What do you expect the output of this class to be?

Step 3. Execute `ModTester` and record the output.

Step 4. Consider the lines of the `allCaps` method of `VectorMod` that read

```
if (vec.elementAt(i) instanceof String) {
  s = (String) vec.elementAt(i);
```

The explicit cast of `vec.elementAt(i)` to string may seem unnecessary, since we've just determined that it is a string. What do you think will happen if we remove the case, and just write

```
if (vec.elementAt(i) instanceof String) {
  s = vec.elementAt(i);
```

Try making the change and recompiling `VectorMod`. Explain what happens.

After writing down your answer, you may want to read the notes on this problem.

Step 5. Many programmers try to shorten their code, using one compound statement rather than many small commands. For example, consider the following lines from the `allCaps` method of `VectorMod`.

```
s = (String) vec.elementAt(i);
vec.setElementAt(s.toUpperCase(), i);
```

One might try to express these steps more succinctly as

```
vec.setElementAt(vec.elementAt(i).toUpperCase(), i);
```

However, there is a problem with this code. What do you think the problem is? After writing down an answer, try making this modification to the `all-Caps` method of `VectorMod`. What do you observe?

You may wish to compare your answer to the notes on this problem.

Step 6. Add the following lines to the end of the `main` method of `Mod-Tester`.

```
// Reset dates to the start of the month.
mod.firstOfMonth(vec);
// Print out the modified vector.
out.println("*** After resetting dates ***");
out.println(vec.toString());
```

What do you think will happen when you run the modified `ModTester`?

Step 7. Recompile and execute the modified `ModTester`. What happens? Explain the results. Note that you may also need to consider the code for `firstOfMonth`.

After writing down your answer, you may wish to consult the notes on this problem.

Step 8. Correct the problem with `firstOfMonth`. Make sure to test your updated code. Summarize the modifications here.

Experiment X2.7: Primitive objects

Step 1. Create a new file, `NumberFun.java`, containing a `NumberFun` class with a `main` method with the following lines.

```
// Prepare for writing output.
SimpleOutput out = new SimpleOutput();
// Create a set of numbers.
Vector numbers = new Vector();
```

Compile and execute `NumberFun`. The program should have no output, but it is useful to make sure that you have it correct to this point.

Step 2. Let's see what happens when we try to add primitive types to the vector. Add the following lines to the `main` method of `NumberFun`.

```
// Step 2.  Add some primitive values to the vector.
numbers.addElement('x');
numbers.addElement(25);
numbers.addElement(3.1415);
out.println("The vector is now: " + numbers.toString());
```

Do you expect the modified `NumberFun` to have an error at compile time, an error at run time, or no error at all? Why?

Step 3. Attempt to compile and execute the modified `NumberFun`. Record and explain any output or errors.

Correct any errors by commenting out erroneous lines.

Step 4. Add the following lines to the `main` method of `NumberFun`.

```
// Step 4.  Add some primitive objects to the vector.
numbers.addElement(new Character('x');
numbers.addElement(new Integer(25));
numbers.addElement(new Double(3.1415));
out.println("After adding primitive objects, the vector contains: " +
          numbers.toString());
```

Do you expect the modified `NumberFun` to have an error at compile time, an error at run time, or no error at all? Why?

Step 5. Attempt to compile and execute the modified `NumberFun`. Record and the output.

Step 6. Add the following lines to the end of the `main` method of `Number-Fun`.

```
// Step 6.  Play with integers.
for(int i = 0; i < numbers.size(); ++i) {
  if (numbers.elementAt(i) instanceof Integer) {
    out.println("Element " + i + " is an integer.");
    out.print("One plus that element: " +
    out.println(1 + ((Integer) numbers.elementAt(i)).intValue());
  } // if
} // for
```

Compile and execute the modified `NumberFun`. Record the new output. What does that output suggest?

Step 7. Add the following lines to the end of the `main` method of `Number-Fun`.

```
// Step 7.  Play with numbers.
for(int i = 0; i < numbers.size(); ++i) {
  if (numbers.elementAt(i) instanceof Number) {
    out.println("Element " + i + " is a number.");
    out.print("  One plus that element: " +
    out.println(1 + ((Number) numbers.elementAt(i)).intValue());
    out.print("  Two times that element: " +
    out.println(2 * ((Number) numbers.elementAt(i)).doubleValue());
  } // if
} // for
```

What do you observe about this code?

Step 8. Compile and execute the modified `NumberFun`. Record the new output. What does that output suggest?

Step 9. Add the following lines to the end of the `main` method of `Number-Fun`.

```
// Step 9.  Play with integers.
for(int i = 0; i < numbers.size(); ++i) {
  if (numbers.elementAt(i) instanceof Number) {
    out.println("Element " + i + " is a number.");
    out.print("One plus that element: " +
    out.println(1 + ((Number) numbers.elementAt(i)));
  } // if
} // for
```

What do you expect the output to be?

Step 10. Compile and execute the modified `NumberFun`. Record the new output. What does that output suggest?

Post-Laboratory Problems

**Problem X2-A:
Default size of
vectors**

Java purports to be platform independent. While it is certainly clear that some aspects of Java, such as the number of bits used for primitive types, are tightly specified and therefore precisely uniform across implementations, others may be less well specified. Look through whatever Java documentation you can find and determine if there is a specified default size and growth rate for Java vectors.

**Problem X2-B:
Implement sets**

When writing programs, it is often useful to have a Set class. Such Sets are a lot like mathematical sets: you can add elements, remove elements, and test for containment. However, a set contains at most, one copy of any element. Using vectors, implement an IntegerSet class that permits programmers to work with sets of integers. Your class should support the following methods:

- size, which gives the number of elements in the set;
- contains(integer), which determines whether the set contains a particular element;
- addNumber(integer), which adds a number to the set (if the number isn't already there);
- removeNumber(integer), which removes a number from the set (if the number is already there);
- smallest, which returns the smallest element in the set.

**Problem X2-C:
Other vector
capabilities**

We have covered only some of the methods provided by java.util.Vector. Find documentation for this class and identify its other methods. For each method, suggest a programming problem that might require the method.

**Problem X2-D:
Implementing
vectors**

Suppose that there were no java.util.Vector class. You might find it advisable to implement your own. Implement a Vector class that supports addElement, elementAt, setElementAt, and removeElementAt. You need not worry about what to do when there are errors, although you can print an error message if you'd like.

**Problem X2-E:
Printing arrays**

Java permits you to print vectors through use of the toString method. Try to determine if there is a way to print out arrays. If not, write a method that one might use to print out arrays. This is a difficult problem, as there are many different kinds of arrays; you may want to limit yourself to printing out arrays of integers.

**Problem X2-F:
A grading
program**

Use the `ClassList` and `Student` classes to provide a more comprehensive grading program. Your program should allow the instructor to

- add students to the class;
- remove students from the class;
- assign a grade for the midterm;
- assign a grade for the final;
- assign a grade for homework;
- look up each grade for each student (midterm, final, homework);
- assign a percentage for each grade component (midterm, final, homework);
- compute a numeric grade for each student; and
- anything else you deem appropriate.

It is likely that you will need to add new fields to the `Student` class (such as separate fields for each component of the grade) and add methods to the `ClassList` and `Student` classes.

Notes

Vectors. Many computer scientists object to the use of the term vector to describe the dynamic data structure that resembles arrays. There are a number of different objections, including the lack of standardization of the name (different languages and different researchers attach different meanings to "vector" as a data structure); the mismatch between the data type and the traditional mathematical or physical meaning of the term; and even the particular's of Java's implementation.

Experiment X2.1, Step 2. As you may recall, floating point numbers are often approximate representations. Hence, when we convert from `Integer.MAX_VALUE-3` (2147483644) to float and back again, Java approximates the result as `Integer.MAX_VALUE`.

Experiment X2.1, Step 3. As the problem says, there is no particularly good way to keep track of the type once you've stored the value in the array, because Java does not keep track of the value. One possibility would be to create a second array and store an indication of type in the second array of booleans, `isFloat`. That is, if the value stored in a place in `stuff` is an integer, you might store <u>false</u> in the corresponding place in `isFloat`; if the value stored in the first array is a <u>float</u>, you might store <u>true</u> in the corresponding place in `isFloat`. For example,

```
stuff[0] = (float) 3.5;    isFloat[0] = true;
stuff[1] = i;              isFloat[1] = false;
```

Of course, this does not do anything about the lack of accuracy.

Experiment X2.1, Step 7. While Java permits you to assign integers to <u>float</u>s because it knows how to coerce integers, it does not permit you to assign arbitrary objects to <u>float</u>s. Your compiler should have given you a message to that effect.

Experiment X2.2, Step 4. As this example suggests, the `java.util.Vector` class provides a mechanism for building string representations of vectors, which makes it possible (one might even say easy) to print vectors. In fact, most classes provide a `toString` method for this purpose. Can you find a way to print arrays?

Experiment X2.2, Step 8. Since the whole vector contains the same elements in the same order, except for the deleted element, and the previous element 2 is now element 1, it is clear that the remaining elements shifted in the vector.

Experiment X2.3, Step 3. You are only allowed to set an element of a vector if you've already placed an element there (typically, using `addElement`).

Experiment X2.3, Step 5. Deleting an element shrinks the size of the vector. Hence, although there was previously an element with index 2, after the deletion there is not, so the replacement is illegal.

Experiment X2.3, Step 6. Here is one possible set of instructions, designed to work in a variety of cases.

```
while (vec.size() < vec.capacity()) {
  vec.addElement("Added");
  out.println("Size " + vec.size());
  out.println("Capacity: " + vec.capacity());
}
```

Experiment X2.3, Step 11. Although vectors expand when you add too many elements, they do not shrink again when you remove elements from them (or at least they don't shrink in typical cases).

Experiment X2.3, Step 12. Just as it is illegal to add elements beyond the end of the vector, it is also illegal to delete them. Remember that the last valid index is one less than the size of the vector!

Experiment X2.5, Step 4. Since "Sam Rebelsky" is already in the class, adding him again should make no difference.

Experiment X2.5, Step 6. We've deleted a student, so that student no longer appears in the class.

Experiment X2.5, Step 7. In order to look for a student, we need a `Student` object. Since we don't have an existing one, we must create a new one. Fortunately, the `Student` class's `equals` method does not try to ensure that two `Student`s are precisely the same object; rather, it just verifies that they have the same name.

Experiment X2.5, Step 9. While we've set the grade of `samr`, a separate `Student` object with name "Sam Rebelsky" is stored in `cs1`. Changes to one do not affect the other.

Experiment X2.5, Step 10. The reasoning is similar to the previous problem. While we've used `samr` to find the student whose grade to set, we've set the grade of a separate `Student` object with name "Sam Rebelsky" is stored in `cs1`. Changes to one do not affect the other.

Experiment X2.6, Step 4. The designers of Java wanted programmers to be particularly careful when assigning and using objects. In particular, when using a general `Object` as a particular type of object, you *must* cast it to that type of object, even if it is obvious what type the object has.

Experiment X2.6, Step 5. This is the same issue as the previous problem. Because the code does not explicitly cast `elementAt(i)` to a string, Java will not treat it as a string, and therefore won't support the `toUpperCase` method. The line should read

```
vec.setElementAt(((String) vec.elementAt(i)).toUpperCase(), i);
```

It is a matter of personal programming style whether you prefer (and use) this more concise code or the multi-line version.

Experiment X2.6, Step 7. Note that `firstOfMonth` does not first check to ensure that the vector elements are dates before casting them. When the program attempts to cast a string to a date, Java reports an error. Since it is not possible to tell the type of an object until the program executes, the Java compiler does not flag this as an error, but the runtime system does.

Session X3: Input, Output, Files, and Exceptions

In this laboratory session, you will implement versions of the `SimpleInput` and `SimpleOutput` classes that we have used in previous experiments. Along the way, you will learn about exceptions, one of Java's key mechanisms for dealing with run-time errors. The goals of this laboratory are to

- strengthen your knowledge of Java by guiding you through the development of important utility classes that you have used and will continue to use;
- motivate the need for run-time error detection and correction; and
- introduce file input and output.

Your instructor will tell you which of the proposed experiments you are to perform.

Prerequisite skills:

- Familiarity with the use of the `SimpleInput` and `SimpleOutput` classes
- Objects and classes in Java
- Arrays (optional)

Required files:

- `SimpleInput.java`
- `SimpleOutput.java`

Discussion

You may have noted that many of our programs and classes depend on two key classes, `SimpleInput` and `SimpleOutput`. `SimpleInput` has been responsible for the inputs to our programs and `SimpleOutput` has been responsible for generating output from our programs.

Are these standard classes that come with all releases of Java? No, they were developed specifically for this lab manual. Then why are we using them? Because the input and output classes that come with Java do not provide many of the key features that beginning programmers need. Java's input and output facilities are designed primarily for experienced programmers.

However, you should now be ready to think about input and output from the perspective of a more experienced programmer. At the same time, you may find it easiest to continue using `SimpleInput` and `SimpleOutput` for most of your programming tasks, extending them when you need new facilities.

Output and `System.out`

How does the computer write to the screen? It turns out to involve a number of complex operations, operations which often differ significantly from computer to computer. In addition, the way you write to the screen differs from the way you write to a file, and the way you write information intended for human consumption may differ from the way you write information intended for computer consumption.

Hence, most programming languages provide a variety of methods and objects, in object-oriented languages, to simplify printing. In addition, most languages have an object or variable that corresponds to the standard output of a program: the output that typically goes to the screen.

In Java, `System.out` is the name of an object of class `java.io.PrintStream` that can be used to print values.

Unfortunately, the designers of Java realized that they had made some mistakes in their original design, and deprecated `PrintStream` in Java 1.1. By saying that `PrintStream` is deprecated, they mean that they are still maintaining the class, but recommend that you use a replacement class (in this case, `java.io.PrintWriter`). We will begin by using the deprecated class, and then consider how we might update code to use the replacement.

How do you print something with a `PrintStream` object? The same way you do with a `SimpleOutput` object. That is, you can call `print` and `println` methods. So, if we have a `PrintStream` called ps, we might print `Hello World` with

```
ps.println("Hello World");
```

How do we print with `System.out`? Since it's an object in class `PrintStream`, we can simply write

```
System.out.println("Whatever we want to print");
```

What if we want to follow the new Java recommendations, and use a `PrintWriter` instead of a `PrintStream`? First, we must convert the `PrintStream` to a `PrintWriter`. Fortunately, Java includes a constructor for `PrintWriter` that does just that. Hence, if we want to convert Java's standard output to a `PrintWriter` named `out`, we would write

```
PrintWriter pw = new PrintWriter(System.out, true);
```

How do we print with a `PrintWriter` now that we have one? We call its `print` and `println` methods, as in

```
pw.println("Even more text");
```

In Experiment X3.1 you will experiment with the different output mechanisms.

Starting to build SimpleOutput

Let us begin to consider how we might write a `SimpleOutput` class. Why might we want such a class, given that `PrintWriter` seems to be able to do most of the work for us? One reason is that it will permit us to more easily add functionality. For example, it is often useful to have a default constructor for an output object that will send output to standard output. `PrintWriter` does not include such a constructor. In addition, `PrintWriter` does not include a `print` method that works on arrays. Given our current state of knowledge, writing a new class is the only way to extend other classes.

What fields will `SimpleOutput` need? Since it is recommended that we print with `PrintWriter`s, it will have a `writer` field that refers to the `PrintWriter`.

```
/**
 * The base PrintWriter that does the real work.
 */
protected PrintWriter writer;
```

Our default constructor will need to initialize this writer. What should we initialize it to? To standard output.

```
/**
 * Build an object that can write to standard output.
 */
public MyOutput() {
  writer = new PrintWriter(System.out, true);
} // MyOutput()
```

Now we need to fill in the `print` and `println` methods. In general, they will be fairly simple, consisting of just a call to the corresponding function in `PrintWriter`. For example,

```
/**
 * Print a string.
 */
public void print(String str) {
  writer.print(str);
} // print(String)
```

Unfortunately, as you will soon realize, you will need to create a `print` method for every primitive type. This means that you will do some busy work. At the same time, you will have the freedom to experiment with the methods. You may also learn that the base class doesn't work quite the way you expected. For example, `PrintWriter`s typically buffer their output (often, just until you tell them to finish the current line with a `println`). This means that you must explicitly tell them "okay, print it *now!*" with the `flush` operation.

```
/**
 * Print a string.
 */
public void print(String str) {
  writer.print(str);
  writer.flush();
} // print(String)
```

In Experiment X3.2 you will start to build your own output class.

Output files

We are now ready to consider one advantage of using our own class: we can extend the class to print to files instead of to the screen. How do we do this? We create a different kind of `PrintWriter`. This time, we'll create one that can write to files. That is, we will use a `PrintWriter` object whose `print` and `println` methods print to a specified file, rather than to the screen.

How do we build such an object and associate it with a file? It is a multiple step process. First, we must build a `java.io.FileWriter` that knows how to write to files. Next, we convert that `FileWriter` to a `PrintWriter`, again using one of the nifty constructors that `PrintWriter` provides. Our constructor might then look like

```
/**
 * Create an object that can write to a file.
 */
public MyOutput(String filename) {
  // Build a FileWriter to write to the given file
  FileWriter fw = new FileWriter(filename);
  // Convert it to a PrintWriter
  writer = new PrintWriter(fw, true);
} // MyOutput
```

Unfortunately, this code has a significant problem. In particular, it is not at all clear what should happen if you call the `FileWriter` constructor with an invalid filename. How does `FileWriter` tell `MyOutput` that there was an error?

In Experiment X3.3 you will consider output to files.

Exceptions

In Java, when a method cannot complete its required tasks, it indicates an error by throwing an exception. An exception is simply an object that is used to indicate errors. In effect, exceptions permit methods to exit in two different ways: they can exit normally, returning a value when appropriate or they can exit abnormally, indicating an error.

Every language provides some facility for dealing with errors. Java's differs from most in that Java forces the programmer to decide, in advance, what to do if an error occurs. Therefore, if you call a method that can throw exceptions, Java requires you to indicate what to do if an exception is thrown. It may be that you know that the method will never throw exceptions (e.g., you always create `FileWriter` objects using a valid file name). Nonetheless, the Java compiler will require you to indicate how to handle the exception.

How do you indicate how to handle the exception? You put the call to the method in a try/catch clause. First, you indicate to Java that you know that an exception may occur by writing

```
try {
  code-that-may-throw-exceptions;
} // try
```

Next, you indicate what to do by catching the exception. A catch clause looks a little like a method definition, except that it has no name and the parameter is an exception. Later, you will learn that there are a variety of types of exceptions. For now, you can just catch generic `Exception` objects.

```
catch (Exception e) {
  what-to-do-if-the-error-occurs;
} // catch(Exception)
```

Putting it all together, we might write

```
/**
 * Create an object that can write to a file.
 */
public MyOutput(String filename) {
  try {
    // Build a FileWriter to write to the given file
    FileWriter fw = new FileWriter(filename);
    // Convert it to a PrintWriter
    writer = new PrintWriter(fw, true);
  } // try
  catch (Exception e) {
    // What should we do?
  } // catch(Exception)
} // MyOutput
```

You may note that we enclosed a number of lines in the `try` clause. This is because we only want the subsequent lines to be executed if the thing we are trying succeeds. In effect, control exits a `try` clause when the first exception occurs. No subsequent statements are then executed. In this particular case, we don't want to create a new `PrintWriter` unless we've successfully created the `FileWriter`.

But what should we do if we catch an exception? In some cases, it may be appropriate to print an error message to output, although such cases are rare. In this case, we're setting up output, so it makes no sense to try to print a message. Instead, we should use Java's specified mechanisms for indicating errors and throw our own exception. Note that we are basically passing the buck. If a method we use fails, then we will most likely fail. If we fail, the method that called us may fail. Eventually, we may reach a method that understands how to handle failure.

To throw an exception, you use the <u>throw</u> command. Typically, you throw a newly created exception. You can create exceptions using strings as parameters. The strings, in effect, describe what went wrong.

If you write a method that throws exceptions, you need to indicate this by writing <u>throws</u> Exception in the function header. For our constructor, we might write:

```
/**
 * Create an object that can write to a file.
 */
public MyOutput(String filename)
  throws Exception {
  // Build a FileWriter to write to the given file
  try {
    FileWriter fw = new FileWriter(filename);
    // Convert it to a PrintWriter
    writer = new PrintWriter(fw, true);
  } // try
  catch (Exception e) {
    throw new Exception("Could not send output to '" + filename +
                        "'");
  } // catch(Exception)
} // MyOutput
```

Instead of creating a new exception, it would also be possible to just rethrow e (the exception thrown by the FileWriter constructor).

In Experiment X3.4 you will reconsider output to files.

Closing files

It is considered good programming practice to close every file that you open. By closing a file, you are indicating that you are done with the file. If you don't close files, Java will close them for you when you are done with the program. However, if you don't close files and then open them again, you may not get the results you expected.

How do you close files in Java? Every FileWriter (and, in fact, every other kind of Writer) provides a close method. All you need to do is call this method when you're done with the FileWriter. How do you know when you're done? You might add a close method to MyOutput or SimpleOutput and make it your practice to close any output object you create.

You can also take advantage of the finalize method to close files when you're done with them. However, this may not be the most reliable solution as finalize is not always called at appropriate times. (If you have not read about this method, don't worry; it's not very relevant to the current subject matter.)

Input

We've looked at some issues pertaining to output. But how do we deal with input? It turns out that some aspects of input are similar and others are different. As in the case of output, in order to do input from the keyword (or, more precisely, standard input), you will use a predefined value, in this case `System.in`. As in the case of output, you will most likely need to convert this `InputStream` to another class, in this case `Reader`.

What are the differences? Recall that there are a large number of `print` methods given by `Writer`s. It turns out that `Reader`s only provide methods for reading individual characters. Hence, we need to use more specialized versions and we need to find a way to convert characters or strings to numbers.

Input and System.in

`System.in` is Java's standard name for the standard input stream. If you read the documentation for Java, you will quickly learn that `System.in` is an `InputStream`. Input streams are intended to be used to read `bytes` rather than characters or strings. As you've seen from the programs that you've written, it is more common to read strings or numeric values.

We'll start with the simplest form of common input: reading strings. Java's `BufferedReader` class provides a `readString()` method that reads one line of text from input. Hence, we need to go from an `InputStream` to a `BufferedInputReader`. How? Once again, you need to do a series of conversions. This time, you will convert the `InputStream` to an `InputStreamReader` and then convert that `InputStreamReader` to a `BufferedInputStream`.

For example, if we use `reader` to refer to the `BufferedReader` that our input class will use, we might write the following constructor.

```
/**
 * Create a new object that can read from standard input.
 */
public MyInput() {
    // First, update System.in to a more modern class
    InputStreamReader tmp = new InputStreamReader(System.in);
    // Then, convert it to something that can read lines.
    this.reader = new BufferedReader(tmp);
} // class MyInput
```

Once we have that constructor, we can add a `readString` method that simply calls `reader`'s `readString` method, as in

```
return reader.readLine();
```

In Experiment X3.5 you will begin creating your own input class.

Converting strings to other types

Unfortunately, `BufferedReader` only provides two input methods: `read`, which reads single characters, and `readString`, which reads one line of input text. What if we want to read an integer or other numeric value?

It turns out that the best solution is to read an input string and then convert that input string to an integer. How do you do conversion? As in many cases before, this will require a series of steps. First, you build a numeric object that corresponds to the string. For example, to build an `Integer` that corresponds to the string `str`, we would write

```
Integer iobj = new Integer(str);
```

Similarly, to build a `Float` that corresponds to the same string, we would write

```
Float fobj = new Float(str);
```

Both of these constructors can throw `NumberFormatExceptions`, so be careful to `try` the construction and `catch` any errors.

Next, we must convert the objects into the primitive types. We do this with the appropriate `xxxValue` method. For example,

```
int i = iobj.intValue();
float f = fobj.floatValue();
```

Putting this all together, we get

```
/**
 * Read an integer on a line by itself.
 */
public int readInt() {
  // Read a line of input
  String str = this.readString();
  // Convert it into an integer object
  try {
    Integer iobj = new Integer(str);
    // Convert it into an int value
    int i = iobj.intValue();
    return i;
  } // try to convert the string
  // Can't convert!
  catch (Exception e) {
    // Return a default value
    return -1;
  } // can't convert
} // readInt()
```

or, more concisely,

```
/**
 * Read an integer on a line by itself.
 */
public int readInt() {
  // Read a line of input
  String str = this.readString();
```

```
// Convert it into an integer object
try {
  return (new Integer(str)).intValue();
} // try to convert the string
// Can't convert! Return a default value.
catch (Exception e) {
  return -1;
} // can't convert
} // readInt()
```

You may have noted that readInt expects each numeric input to be on a line by itself. In the problems we explore a readInt method that can read an integer from part of a line.

In Experiment X3.6 you will experiment with reading integers.

Experiments

Name: _____

ID: _____

Experiment X3.1: Using `System.out`

Step 1. Using our reliable `SimpleOutput` class, write a program that prints your name. Enter your code here.

Step 2. Using `System.out`, write a program that prints your name. Enter your code here.

Step 3. What, if any, advantages do you see to using `SimpleOutput`? Why do you think we provided such a class?

After entering your answer, you may want to read the note on the subject.

Step 4. Using a `PrintWriter`, write a program that prints your name. It is likely that you will need to convert `System.out` to a `PrintWriter` with

`PrintWriter out = `<u>`new`</u>` PrintWriter(System.out, `<u>`true`</u>`);`

You will also need to import `java.io.PrintWriter`. Enter your code here.

Step 5. What do you see as the relative advantages and disadvantages of using `PrintWriter` objects versus using `SimpleOutput` objects?

Step 6. Create an `ArrayPrinter` class with a `main` method that contains the following lines:

```
int[] stuff = new int[4];
stuff[0] = 1;
stuff[1] = 2;
stuff[2] = 4;
out.println(stuff);
```

Try to compile and execute the `ArrayPrinter`. If you succeed, record the output. If you fail, record and explain the error messages.

Experiment X3.2: Building your own output class

Step 1. Create a new class, `MyOutput`, that contains

- one field, `writer`, of class `OutputWriter`;
- a constructor similar to the one we developed earlier;
- a `println(String)` method.

Step 2. Create a new class, `OutputTester`, that will be used to test your `MyOutput` class. Your class should contain a `main` method with the following lines.

```
MyOutput out = new MyOutput();
out.println("Hello");
```

Compile your two classes and execute `OutputTester`. Record the results.

Step 3. Add the line

```
out.println(7.2);
```

to the `main` method in `OutputTester`. Try to compile and execute the program. Record any error messages you receive.

Step 4. What do those messages suggest?

Step 5. Add a `println(double)` method to `MyOutput` and recompile both classes. Do you still receive the same error messages? If so, why? If not, why not?

Step 6. Add the line

```
out.println(6);
```

to the `main` method in `OutputTester`. What do you expect to happen when you compile and execute your program?

Step 7. Try to compile and execute the program. If compilation and execution succeed, record the output. If either fails, record the error messages.

Step 8. Did what happened in Step 7 correspond to what you suggested in Step 6? Explain what happened in Step 7.

Step 9. What do you expect would happen if we added the following lines to the `main` method in `OutputTester`?

```
int[] stuff = new int[4];
stuff[0] = 1;
stuff[1] = 2;
stuff[2] = 4;
out.println(stuff);
```

Experiment X3.3: Output to files

Step 1. Add the following constructor to your `MyOutput` class. Note that you will need to import `java.io.FileWriter`.

```
/**
 * Create an object that can write to a file.
 */
public MyOutput(String filename) {
   // Build a FileWriter to write to the given file
   FileWriter fw = new FileWriter(filename);
   // Convert it to a PrintWriter
   writer = new PrintWriter(fw, true);
} // MyOutput
```

Try to compile `MyOutput` and record the results.

When you are done, read the notes on this experiment.

Experiment X3.4: Output to files, revisited

Step 1. Update the `MyOutput(String)` constructor from the previous experiment to use `try` and `catch`. The body of the constructor will now be

```
try {
   // Build a FileWriter to write to the given file
   FileWriter fw = new FileWriter(filename);
   // Convert it to a PrintWriter
   writer = new PrintWriter(fw, true);
} // try
catch (Exception e) {
   // Do nothing
} // catch(Exception)
```

Try to compile the revised `MyOutput` and record the results.

Step 2. Add the following lines to the `main` routine of your `OutputTester` class. Recompile and execute `OutputTester`. What are the contents of the file `stuff.txt`?

```
// Write some information to a file.
file = new MyOutput("stuff.txt");
file.println("Hello");
file.println(2 + 3);
```

Step 3. Change the file name in the code from Step 2 from `stuff.txt` to the empty string or to another illegal filename specified by your instructor. Recompile and execute `OutputTester`. What happens?

Step 4. Add the line

```
throw new Exception("Cannot write to '" + file + "'");
```

to the `MyOutput(String)` constructor. Recompile `MyOutput`. If you are successful, execute `OutputTester`. Record either results or error messages.

Step 5. Change the method header for the `MyOutput(String)` constructor to read

```
public MyOutput(String filename) throws Exception {
```

Recompile `MyOutput` and `TestOutput`. If you are successful, execute `OutputTester` and record the results. If you are not successful, record the error messages.

Step 6. Update the `main` in `TestOutput` to use appropriate try/catch clauses. Summarize your changes.

Experiment X3.5: Starting to build your own input class

Step 1. Create a new class, `MyInput`, that contains

- one field, `reader`, of class `BufferedReader`;
- a constructor similar to the one we developed earlier; and
- a `String readString()` method using the body we developed earlier.

Here is the constructor we created earlier.

```
/**
 * Create a new object that can read from standard input.
 */
public MyInput() {
    // First, update System.in to a more modern class.
    InputStreamReader tmp = new InputStreamReader(System.in);
    // Then, convert it to something that can read lines.
    this.reader = new BufferedReader(tmp);
} // class MyInput
```

Here is the body of the `readString()` method we developed earlier.

```
return reader.readLine();
```

Compile your class. What error messages do you receive? What do these error messages suggest?

After answering this question, you may want to look at the notes on this step.

Step 2. Update `readString` so that it uses `try` and `catch` appropriately. Return the empty string if you catch an exception. Compile your class and correct any compilation errors. Record the code for your method here.

Step 3. Create a new class, `InputTester`, that will be used to test your `MyOutput` class. Your class should contain a `main` method with the following lines.

```
SimpleOutput out = new SimpleOutput();
MyInput in = new MyInput();
out.println("Enter your name: ");
String str = in.readString();
out.println("You entered " + str);
```

Compile your two classes and execute `InputTester`. Enter your name when prompted to do so. Record the results.

Step 4. How would this code differ if you used `SimpleInput` rather than `MyInput`?

After writing your answer, you may wish to look at the notes on this step.

Step 5. Update `InputTester` to read two lines of text, such as a name and a major. Recompile and execute the program. Summarize your changes and record the output.

Step 6. Add the lines

```
int i;
i = in.readInt();
```

to the `main` method in `InputTester`. Try to compile and execute the program. Record any error messages you receive. What do these messages suggest?

Step 7. Try to update `MyInput` to include a `readInt` method that calls a corresponding method in its base reader. Try to compile the updated class. What do the error messages you receive suggest?

Experiment X3.6: Reading numeric input

Step 1. Add one of the `readInt` methods described above to your `MyInput` class. Recompile the class and correct any compilation errors. Here is one possible definition of `readInt`.

```
/**
 * Read an integer on a line by itself.
 */
public int readInt() {
  // Read a line of input
  String str = this.readString();
  // Convert it into an integer object
  try {
    return (new Integer(str)).intValue();
  } // try to convert the string
  // Can't convert! Return a default value.
  catch (Exception e) {
    return -1;
  } // can't convert
} // readInt()
```

Step 2. Add the following lines to the `main` method of `InputTester`.

```
int i;
out.println("Enter an integer");
i = in.readInt();
out.println("Read " + i);
```

Recompile and execute `InputTester`. Enter the value 3. Record your results. What do those results suggest?

Step 3. Rerun `InputTester` using the following inputs

- `-1`
- `004`
- `3.5`
- `three`
- `10 20`
- `9876543210987654321 0`

Record the results for each case. What do these results suggest?

Step 4. Add a `readFloat` method to your `MyInput` class. The design of this method is left to your imagination. Enter the code for the method here.

Step 5. Update `InputTester` to read in and print out a <u>float</u>. Run your program with the following inputs.

- -1
- 004
- 3.5
- three
- 10 20
- 98765432109876543210

Record the results for each case. What do these results suggest?

Post-Laboratory Problems

Problem X3-A: Printing integer arrays

Add a `println(int[] ints)` method to the `MyOutput` class. This method should print the array nicely. For example, the code

```
SimpleOutput out = new SimpleOutput();
int[] stuff = new int[4];
stuff[0] = 1;
stuff[1] = 2;
stuff[2] = 4;
out.println(stuff);
```

should print

```
[1, 2, 4, 0]
```

Problem X3-B: Printing string arrays

Add a `println(String[] strings)` method to the `MyOutput` class. This method should print the array nicely.

Problem X3-C: Redirecting output to a different file

Add a `setOutput(String filename)` method to your `MyOutput` class that redirects output to a file. If the object was previously writing to standard output, it should now write to the given file. If the object was previously writing to another file, it should close that file and begin writing to a new file.

Problem X3-D: Redirecting output to standard output

Add a `setOutput()` method to your `MyOutput` class that allows one to stop writing to whatever was previously being written to and then begin writing to standard output. If the object was previously writing to a file, it should close that file.

Problem X3-E: Reading input from files

Update `MyInput` so that it can also read input from files. As in the case of `MyOutput`, you will need to add a constructor that takes a file name as a parameter. You will turn that file name into a `FileReader` and then into a `BufferedReader`.

Problem X3-F: Reading parts of lines

You may have noted that one significant difference between `MyInput` and `SimpleInput` is that `SimpleInput` objects allow you to read multiple numeric values from one line. Update `MyInput` to support these additional methods.

How will you do this? You'll need to keep track of the line most recently read. You can identify the positions of the spaces on that line, split the line at each space, and convert the substrings individually.

Problem X3-G: Redirecting input

Add `setInput` methods to `MyInput` that behave similarly to the `setOutput` methods described in previous problems.

Notes

Experiment X3.1, Step 3. Why did we provide a `SimpleOutput` class? Primarily because it seemed like a good way to introduce objects. Note that the first program we gave you used a `SimpleOutput` object. In addition, as you will see later, by using `SimpleOutput` objects, we can easily change our programs to write to files rather than to the screen. It is also possible to extend the `SimpleOutput` object to provide additional capabilities. For example, we can add a method to print arrays. Finally, by relying on a single class that we developed, we can easily update all of our programs when Java incorporates a new output mechanism.

Experiment X3.3, Step 1. It is likely that the compilation will fail. If your error message indicates that it did not understand about the `FileReader`, then you forgot to import that class. Once you've fixed that error, you will now receive an error about an exception that must be caught. We discuss this error in the section titled "Exceptions".

Experiment X3.5, Step 2. It turns out that `readString` throws an exception. Exceptions are typically caused when you attempt to read from beyond the end of input. Hence, we need to `try` the call to `readString` and <u>catch</u> an exception.

Experiment X3.5, Step 4. As long as the program only reads and writes lines of text, there should be no difference between a program that uses our newly developed classes and one that uses `SimpleInput`. On the other hand, since we have not yet written methods to permit reading of numeric values, there will be some differences.